# Complexity, Learning and Organizations

# ONE WEEK LOAN

ve

at we ho

ooking at the world and at human systems, in organizations society as a whole. He proposes a holistic management approach which is in direct opposition to the short-term shareholder value-driven approach which dominates much management practice. The aim is to encourage the emergence of a new type of learning within organizations. To illustrate this, he discusses self-organizing systems; the complexity paradigm; the nature and use of knowledge; management learning at both the organizational and the individual level; and personal development. Finally, he argues in favour of considering business and economics as a network of agents that operate on the basis of synchronicity – the quantum structure of business.

Encouraging readers to reflect on their own experiences, and drawing on examples from a number of real-life company cases, Walter Baets delivers a readable and thought-provoking book. For students and managers interested in complexity, knowledge management, innovation and organizational learning, this book is an invaluable guide.

**Walter R. J. Baets** is Director Graduate Programs at Euromed Marseille – Ecole de Management and Professor in Complexity and Knowledge.

# Complexity, Learning and Organizations

## A quantum interpretation of business

Walter R. J. Baets

Routledge
Taylor & Francis Group

LONDON AND NEW YORK

First published 2006 by Routledge
2 Park Square, Milton Park, Abingdon, Oxon OX14 4RN

Simultaneously published in the USA and Canada
by Routledge
270 Madison Ave, New York NY, 10016

*Routledge is an imprint of the Taylor & Francis Group, an informa business*

*Originally published as 'Wie orde zaait, zal chaos oogsten' by
Koninklijke Van Gorcum BV, Postbus 43, 9400 AA Assen, 2002 & 2004*

© 2006 Walter R. J. Baets

Typeset in Times by Keystroke, Jacaranda Lodge, Wolverhampton
Printed and bound in Great Britain by MPG Books Ltd, Bodmin, Cornwall

*British Library Cataloguing in Publication Data*
A catalogue record for this book is available from the British Library

*Library of Congress Cataloging in Publication Data*
Baets, W. R. J. (Walter R. J.)
Complexity, learning and organizations : a quantum interpretation of business /
Walter R.J. Baets.– 1st ed.
p. cm.
Includes bibliographical references and index.
ISBN 0–415–38178–9 (hard cover) – ISBN 0–415–38179–7 (soft cover)
1. Organizational learning. 2. Knowledge management. 3. Industrial
management. I. Title.
HD58.82.B32 2006
658.3'124–dc22                                   2005030033

ISBN10: 0–415–38178–9     ISBN13: 978–0–415–38178–9 (hbk)
ISBN10: 0–415–38179–7     ISBN13: 978–0–415–38179–6 (pbk)

**Disclaimer**
We were unable to locate the copyright holders of the poems
by Machado and Tagore. Anyone wishing to claim ownership
should contact Routledge.

To those of us who can still marvel and who believe that one can make a difference

# Contents

 # Illustrations

## Figures

## Tables

# About the author

**Walter R. J. Baets** is Director Graduate Programs at Euromed Marseille – Ecole de Management and Professor in Complexity and Knowledge Management. He is the coordinator of E<sup>c</sup>KM, the Euromed Centre for Knowledge Management. Previously he held the Philips Chair in Information and Communication Technology and was Director of Notion (the Nyenrode Institute for Knowledge Management and Virtual Education) at Nyenrode Business Universiteit (the Netherlands). As Dean of Research he co-created the Euro-Arab Management School in Granada, Spain. He graduated in Econometrics and Operations Research at the University of Antwerp (Belgium) and did postgraduate studies in Business Administration at Warwick Business School (UK). He was awarded a PhD from the University of Warwick in Industrial and Business Studies and an Habilitation from the University Paul Cezanne, Aix-Marseille III (F).

He pursued a career in strategic planning, decision support and IS consultancy for more than ten years, before joining the academic world, first as managing director of the management development centre of the Louvain Universities (Belgium) and later as Associate Professor at Nijenrode University, The Netherlands Business School. He has been a Visiting Professor at the University of Aix-Marseille (IAE), GRASCE (Complexity Research Centre) Aix-en-Provence, ESC Rouen, KU Leuven, RU Gent, Moscow, St Petersburg, Tyumen and Purdue University. Most of his professional experience was acquired in the telecommunications and banking sector. He has substantial experience in management development activities in Russia and the Arab world.

His research interests include: innovation and knowledge; complexity, chaos and change; the impact of (new information) technologies on organizations; knowledge, learning, artificial intelligence and neural networks; online learning and workplace learning; besides, of course, his passion for the quantum interpretation of business.

He is a member of the International Editorial Board of the *Journal of Strategic Information Systems, Information and Management* and *Systèmes d'Information et Management*. He has acted as a reviewer/evaluator for a number of international conferences (e.g. ECIS and ICIS) and for the EU RACE programme. He has published in several journals, including the *Journal of Strategic Information Systems*, the *European Journal of Operations Research, Knowledge and Process Management, Marketing Intelligence and Planning*, the *Journal of Systems Management, Information and Management, The Learning Organization* and *Accounting, Management and Information Technologies*. He has organized international conferences in the area of IT and organizational change.

Walter Baets is the author of *Organizational Learning and Knowledge Technologies in a Dynamic Environment*, published in 1998 by Kluwer Academic Publishers, and co-author with Gert van der Linden of *The Hybrid Business School: Developing knowledge management through management learning*, published by Prentice Hall in 2000. Along with Bob Galliers, he co-edited *Information Technology and Organizational Transformation: Innovation for the 21st Century Organization*, published in 1998 by Wiley. In 1999 he edited *Complexity and Management: A collection of essays*, published by World Scientific Publishing. Recently he co-authored *Virtual Corporate Universities*, published 2003 by Kluwer Academic, and he edited *Knowledge Management and Management Learning: Extending the horizons of knowledge-based management* (Springer, 2005).

**Erna Oldenboom**, MA, author of Chapter 10, obtained degrees in Management Development and Human Resources Management in the Netherlands, and a Master's in Political Sciences (Peace and Conflict Management) at the University of Granada (Spain). She has long-standing corporate experience in the different aspects of human resources management and organizational development, and in particular in coaching and personal development. She is currently Professor of Human Resources Management and Personal Development at Euromed Marseille – Ecole de Management, and a freelance coach and trainer.

# Preface

Caminante, son tu huellas
El camino, y nada mas;
Caminante, no hay camino,
Se hace camino al andar.
Al andar se hace camino,
Y al volver la vista atras
Se ve la senda que nunca
Se ha de volver a pisar.
Caminante, no hay camino,
Sino estelas en la mar.
                          Antonio Machado,
                          Chant XXIX,
                          *Proverbios y cantares*,
          Campos de Castilla, 1917

Science cannot solve the ultimate mystery of nature . . . because in
the last analysis we ourselves are part of the mystery we are trying
to solve.

                                                    Max Planck

There is no path; you lay down the path in walking. The path is made
while creating one's life, just as it is while shaping one's academic career.
This book is evidently linked to my path, of course; how could it not be?
This path, this book, also allows us to take a moment to step back and
identify today's major stakes in the science of management, so that we
can make a choice between the many possible paths to be discovered, to
be created, to be laid down by walking further. This book explores a new
paradigm in a way that has not yet been undertaken in any other book,
I think. I feel it to be important that more people are willing to explore
these ideas and leave the well-trodden path. This book illustrates and

proposes a range of choices for a research agenda, for multiple research agendas, which are, at one and the same time, pertinent and interesting, and in any case innovative, I hope.

I willingly refer back to the invitation from Jean Louis Le Moigne, Edgar Morin and Magali Roux-Rouquié to attend their conference in June 2005 entitled 'Intelligence of Human Complexity, Epistemology and the Potential of Complexity in Practice'. I would not have been able to describe better the stakes our society faces for our science and managerial practice, as I observe them today. But don't forget: beauty is in the eye of the beholder, and so is truth. Beauty, truth and meaning are what we should strive for and what will eventually lead to more respectful solutions for our world. Beauty, truth and meaning are elements that will come up a number of times in this book. But to continue, Le Moigne, Morin and Roux-Rouquié proposed that this conference aimed at making a kind of state of the art targeted at 'transforming our experiences of action into complex situations in science with consciousness'. I hope to be able to contribute to this goal, which is dear to me.

I have not walked this path alone, fortunately. On numerous occasions I was able to meet up with other scientists who are in the process of exploring similar subjects. They were always happy meetings, passionate and productive. The path which has been walked today is not only mine, but that of a growing number of researchers and practitioners from all sorts of disciplines. I am happy to be able to make a modest contribution to their work and to their path.

Before developing the theme itself in the different chapters of the book, I want to make a short summary, allowing readers at each moment to position themselves in relation to the work as a whole. I would like the reader to enjoy discovering the details through what follows.

In Chapter 1 I express the promises, the objectives and the open questions with regard to our managerial practice of today. I deliberately introduce the human being with his weaknesses and his potential. Anecdotal evidence allows me to prepare the more conceptual work in the following chapters. But that conceptual development serves only one aim: to highlight and explain a manager's daily practice. Better understanding, or should I say broader understanding, is what we need in order to be able to give a deeper meaning to our daily practice – not just for the fun of broadening our understanding, but mainly through the necessity of better understanding what we observe. This first chapter gives some case material to keep the following chapters more down to earth. Having practised quite a lot, and having discovered the limits by experience, I am well qualified to highlight the underlying problematic of our rational approaches.

In Chapter 2 I take the step of trying to explore the beginning of an underlying theory. Why should we be interested in questions posed by the philosophy of science, or philosophical questions more generally? The reason is that what we accept as true in advance has a strong influence on perception itself and on the search for truth, or deeper knowledge. If we think that the world is at the centre of the universe, our research will be influenced by our belief that all the other planets rotate around the Earth.

Effectively, in research we will again find the facts which, the evidence shows, confirm this hypothesis (let's call that a research hypothesis). Therefore, the starting position plays a crucial role in what we will find.

Let us use the metaphor of rose-coloured glasses. If we look through rose-coloured glasses the world seems rose-coloured. It is what you really see. Except that it is not the reality. A pair of blue-coloured glasses would give the idea (even the observation) that the world is blue. That is not true either. Philosophers of science look for an exact representation of the world, just as each manager is in search of an exact representation of the way the market works.

I am exploring a more holistic approach to management, and therefore ask the question, 'Is there a common notion of holism?' In this thesis I comment on one of Ken Wilber's concepts, which is, I think, very rich and usable. He visualizes something that we can call different dimensions of the image of the holistic world. Wilber's model gives me the necessary epistemological base to continue my investigation.

We hoped that the computer would come to support human thinking. In view of the growing knowledge about how the brain functions, that created a dilemma for us. We asked people to start to think like machines (in symbols), and here I notably refer to the success of quantitative methods. In parallel, we hoped that machines would think like humans (in holograms and 'photos'). However, what we were hoping for resembled an upside-down world. It is not surprising that it has not really worked well.

But the consequences are more serious. At the heart of the general trend of a rather rational practice of science, we tried to apply the same type of thinking to economy and management. Economic theory, as well as the theory of management, is based almost exclusively on an intellectual framework which is not ours. If we try, using this symbolic and rational approach, to simulate or understand reality, which is actually dynamic and non-linear, the chances are high that we will fail. In fact, we can optimize production chains perfectly, for the simple reason that they are created on a mechanical principle. The problems start when there is interaction between humans, markets, the organization of companies, the choice of clients, etc.

Chapter 3 continues to develop the necessary underlying theory and is dedicated to the theory of complexity and the automatic learning behaviour of systems (based, among other things, on the theories of Varela). These theories serve to justify the importance of the personal development of the manager. Only a 'learning' manager will be in a position to play the spider's role in the web, to be the inspirer and the creator of good conditions for others.

If we are therefore going to look into the heart of contemporary theories of artificial cognitive intelligence to try to find how we think about the subject of reasoning, we are going to have to develop an attitude which distances itself from the rather positivist approaches adapted hitherto. Reason (intelligence) is considered to be a behaviour: behaviour is what counts. The link between the brain and reason (intelligence) is broken: reason is not seated only in the brain but throughout the whole body (distributed intelligence).

Despite the two great revolutions in science – the theory of relativity and quantum theory – most of today's thinking is still Newtonian, wherein we observe a fixed time and space continuum. In Newtonian thinking, time is reversible and one can therefore predict the future from the past, but therefore the opposite is also true. In effect, one can determine the past from the future, therefore past and future are immutably linked through causality. In practice – and here I refer to company practice – that is not generally the case. In fact, no one has ever succeeded in predicting market potential, or market share, or future relationships with competitors. The financial markets are the most eloquent example of this, but no matter in what market (at least, in dynamic markets), it is equally impossible to make a diagnosis other than for the short term. The more dynamic a market, the more difficult it is to predict, for in this case time plays a more 'constructive' role.

This chapter discusses the theories of Prigogine, who also investigated the behaviour of systems far from equilibrium in comparison with that of systems near to equilibrium.

Another big current of ideas in relation to the theory of complexity is that of John Holland, the father of genetic algorithms. Holland's theories, along with those of Prigogine, will be accepted by the majority of people in the Anglo-Saxon world as the theory of complexity. The development of genetic algorithms cannot be seen disconnected from research into 'artificial life', with which Chris Langton's name is closely linked. The research on artificial life gave us new ideas to examine. This research highlighted remarkable characteristics of systems, notably the functioning of so-called complex systems on the basis of a number of simple rules. It is therefore possible for a system with simple agents (for example, people), in which everyone follows their own simple goal (to survive, for example) and where everyone follows rules of simple interaction, to produce complex behaviour.

The basis of these developments, and the interesting applications which come from them, imply that where hierarchical and organized structures are not capable of completely understanding this type of system, it is no longer necessary to look in the classical direction: there are a number of alternatives. We can therefore consider companies, or some other form of network of social entities (society, country, international community), as networks of agents. These networks of agents show an emerging behaviour (or a self-creating behaviour) which is produced again each time in the network (we can make a comparison with what Prigogine showed us).

The role of a manager of a particular network is therefore no longer to come up with good solutions (if that was the case before), but only to create optimal conditions and circumstances so that the network can function in the best possible way with total freedom of action. These networks are self-creating and self-organizing, based on principles that we have already found in neurobiology. The networks show a behaviour which is sometimes very complex, but the rules of piloting are very simple. The strength is not even found in the 'knots' of the network (agents), but rather in the quality of the interaction of agents in a company, which rather than the quality of the individuals, is what will then make up the quality of the company.

These ideas present us with a paradox in management: we are trying to direct and control what is not controllable or manageable. That would not be so terrible if we were not astonished when it did not work. In fact, it is impossible for management to ensure its success (in markets and/or dynamic companies) through control and forecasting. In consequence, we must fundamentally call into question the way of facing such dynamic systems.

If it seems that the future is unpredictable, and a management oriented to control does not address problems because the 'better' way does not exist, what is there left for a manager? If the construction of bigger and bigger models (axiomatic systems), or use which is more and more constrained by more complicated rules, does not improve our understanding, what is left for us?

In Chapter 4 I add another concept, namely the one of self-reference. Autopoietic systems appear promising, as argued in the previous chapter, but they also need, and possibly often suffer from, a quality which is called self-reference. In order for an autopoietic system to flourish, it creates its own self-referential frame. As such, that should not be a problem, as long as that self-referential power does not lock in the autopoietic system. A self-referential system could become completely distant and strange from its environment, of which it should be an integral part. In such a case, self-reference is devastating (as illustrated in Chapter 7). But self-reference is equally the basis for communication within the network that each dynamic system appears to be. Potential power and potential danger that self-reference is, the reader should understand it correctly. That is what we aim for in this chapter. Using, *inter alia*, Gödel's famous theorem to illustrate self-reference, it is an open-ended introduction to the concept of self-reference.

The theory of complexity, developed thus far, gives us the necessary framework to be able to investigate, in Chapter 5, knowledge and learning. The idea that organizations must constantly learn, and therefore become 'learning organizations', is not new. As a result of theories formulated in the 1970s and 1980s, attention moved away from individual learning (pedagogy) towards organizational learning.

The question we can ask is not really whether groups, after a while, have learned something. Evidently that is possible. The question that I want to ask myself here is: How does that work? What is the mechanism of this organizational learning? And next, if, as a manager, you want to introduce a learning organization, how can you do it? Should you look for it in group processes, or rather in individual processes? This chapter explores existing theories of knowledge and learning, and also develops a new theory based on the paradigm of complexity.

There are support techniques for the manager who wants employees to learn. What the manager must avoid is thinking again that a definite, prescribed path exists and that you only need to follow this route. Worse still, this could be the way to failure and disillusion. A proposition for a knowledge and learning infrastructure is made within the framework of the proposed paradigm.

Once we have developed the concept of knowledge and learning within the new paradigm, Chapter 6 aims to identify and formalize the tasks for a learning manager; at the end of the chapter we will clarify why and how these tasks contribute and how they can be done.

- The main need for the learning manager is to continually learn. Any fixed scheme must always be re-examined.
- Instead of directing people, the learning manager stimulates individuals to learn. In practice, this means not bolting everything down from the beginning, but leaving space for improvement, learning and innovation.
- The learning manager is a key point in the network of colleagues and learning clients. The rules of interaction deserve the manager's attention.
- The rules of interaction in the network must be stimulated so that the network is creative. To restrain and correct are not priorities.
- Finally, the learning manager can make the context as rich and vast as possible.

After considering the learning individual in the previous chapter, Chapter 7 explores the pitfalls for organizations and their learning. It uses our legal system as an illustration of how organizations can get in the way of their own learning, fall into the trap of self-reference, and eventually completely bypass their social relevance. Though this chapter could easily be misunderstood as a criticism of bureaucratic management (e.g. of government-related activities), it is a much broader warning about the potentially devastating power of self-reference hiding round the corner of any company. This chapter is an illustration, not a case study.

Once we accept holism, constructivism and emergence as fundamental to a new paradigm, we cannot avoid touching on a paradox, perhaps the most important one in science, as I have already said. Chapter 8 will introduce the reader to the world of quantum interpretation. Almost the whole of scientific society is still centred on Newtonian principles: in other words, fixed time and space. If we know what happened yesterday, we therefore also know what will happen tomorrow (and also what happened the day before yesterday). Science cannot progress easily with the time–space continuum that the scientific revolutions of the last century offered us. In the economic and managerial sciences this revolution seems to have been completely sidelined. Our economic thinking is still Marshallian, the economic thinking of the nineteenth century (Arthur, 1998).

Causality is a deeply rooted concept in Newtonian thinking. Since complexity theory and, even more so, quantum mechanics have fundamentally questioned that causality, what could be the organizing principle behind corporate or market behaviour? What can quantum mechanics – its philosophy and interpretation – offer us in order to clarify the organizing principles of management, markets and companies?

In this chapter we introduce the notion of synchronicity, which is interesting in management and which this chapter will investigate through a number of other authors working principally in other sciences. This could be key to a different understanding of causality in the science of management.

Synchronicity (being together-in-time) (according to Pauli) appears in all the sciences and techniques in which simultaneity plays a role. It is necessary to take into account that we are not speaking about a *causal* coherence (from cause to effect) but a *coincidence* (= a going together), which must be considered useful even if we cannot explain the deepest cause of this simultaneity. We must remember that we always speak about synchronicity if the events concerned occur within the same time period. The notions of statistics or the theory of probability are of another order. Probability can be calculated with mathematical methods, which is impossible when speaking about synchronicity.

An alternative proposed by a few authors in other sciences, and the quantum approach to energy, information and communication, allow me to strongly propose causality at a much lower level of aggregation, that is to say the quantum level. In fact, we should really speak about synchronicity or coincidence rather than causality. It is important that it is this structure which allows humans to realize what we can realize; which could be: to heal yourself, to simply survive or to innovate in companies. It is therefore a question of elementary particles (let us say people's characteristics), linked in solid networks with all sorts of other matter (the entourage), which interact, and in doing so make up part of larger energetic fields (morphogenetic fields) which contain knowledge and information. When more members of a team (or a company) are 'entrained', their actions will be more successful, for example in product innovation teams. The scientific approach set out in this book is that the understanding of innovation must therefore be based on 'entrainment', quantum interpretation, synchronicity, morphogenetic fields and individual space for self-organization.

Innovative research by definition never follows paths already laid out, but it is valid to ask whether we can speak here about a change in the paradigm. This is, in any case, what I want to suggest.

All this leads to the theme of my current research: based on the metaphysical question of knowing whether matter has a 'consciousness', in what way can we obtain understanding of the 'logic' of economic behaviour? Is this logic a quantum logic and how therefore does it present itself? For practical reasons, we limit ourselves in the first place to the problematic of innovation, but we can, of course, ask ourselves the same questions concerning the functioning of the whole economy. What are the basics, the principles of construction and the role of consciousness? Where is the centre of causality and how does the organizing principle function? Is there still any causality by comparison with non-locality and synchronicity? If we can obtain a new understanding of economics and management behaviour, is it this understanding which lets us develop a new economic theory, or at least a theory of innovation? Can we develop a quantum interpretation of economy?

From this comes a research agenda that is challenging for the academic community, relevant for the managerial community. The scientific proposition on which I would like to do research is the following: in order to be able to understand the phenomena of management better, we must research the quantum interpretation of the economy. Synchronicity, non-locality, entrainment and entanglement create, via energy in the network of individual interaction, an emerging behaviour. With 'complex adaptive systems' it should be possible to begin to understand these phenomena. In current companies this emerging behaviour makes a difference in the strategic triangle of knowledge, learning and innovation.

The research agenda can be summarized as follows:

- What is the quantum interpretation of management phenomena (what are the roles of consciousness, synchronicity, morphogenetic fields, etc.)?
- Can we create evidence of an emerging character of management phenomena, and in particular of innovation?
- Can 'complex adaptive systems' visualize emergence, synchronicity and morphic fields?

- Can we clarify the crucial role of knowledge, learning and innovation for companies by answering the previous questions, but especially by improving the application of these concepts in companies? Research is therefore limited at first to knowledge, learning and innovation.

In Chapter 9 the way in which we can confront this research agenda will emerge. Obviously, this chapter is, among other things, an illustration of the potential of complex adaptive systems (CAS). But above all, it aims to explore business economics within the framework of this new paradigm. What are the assumptions of classical business economics and to what extent do they really hold? On the basis of the quantum interpretation developed in this book, can we illustrate the existence of a quantum interpretation of certain crucial managerial processes? Does it exist, can it be visualized, and does it give a richer interpretation for management? Though the chapter starts off with a theoretical positioning, the bulk of the contribution is a number of real-life projects that have been undertaken in companies, providing first-hand insights and indeed illustrating the existence of a quantum interpretation leading to a different understanding.

As the whole text demonstrates, the accent on the problematic for companies is placed, in my view, in the junction between the management of knowledge, (continuous) learning and innovation. For this reason the projects reported on are focused on:

- the management of knowledge;
- learning;
- innovation;

but also, and especially, on the interaction between these three.

Based on the underlying theory developed, CAS, principally artificial neural networks (ANNs) and agent-based simulations, seem to be ideal research tools for investigating a quantum interpretation of management.

Years of experimentation, mainly with ANNs, have comforted me with the idea that ANNs appear very interesting if we use them for their learning qualities. In this case they are capable of resolving real problems which are insoluble using 'classic research methods'. An ANN therefore appears to have added value through dynamic characteristics (therefore learning characteristics) and non-linearity. Next, it seems interesting to study more deeply the groups of non-linear dynamic methods. These methods, which are called complex adaptive systems in Anglo-Saxon literature, include, among other things besides ANNs, fuzzy neural networks, agent-based simulations and genetic algorithms. In our work, we have concentrated on ANNs and agent-based simulations.

We must understand better not only what these CAS have to offer in support of management, but also how they help our understanding of the management of knowledge and learning, and, eventually, how to reach emergence. Do CAS allow us to visualize a quantum interpretation of markets and companies? To be able to then apply these methods successfully, we need an adapted theory (as developed in this book), necessary for the subject of knowledge and learning which goes beyond the purely symbolic nature of artificial intelligence.

As yet, there have been few publications about the process of innovation as a learning and emerging concept. And neither are there many publications about emerging behaviour and how to study it. However, two exceptions have greatly inspired me and have led me to experiment with agent-based simulations and neural networks, other than my own research.

Epstein and Axtell describe in their book *Growing Artificial Societies* (1996) how artificial societies can emerge, how they self-organize, how they grow, how they learn and even how they enter into conflict (and how they resolve these conflicts). Another remarkable book is Wolfram's *A New Kind of Science* (2002). This long and impressive book gives very detailed (perhaps too detailed) examples of emerging behaviour, in the sense of where an organization finds itself suddenly in disorder. It is a hugely detailed piece of research towards a scientific approach which is constructivist – which builds from minuscule particles. The approach of these two books entirely suits the theoretical framework which is developed here.

With six different research projects, all done in companies, the beginning of evidence for the theory developed here is created. Evidently, these six projects do not give definitive responses, either for the theoretical concept presented or for the possibility of simulating the concept with CAS. What we can say is that this first result, this first evidence, is encouraging. We develop, on the basis of this new theory, and by making use of simulations, situations which are at least recognized as real. That is encouraging and suggests that we can at least show what happens in practice. First of all, more research is necessary in these sorts of simulations and, if possible, also in the approaches based more on human techniques (such as brainstorming) in order to be able to verify the theoretical framework. This refers to my concern, already expressed, for obtaining the best possible understanding of the emergence of markets and more general managerial phenomena. A second aspect which requires more research is the use of CAS. But above all, this research must be specifically oriented to the applicability of these approaches in companies. If we get to the point where companies are starting to use these approaches, the change in paradigm is going to gradually happen.

No book can claim validity for managers, or even claim to be a management book, if it only addresses theoretical and conceptual matters. Chapter 10 closes the circle. How could a manager who does indeed understand the potential of this new paradigm start managing accordingly? A new paradigm needs an adapted set of competencies for managers who want to manage in this new paradigm. Management *in* complexity (not *of* complexity), management *in* diversity, management *in* respect for multiple solutions and multiple truths, and management *in* paradoxes – those are the necessary skills for the manager of today. 'Wave or particle?'; it only makes a difference in the eye of the observer, the manager. Machines cannot realize values and cannot make intuitive choices. Machines cannot choose between multiple possible truths; managers who behave and think as machines cannot, either. Personal development is what we want to discuss in this chapter.

\* \* \*

This path is not laid down in walking alone. Many people, over many years, have walked part of that path together with me. I am afraid I cannot mention them all, not even the most important ones. However, I would just like to mention a few crucial ones, since without them this book would never have existed. First of all I would like to thank the many groups of students, in different universities and business schools around the world, who have been willing to listen, to react and to enact in my courses. A course and a book, if they intend to be useful, should be an act of co-creation. A number of academic scholars have been extremely helpful to me in drafting the ideas of this book and, though the list is endless, a few key names are Jean-Louis Le Moigne, Bob Galliers, Jacques-André Bartoli, Venu Venugopal, Gert van der Linden, Machiel Emmering, Bernard Paranque, pretty much in that chronological order.

On a more practical level I would like to mention Claude Amenc, Claude Spano, Peter van Leeuwen and Karen Ray, all of whom were crucially important for getting the message over.

But above all, it is Erna, my wife, who has facilitated, encouraged and managed my mind-breaking exploration of theories further away from equilibrium (as Prigogine would have said). Not only did she contribute the last chapter of this book, but she is responsible for the breadth that I have been able to finally achieve in this book. The course we co-teach, entitled 'The quantum interpretation of business: from rational to non-rational forms of knowledge', is a unique and fascinating exploration of the frontiers of managerial knowledge today. The students appreciate it, we enjoy it, and I hope it is the beginning of an even more exciting path to be laid down in the coming years.

I hope you enjoy reading this book.

Walter Baets
Aubagne, September 2005

# 1  We humans

During my years in the Netherlands I became acquainted with one of the events that is very dear to the Dutch: Queensday. It is indeed the commemoration of the Queen's birthday (though in fact it is the Queen Mother's birthday), and as such it is a bank holiday. In every town and village in the country, people sell whatever they want to sell on the streets; very often they sell their old stuff. Surprisingly, in the major towns (like Amsterdam and Utrecht) people sleep in the streets the night before, on the specific (strategic) spot where they want to sell their stuff, in order to make sure that they have that specific spot for their little shop. The phenomenon is called the 'free market'. In a city like Amsterdam this is a huge scene of chaos, or should we say a perfect self-organization that, despite the presence of millions of people in town (many people come from all over the country to Amsterdam), passes more or less smoothly. But . . .

Queensday 2001. As in every other year, millions of visitors came to Amsterdam for the free market. As in every other year, most people came to Amsterdam by train, and, as usual, many additional trains were laid on. The increase of preventive alcohol testing seems to have had an unanticipated effect, in the form of a shift from private to public transport. Only in 2001 things went seriously wrong. All trains were stopped in the evening hours. The central railway station was closed down. Lots of people gathered in front of the railway station, some of them rather drunk. For the first time in Dutch history (the Dutch are known to be correct people) a real riot broke out. The newspaper headlines read 'Civil war in Amsterdam' or 'Revolution'. In short, everything went seriously wrong.

The next day, everybody was looking for 'things' that went wrong, and especially for somebody to blame for this riot. And if one looks very hard, for sure one is going to find something (or someone). Don't the French say 'for a hammer, everything resembles a nail'? The trouble is that one never knows whether the people identified are indeed to blame for what happened, but in fact most often that is not the most important consideration. We have to find somebody who is guilty, or do we just look for a victim? Maybe we should beef up the procedures; that always sounds good. After all, if the procedures are clear-cut, they can easily cut wood, can't they? Most medals, however, have a reverse side. In fact, I do not really think there are any medals with only one side, despite the fact that science is working very hard to find such kinds of medals.

Is it that the Dutch Railways (NS) is badly organized? Didn't they have procedures for such cases? Weren't the procedures put into effect with rigour? None of this has to be true. One can attempt to organize a system in all its details, but once humans are involved, mistakes are unavoidable. People are not machines. People make errors, they innovate, they experiment, they anticipate and they do a lot of other very positive things that a system can never anticipate. Systems are made for controllable, mechanistic applications, such as a watch. They operate in an ordered and organized way, at least if there are no outside forces to influence them (such as if you throw a watch on the ground). In other words, one can attempt to organize a human system, but there is no point hoping it will work. Somewhere, somebody will do something that has not been foreseen in the procedures, and that tiny different behaviour can eventually cause huge effects. That is what was seen on Queensday 2001. Can we find somebody who is to blame? Maybe. Can we anticipate this kind of event? No!

Another, more painful example in Dutch history is the explosion of a fireworks factory in the centre of Enschede (a medium-sized town in the east of the Netherlands). Despite the detailed rules about security in fireworks factories, a catastrophe could not be avoided. Should we refine the rules (even further)? Maybe. In the meantime, we invest a lot of money to find somebody who is guilty. But how come we learn so little from this kind of catastrophe? A comparable disaster had taken place roughly ten years earlier. Detailed suggestions were formulated and, to our surprise, they had not been put into effect. Is it that they were not applied, or didn't they help? Or do we look through the wrong pair of glasses and consequently see the wrong things? Don't be surprised that if you look at the world through a pair of rose-tinted glasses, the world will appear to be rose-coloured. The world is not really that colour, but for you it is, of course. And we are both right. For you the world is rose, but for everyone else it isn't. It all depends on the pair of glasses you wear.

If we now introduce a somewhat more complex world and do not limit it to only one country, we see the most remarkable things. On 11 September 2001 two aeroplanes with passengers on board are flown into New York's twin towers. Thousands of relatives of the victims of these (undoubted) terrorist activities cry out for justice. In fact, a nation should do everything in order to protect its citizens against this kind of terrorist attack. Let there be no doubt about this, and let us not ignore the fact that it will be a long and difficult road to follow. Thus far, everybody agrees. Then we start organizing. Being very organized, we are going to 'seed' actions, and what we get as a result is a lot of chaos and misery. Don't we humans ever learn? What seems a long time for one person (a few weeks for Bush and his compatriots) seems very short for others. How is it possible, in such a short period of time, to find out what really happened, who was really behind it, and how we could prevent such events? But maybe we don't need to; we could also 'invent' these details. Proof was not really necessary in this case (as it proved to be unnecessary in more recent dreadful cases). It was clear to everybody that bin Laden was guilty and no error could have been made. It was decided to follow a proven way of creating disaster: a regular war of an impressive media quality. Not surprisingly, we have harvested the well-known fruits from this tried and tested approach. A country was destroyed and many thousands of innocent people were killed. In the meantime, another country is added to the hit list. We have created yet another vacuum of power, we arm certain parties (and not others), and then we are surprised that the armed parties fill that vacuum, just as has happened many other times in history. Wasn't it the United States that armed Saddam Hussein in order to fight Iran? Afterwards we are surprised when we get the very reaction we have provoked. Wasn't it also the United States that armed and trained the bin Laden fraction in order to get the Russians out of Afghanistan? Wasn't it Churchill who found it an interesting idea that the Russians and the Germans would kill each other on the Eastern Front in the Second World War? That would avoid the Allies having to take action. And suddenly we were again surprised that Stalin wanted to continue and 'liberate' Germany himself. Don't we ever learn? If a journalist asks Madeleine Albright (ex-Secretary of State of the United States) whether she feels responsible for the millions of children dying as a result of the economic blockade of Iraq (before the recent war), she can only say that this is the price 'we' have to pay for the defence of democracy; collateral damage. Who is 'we'?

Within a part of the world, or even within a country or a cultural community, we have co-created throughout history a pattern of values and norms that is based on different aspects of life. For convenience we refer to this as culture, science, or religion, each of which has many subordinate details. The prevailing culture, science and religion (or spirituality in a larger sense) has an important impact on people's daily reality, even though often we are not really aware of this. These values are passed on very young via the family, and further developed during school life and the other contacts during our youth. For those who continue their education at university, strict rules are taught about how we should consider reality (in this part of the world). Imagine my surprise at finding a book titled *The Islamic Approach to Doing Scientific Research*. No doubt this will lead to Islamic findings. There seems to be one correct way of doing scientific research (in different parts of the world) that guarantees scientifically sound results. Our society is based on, and organized according to, generally accepted values – at least in what we call democratic countries. After years of being submerged in those values, it should not surprise us that many things are implicitly absorbed and transformed into our acts. We are not explicitly aware of these any more. Understanding (science), significance (spirituality) and design (art) are all important aspects of our behaviour.

What this book aims to do is to explore the split in the Western individual between, on the one hand, scientific thinking (understood as the positivist, reductionist scientific approach) and, on the other hand, the limited support that this approach gives for the necessary significance and design in human activities. If we were able to be aware of the underlying assumptions in our thinking, we might be able to deal better with issues of significance and design in an enriching and hence learning way. Eventually I would like to address in this book how to improve our learning capacity, as well as how to improve our capacity to create significance and art, all with the aim of enriching our actions. We explore how understanding (science) stands in the way of learning action. Who preaches order will spawn chaos (as the title of the Dutch edition of this book says). The more we organize things (by means of strict rules), the easier it becomes to ignore those rules. But worse, it is often sad to see how people became unable to deal with circumstances that are not described in rules. People seem to have lost their creative power. The means (the rules) become the target, and the real aim, to which the rules should contribute, becomes subordinate, or disappears completely. If we want to be able to learn, we should sacrifice blind rule-following.

When I was still living in Spain we flew back to the Netherlands for a few days. In Madrid (we lived in Granada) we had to transfer to a KLM flight to Amsterdam. My wife had an economy-class ticket (booked well in advance), but my own ticket (booked entirely too late) was a business-class ticket (there was no economy seat available). Fortunately it was being paid for by an assignment, but I wanted to fly with my wife. Since economy class was fully booked, I proposed to swap my ticket with any economy passenger (without a refund and without going through any other administrative procedure). The value added of this is clear: two happy people. I would be able to travel with my wife; the other passenger would suddenly get a business-class upgrade for free. However, this was impossible; it was against all rules. But since KLM is client-friendly they suggested waiting. Maybe a business-class seat would become available (the plane was fully booked; better times for the airlines) and then they could upgrade my wife. The rules did allow that. The proposal did not appeal to me, since it could always go wrong, whereas my proposal was simple and immediate. The story ends as might be expected. All the passengers showed up. One of us flew business, one economy. KLM had made two unhappy clients instead of three happy ones. The rules survived; my preference for KLM did not.

The underlying question of this book deals with my feeling about an ethical dilemma. Is the human still the centre of our action or are we rather trapped in the predominant power of the system? By system I do not only refer to a government, a state, a multinational company, as Marcuse suggested in the 1960s, or Orwell's Big Brother, but very simply to any mechanistic procedure, on any possible level. Who preaches order will spawn chaos, and chaos does not necessarily need to be equal to a catastrophe. This book elaborates on the latent tension between the role and the power of the image, what we can call for simplicity an Eastern way of thinking, and the more rule-based and rational character of our Western society. People feel this tension, but there is not enough space in daily work and living conditions to deal with it differently. This creates a lot of tension in society, and especially on an individual level it creates frustration, stress and demotivation. If your boss, or your company, or the procedures have already decided everything for you, then there is little room for creativity. Fortunately, we have some ways out in our 'free time', at least in this part of the world.

The aim of this book is not to achieve scientific correctness as it is understood in this part of the world. I would prefer to share some insights and experiences with readers able to learn from it. A scientifically correct book would contain more references than is desirable, which would guarantee that everybody would accept it, and there would most likely be little criticism of it. But why would you read such a book, if it only repeats what others have already written? Maybe I should label this book as one that attempts to give insight into what is scientific in the first place. There will not be many references to other books (other than for intellectual respect). I will, however, suggest some further reading for the interested reader. The book is discovering, exploratory, with the aim that readers can themselves make sense out of it and identify what is important. Maybe I shall sometimes allow myself some 'poetic licence'. I do use some allegories and symbolic stories. Often I use metaphors in the form of pictures and stories instead of observable facts. My aim in doing so is to write a readable book, usable by everybody who wants to learn and who wants to understand why they feel the tension I mentioned. We talk about a gap between rationality and control on the one hand, and creativity and development on the other hand.

Though this book addresses the learning human, rather more attention is given to the learning manager and the learning teacher and/or researcher. In English at least, we correctly use the term 'teacher' for somebody who attempts to teach. In other languages this is sometimes different. In my native language (Dutch) the word *leraar* is used (this would probably correctly translate as 'the one who allows learning'), in order to refer to somebody who in fact teaches. The correct word, which does not in fact exist, is '*onderwijzer*' (this literally means teacher). Anyway, and in practice, in many languages we often do not correctly distinguish between teaching and learning and related words. We will discuss this later in detail, while talking about knowledge and learning. For the manager (and more generally for anybody who holds a position of responsibility in our society), this book aims to illustrate why we always reinvent the wheel, why we are so keen on power (and control, or should it be the other way round?) and why it is so difficult to share. The rational, control-oriented character of our society gives us the perfect context (and excuse). For the researcher, this book seeks to give insight into why there is so little breakthrough research going on these days. If one searches where others already searched (the word is 're'-search, isn't it?), one should not be surprised to find what others already found. If one would like to find something new, one should search either in a different direction, or with a different pair of glasses. The word 'research' (searching for what has already been searched for) suggests continuing to search in already known directions. In order to allow the reader to acquire the necessary insight (which is the only ground for possible change), some attention is given in the book to both traditional philosophy of science and somewhat more innovative trends. The reason for this is not that this book aims to address that issue, but rather because our epistemological choices are very often the cause for most of what we do and believe on a daily basis. If we aim to better understand the daily practice of 'taking responsibility' (what I will translate further as management), or if we want to understand why science often confirms what we already (commonly) know, we have to pay attention to questions of significance (truth, knowledge, etc.).

We already touched briefly upon the components of significance and understanding, but we should not forget a third important component: the form. While it seems difficult for most managerial thinking to contribute to a 'better world' (a fair world, a world in which more people could enjoy themselves), some forms of artistic expression (literature, poems) deliver added value more easily. Literature and poetry in fact make it much easier for people to learn and, something that is not completely unrelated, those artistic forms are less restricted by rules. It could be 'coincidence'; however, I shall argue later that coincidence does not happen by coincidence. The free format of poetry, for instance, probably allows more space for spirituality and significance but also for understanding. As rational human beings we are somewhat dissociated from this capacity, but see how liberating it is if we manage to share some of our inner feelings, either on paper or with other people. Who has never experienced such liberation?

An impressive poem that perfectly illustrates the modern human's split is Antonio Machado's famous poem (which I have translated):

| | |
|---|---|
| Caminante son tus huellas | Wanderer, your footprints are |
| el camino, y nada mas; | the path, and nothing more; |
| caminante, no hay camino, | Wanderer, there is no path, |
| se hace camino al andar. | it is created as you walk. |
| Al andar se hace camino, | By walking, |
| y al volver la vista atras | you make the path before you, |
| se ve la senda que nunca | and when you look behind |
| se ha de volver a pisar. | you see the path which after you |
| Caminante, no hay camino, | will not be trod again. |
| sino estelas en la mar. | Wanderer, there is no path, |
| | but the ripples on the waters. |

Antonio Machado, Chant XXIX, *Proverbios y cantares*,
Campos de Castilla, 1917

You walk through the desert and you can see the path that you have created, a path that you will never walk again, but that nobody else will ever walk either. That path brought you to where you are and it allowed you to learn what you wanted or needed to learn. The walk has produced its contribution – that is, it has created a lot of experiences. However, the path does not exist; you made it yourself while walking. The walk is important since it gives you experiences, but the path itself is not important. The walk allows everybody to learn, independent of the specific path followed.

But then you turn round and look into the desert. In no way does the path behind you help you to choose which direction to take. The walk can help you, your experiences and your learning can help you, but not the path. And again you will have to create a new path by walking. And again there is no path, because a path gets laid down by walking. That walk is the path of learning. Every path allows learning and everybody learns what they want or are able to learn. Generally validated paths that would always be good do not exist. But that is what we are looking for while identifying methods, techniques and approaches, independent of the experience itself, as if a walk is something that takes place outside ourselves. It refers again to the eternal division between us and what we observe, between the object and the observing subject. On the whole, our society is still convinced (at least implicitly) that this division really exists. That would be a subject on which we would all be able to agree. But do not forget that if we put on rose glasses, the world appears to be rose; it does not really become rose-tinted. If you choose to use glasses that purport to show the world as it objectively is, then that is fine, as long as you do not imagine that indeed the world is then really objective. It is like the fairy tale about the emperor's new clothes. That is what this book attempts to deal with. Why doesn't this objectivity exist and why do we think so strongly, specifically in the West, that this objectivity does exist? What are the consequences of this acceptance?

Does this mean we do not have to do anything or that we are unable to do anything? If you do not know where to go, then any path is a good one. That is what Alice in Wonderland has shown us. When Alice asks the cat which road to take, the Cheshire Cat asks Alice where she wants to go. Alice does not really know, hence the cat can only answer that if you do not know where you want to go, any road is a good one. If you drive a car but you have no idea where to go, you will be stuck at the first roundabout for the rest of your life. Knowing where to go does not necessarily mean that you should also arrive there. Our culture is oriented to first identifying and then optimizing the path, with the aim that everybody can follow the path afterwards. We fix the path, and practice will show where it leads to. Such a fixed path does not allow a lot of space for the 'learning' individual. It is all fixed up front.

What we should decide is where we would like to go and then leave the path as free as possible so that everybody can identify their own most attractive path, ideally using their own learning experiences. We think entirely too much in terms of plans, budgets, rules, controls, without any decent debate about what we would like to realize and what we share as a potential goal. Most debates boil down rather quickly to the identification of a path. But as we have known for a long time: all roads lead to Rome. We seek order, but we get chaos. Often we respond to that chaos with more rules and more order, and very often we indeed get more chaos.

Now that I have introduced the theme of chaos and order, and we have briefly touched upon the 'learning' human, I would like to introduce this latter theme using a poem by Rabindranath Tagore:

> A very great musician came and stayed in our house.
> He made one big mistake.
> He was determined to teach me music,
> and consequently, no learning took place.
> Nevertheless, I did casually pick up from him
> a certain amount of stolen knowledge.
>
> Rabindranath Tagore

Can we teach children how to cross a street? Can we teach children to become a professional soccer player? Can we teach people how to become managers? Can we teach a car driver how to control a skid?

You could teach the rules, and as far as those rules cover all aspects of mastering a particular competency, you should be able to teach that competency. However, that would mean that the competency is not in fact a competency (or, if it is, it is an extremely simple one). A competency is seldom based on simple 'rules' rather, it is acquired via much exercise and experience. In order to become a good soccer player, one really has to play a lot of soccer. A coach could be a mirror for the athlete, but rules cannot. If you would like to open your own shop, I could explain some basic rules to you and tell you about some of my or other people's experiences, but you would eventually have to experience for yourself how to set the shop up and how to deal with your customers. Coaching helps, but can never replace one's own learning. Here again we see the path that you will have to lay down in walking. By practising, you will have to find out how to make music. The metaphor of the path, the exploration and how to deal with experiences that are always new is a strong one, and will regularly reappear throughout the book.

In our daily life, we want to limit as much as possible the risk of such a journey. That is what we have control mechanisms for and why we use rules. If we leave on a trip, we take a travel guide. We check the car and take out some travel insurance. If we do not choose a completely organized holiday (control, the fixed path), we at least book the hotels. There is nothing wrong with this approach, but don't be surprised when you fail to discover the unexpected charm of the country. Most probably you will end up surrounded by your compatriots (or people of related nationalities), in organized places (five-star hotels, luxury camp sites, etc.) and you will say: nice country indeed, but we had a lot of fun with our neighbours or the travel company. Again, there is nothing wrong with this, but don't be surprised not to discover something that has not yet been discovered by others. On holiday, we are in a 're-search' mode: we search what others have already searched and hence we will find what others have already found.

It is a choice. Once the choice has been made, we should not be surprised by the consequences. When Mark Twain had acquired all the analytical knowledge necessary for becoming a pilot on the Mississippi, he discovered that the river had lost all its charm and beauty. There is always something that dies. An important focus on analytical understanding does not leave a lot of space for paramount impressions (such as what it is like to travel down the Mississippi). What is less known in daily life, but more in the performing arts, is that each time something new also gets created. Every piece of art is an artistic creation. It is this continuous re-creation (to be understood in the sense of creating anew each time and not doing the same thing again) that will lead to the essence of learning and to what a learning human can do in order to progress out of chaos.

I would like to add another metaphor to the travel metaphor developed earlier, and that is the one of the motorbike. For the purpose of this chapter (and only for that purpose), I would like to define the motorbike as a prototype of intelligent technology that can be almost completely controlled. The combination of this 'wonder of technology' with the travelling metaphor gives an interesting dimension that is brilliantly described by Pirsig in *Zen and the Art of Motorcycle Maintenance* (1974, p. 12).

You see things vacationing on a motorcycle in a way that is completely different from any other. In a car you're always in a compartment, and because you're used to it you don't realize that through that car window everything you see is just more TV. You're a passive observer and it is all moving by you boringly in a frame.

On a cycle the frame is gone. You're completely in contact with it all. You're *in* the scene, not just watching it anymore, and the sense of presence is overwhelming.

The manager in the pilot's seat (of the plane, or the car) is the idea we usually have when thinking about management. The pilot plots the course, and then it is executed mechanistically and with high precision. We develop rules and procedures in order to also be able to delegate 'difficult' things and afterwards to be able to control them. We construct a difficult control panel (the French call it a *tableau de bord*) and we get our appreciation out of the quality of the control. Just look into the cockpit of a plane; it is clear that a good pilot (manager) really needs to be a walking computer. The tremendous joy and pleasure of piloting is no longer part of management. Therefore, we indeed regularly (too regularly) use the automatic pilot. Mark Twain, being a Mississippi pilot, does not appreciate the Mississippi as a continuous discovery any more. If we want to take our development seriously, we will have to continue learning, though. Control, based on a good cockpit, can be taken over by almost anyone, after decent training in using the instruments of the cockpit. Flying without instruments, arriving at airports (or even on fields) that are not discovered yet, needs other skills and competencies. Significance (why are we doing this?) and form (creation out of nothing) become significant success factors in that case. And independent of all this: is it more fun to make the everyday crossing by ferry from Marseilles to Corsica, or to explore the Atlantic coast in a sailing boat?

Do you recognize all this? Let's take another example, to paraphrase from Pirsig's book. My friend and I are on a motorcycle trip. It is still rather cold in the morning and after a short morning trip we have stopped at a café in order have something warm to drink. Half an hour later we leave again and discover that my friend's motorbike does not seem to be very willing to start. I suggest that the choke might help. Surprise, and a question about whether this is mentioned in the manual. Yes, if the motor is cold, one should use the choke while starting the bike. But the engine is not cold, is it? Yes it is; we have been in the café for half an hour. *But why doesn't the manual say so?*

Xerox did lots of research into the behaviour of sales reps (people who repair copying machines) and in particular why they so infrequently use the manuals, which are updated twice a year and mailed around the world (at a high cost). To their surprise, the answer was very simple. Either the problem is so easy that you do not need a manual; or the problem is complicated and then it is not in the manual.

> 'Sometime look at a novice workman or a bad workman and compare his expression with that of a craftsman whose work you know is excellent and you'll see the difference. The craftsman isn't ever following a single line of instruction. He's making decisions as he goes along. For that reason he'll be absorbed and attentive to what he's doing even though he doesn't deliberately contrive this. His motions and the machine are in a kind of harmony. He isn't following any set of written instructions because the nature of the material at hand determines his thoughts and motions, which simultaneously change the nature of the material at hand. . . .'
>
> 'Sounds like art', the [art] instructor says.
>
> (p. 167)

This rather sums up the problem of our time. The reach of human knowledge is so wide that we have all specialized in something, and the distance between specialists only increases. Specialization (in-depth knowledge) often comes at the price of failing to broaden one's knowledge and views, sharing, meeting. Isn't knowledge management precisely the management of the 'holes between disciplines'? Western civilization has smartly introduced the subject–object division as a kind of answer, but that does not mean that such division necessarily exists. Is a person ill only if they have a fever? Or is the fever only the consequence and do we need to search for the cause? Is it possible that less favourable social conditions can make people sick? How can we support general practitioners in our Western, symptom-oriented medical science in their role as first-line help? Somewhat more experienced (older) medical sciences, like the increasingly popular Ayurveda (of Indian origin), have different answers.

This book does not aim to search for Eastern wisdom. Many others have done that. On the contrary, those of us who live in a Western society will have to acquire an insight and an understanding about our own society, given the culture and history we are part of, and in which we live daily. But as Columbus did, we want to discover the East by going West. If he had continued to search for the Eastern countries by going in an easterly direction (doesn't that sound familiar and logical?), Columbus would never have discovered America.

> [W]hat struck me for the first time was the agreement of those [computer] manuals with the spectator attitude I had seen in the [motorcycle repair] shop. These were spectator manuals. It was built into the format of them. Implicit in every line is the idea that 'Here is the machine, isolated in time and in space from everything else in the universe. It has no relationship to you, you have no relationship to it, other than to turn certain switches, maintain voltage levels, check for error conditions . . .' and so on.
>
> (p. 34)

Not by accident, Pirsig refers to the pragmatic philosopher John Dewey. In his book, Pirsig pays a lot of attention to the environment with its ever-changing processes and how one could have the slightest idea whether everything is still going well. Dewey does the same in his extended work. Isn't usability a good measurement for quality?

There are no perfect parts, either for a motorbike or for anything else, and there never will be. But if you really get as far as those instruments can bring you, then marvellous things happen, and you 'fly along God's road with a speed that you can easily call magic'.

This book aims to give an insight into the underlying reasons why all this is so difficult for Western managers, and people. Suggestions are given concerning the art and form of management. But the reader is the only one who can create its significance, 'laying down the path in walking'.

# 2 Paradigms, truth and postmodernism

- What can we learn from the philosophers of science?
- Postmodernism in fact comes from architecture
- An extended taxonomy of the theories of the philosophy of science applied to management
- The wider view: a vision of humankind and the holistic world

We often think that philosophers deal with philosophical problems. Of course they do. But it is not that simple. In the first place, what are philosophical problems? Are they less existent and real than other problems? Are they of a different nature? As in other social sciences, philosophers thought at a certain moment that in order to be a real philosopher, one should be educated as a philosopher. Hence, are philosophical problems disconnected from reality? In the meantime, philosophy became a discipline in its own right, which has not always been the case in history. Among the philosophers, philosophers of science deal with the conditions under which knowledge can be judged trustworthy. In our everyday language, that is what allows us to understand what is right or wrong. Philosophy cannot be seen independently from the aim of discovering the final truth, a general understanding of values, and philosophers have oriented themselves towards concepts rather than towards empirical research. Some even pretend that philosophy is searching for knowledge, but many other scientists would doubt that. Both points of view are no doubt correct.

Philosophers of science research things we call epistemologies. An epistemology is a theory, or an attitude about 'reality', the sources and limitations of knowledge. It creates a framework that aims to transform intuition into knowledge, and in doing so, it creates expressions that are generally true. There is, however, a previous stage, in which philosophers accept what exists and what is necessary in order to be able to develop a theory. Within the framework of science, we call that an ontology: that is, a theory of the things that need to exist, or the conditions that need to be fulfilled, in order for the theory to be proved, to be true. Maybe these definitions are somewhat difficult, but they are also very important for the researcher or the manager who is interested in working with science or comprehension.

Why do we need to be interested in the questions of the philosophers of science, or, more generally, why should we be interested in philosophical issues? Because what we accept as true to begin with has an important impact on what we perceive, and on the research for truth and knowledge afterwards. If we believe that the world is the centre of the universe, we are going to research 'knowing' that all the planets circle around the Earth. In general, we will even find evidence that confirms our (wrong) hypothesis (what we could call a research hypothesis). Hence, the starting point of our investigation has an important impact on what we can find. If we are searching for something by the light of a lamp, so that we can see, but what we are looking for was lost elsewhere, then we should not be surprised not to find it. Now, before you say 'that is evident' too quickly, I would like to draw your attention to the fact that this is precisely what we often do in scientific research.

For instance, we believe that a promotional campaign has an influence on the buying behaviour of people, and indeed we find a strong correlation. Other variables that we find less interesting are of course not present in our equations, and therefore cannot show any effect. There is nothing wrong with that, so long as we do not claim that the research 'proves' in a scientific (and therefore correct) manner that there is a positive correlation between campaign and sales results. The only thing one can say is that these results are correct for this particular study, and given the problem as it was defined (in the absence of certain possible variables). It would be a mistake to extrapolate this particular study to a theory that claims general validity. A researcher researches a specific problem in a scientific way and afterwards extrapolates it into a general theory. Reducing a problem to something smaller and easier to study is not an error, but then it becomes impossible to draw more general conclusions.

Let us use the metaphor of coloured spectacles again. If we look at the world through rose-tinted glasses, the world will appear to be rose. That is what we really observe. But, of course, it is not reality. A blue pair of glasses would give the idea and also the observation that the world is blue. And that is not correct either. Philosophers of science are interested in the correct representation of the world, but also each manager is in search of a correct representation of the behaviour of markets.

The metaphor of the glasses shows that the choice made when starting research determines what we see and find in the research. Each person has, through their education, their schooling and their culture, a vision about how to do research and, more widely, about what truth would be.

What are the different views on science and how do they influence our thinking and observation? The latter, the way we observe, is indeed even more important for us. How do philosophical choices have an impact on how to undertake research, what we call the methodological consequences? How do the choices determine the way of observing, for instance, the company or its management processes?

In this chapter we are not going to simply explore the philosophy of science. Many books have been published on that subject. Rather, it is important to position oneself in the ideas of the major schools of thought, within a certain social context and with a particular social aim. I would say that the chapter attempts to reinforce the importance of philosophy of science for social systems and, in particular, in order to improve management.

Any person and any manager *per se* is developing an image of science that fits the temporal and geographical context. Does it make sense to talk about an 'Islamic way of doing research', as some books suggest? The scientists of medieval times certainly had a different view of science from the one we have today. Science without any context, as one could say *ins blaue hinein*, done haphazardly, doesn't make a lot of sense, and in practice is impossible. With a contextual embedding of research we are assuring a kind of thinking, an intellectual reference framework which will allow us to judge the true value of any new research (or its application). Just as with philosophy in general, the philosophy of science is embedded in the current sociology of its society and in the history of that same society. The different view of science in medieval times as compared with today illustrates this clearly. Another illustration is the attitude of a pharmaceutical researcher working for a pharmaceutical giant like Glaxo, compared to that of a researcher working for the WHO. The Ayurvedic medical approach (a classical Indian medical approach), is different in diagnosis, focus (it is holistic) and therapy from what we consider as medical treatment in the Western world. These different starting points cause a different attitude and a different treatment.

Different images of science often remain very underexposed, or, worse still, many people are not even aware of those differences. Therefore, it is very difficult to compare different research, since each piece of research could have been undertaken within different reference frameworks – sometimes radically different frameworks.

In this chapter I shall give an overview of different philosophical schools that, because they lie within a particular historical framework, generate different images of science: I have labelled the result a taxonomy. Within this context, a taxonomy is nothing more than an overview of different ideas, but a rather broader overview than is often found in the literature.

Let us start with an overview of what we classically consider the philosophy of science. Then, we will take a look into theories that originate from architecture and the arts and that have gradually entered the area of research methodologies that we often label postmodern. We will investigate what neurobiologists have researched concerning cognition and the functioning of the mind. A last source of input is the developments in artificial intelligence and their contribution to the understanding of thinking and learning. Working with 'learning' artificial intelligence, one is rapidly confronted with the fundamentals of what thinking and truth are.

As learning individuals we cannot avoid what I would like to call the dilemma of the researcher – though it is not limited to researchers. If you have the feeling that we are going too deeply into academic research, it is enough to replace 'researcher' by 'searcher' or even 'learner'. What is this dilemma of the researcher?

A researcher needs to work in harmony with the environment – the context, such as it is known to the researcher, and such as it appears to be in society. The researcher is part of a socializing process (within a network of peers) within social, intellectual and political traditions, values and norms. In order for the researcher to have their research validated afterwards, they have to work within a prevailing context that allows such eventual validation (by their peers). 'Validation' is a protected word that already presumes a certain conception of, and choice within, science. Let us for the time being use the word 'visualization', instead of validation. In order to validate their research, the researcher is confronted with a dilemma that forces them to make choices. This does not need to be wrong, or even very important, provided the researcher is aware of it.

The 'pair of glasses' we put on, the choices that we make, will determine what we are able to see and hence what we are going to find as a result of our research.

Let us detail these problematic choices. First of all there is what the researcher accepts as ethical. Is the researcher responsible for the possible (mis)use of the results of their research? As a further consequence, is the researcher responsible for human behaviour and human dignity?

Can we only research the observable behaviour of humans, without considering their emotions? To what extent is what is observed due to the reference framework of the researcher? The political context within which the researcher operates also forces the researcher to make choices. Unfortunately, lots of examples exist where mainly totalitarian regimes use 'scientific research' in order to justify inhuman behaviour or to glorify the system. What role does a researcher want to play and how does this influence their research results?

Another problematic choice is the relationship with the unforeseeable. To what extent are we able to, and do we want to, exclude this from our research? Is this a problem, or rather an opportunity? Finally, the researcher also has budgetary constraints, or time limitations. Resources are limited and choices need to be made.

All these are problematic choices that play a role in research, but also, consequently, in the results of that research. None of the choices is good or bad, but they all have consequences.

Now let us consider the last dilemma. What epistemological choices does the searcher (and not the re-searcher), the learner, make concerning the subject of truth, the observation, the quantitative nature of things, the possibility to generalize? These are all problematic choices in which there is again no good and bad, but certainly all choices have their impact. Certain scientific ideas are typical of a certain time period. What interests us here is the importance of those choices and their consequences for what is good research and the choice of the research methods adopted. Translated into management, we refer here to how we want to consider management processes if we want to improve them. What do we accept as being the best and how can we measure and compare? Next, the question is how to control those processes, how to manage them, and, if possible, which variables to influence.

# What can we learn from the philosophers of science?

The philosophy of science is a discipline that became independent of its object of study, namely the practice of science. It is not very old, though philosophers such as Plato or Aristotle, for instance, dealt explicitly with science-related problems. Philosophy itself is as old as the world, and scientific investigation has always been very close to philosophy in the past. In the beginning, philosophy was positioned as a 'proto-science'. When other fields became increasingly important, such as astronomy or later psychology, the different domains started to shift away. The next step that each of the (sub)domains made was to develop its own scientific tradition. In general, sciences are a product of philosophical practice. It is interesting to explore the question of when the philosophy of science became a separate discipline and the 'why' and 'how' of that. That is what I would like to explore next.

Before the seventeenth century, say before René Descartes (1596–1650) and Galilei Galileo (1564–1642), the Church, or let us say religion more generally, was the seat of science in the world. In certain parts of the world this is still the case. Science aimed to justify religion. Just remember the struggle that Galileo had to convince the world that the Sun is at the centre of what is consequently called our solar system and that the world rotates around the Sun. The opposite idea, of the Sun and planets revolving around the Earth, was comfortable for the Church, as it could help the Church keep its power, or, even worse, justify the Church's power. In that period science dealt with what was commonly accepted.

From the seventeenth century onwards, Descartes launched rationalism to a degree that was unknown before: 'I think, therefore I am.' It was the beginning of modern philosophy: thought itself was defined as the subject of philosophy. Science became increasingly interested in experimentation. It might seem strange to the researcher of the twenty-first century, but the researcher in those days was involved and responsible. He took responsibility for the direction of research he was undertaking, for his involvement and all that was not under discussion. It was accepted that the researcher researches on the basis of his values, his beliefs and his hypothesis. This period is identified by what we know today as a typical Newtonian concept: time and space are fixed, known and absolute. (Much later, Einstein caused a revolution by showing that time and space are relative, hence no absolute truth exists. What exists is a relationship with a subset of the whole world.) At that time, an important interest in quantitative research developed. Therefore, Cartesian thinking is often referred to as an approach whereby everything should be measurable. This more rational approach to science was considered a reaction against a more metaphysical religious thinking. Often we forget that this metaphysical approach was at least holistic, but more by accident than on purpose. Since we could not yet separate correctly, we considered the whole. Cartesian thinking does not reject the existence of God, but does want to give a more profound backing to metaphysical thinking.

If we can distance ourselves, from the religious goals that were behind research prior to the seventeenth century, we observe the contours of a discussion about science that is still going on:

- On the one hand, we have researchers who consider reality to be essentially a holistic concept: only within the whole can a part be studied. All depends on everything, and hence one cannot deduce simple causal relationships from a larger whole without doing injustice to that whole. All kinds of observations, even highly subjective ones, can be valuable inputs for research.
- On the other hand, we have researchers who feel that this approach is too metaphysical and too vague. They believe only what can be measured 'objectively', and believe that from those observations general laws can be deduced. Even if these laws represent only part of reality, they are still useful, since generally applicable. This last point is of course argued against by the other group. What does it mean to say 'generally applicable' if one only talks about a small part of a more general truth? For this group of researchers, repetition and control of research is crucial.

Holistic researchers do not argue that one can reduce reality in order to study it. Holism also accepts that a whole is constructed out of many smaller parts, but it considers that those smaller parts create, via interaction, more than the sum of the separate parts. According to holistic thinkers, the problem with reductionism occurs when afterwards conclusions are drawn concerning problems larger than those particularly studied. They argue against drawing conclusions on a whole on the basis of studies of parts. There is nothing wrong with a detailed study of the stomach, say. A stomach can indeed hurt a lot. It is certainly possible to find remedies against a stomach that hurts. The problem appears if one wants to draw conclusions concerning the general health of a patient based only on research on the stomach. For instance, it is not automatically true that if the stomach is cured, the person will feel better.

That still needs to be observed and proved. A reductionist is going to try to cure the stomach by researching on the stomach and immediately around it. A holist will research the entire body and even external influencing factors in search for a disequilibrium that could have arisen in the body (the body considered as being a whole). People are more than the correct operations of all their organs.

As already suggested, the relativity theory of Einstein came as a real break point. It became clear that absolute observation did not exist. It equally became very clear that in order to compare different theories, one should use different methods. Moreover, in 1931 Gödel (1906–78) proved his theorem, which opened up a kind of Pandora's box without his really wishing it to. According to Gödel, no axiomatic system can ever validate or reject all possible hypotheses. In other words, there will always be a hypothesis about which we cannot say or, better, prove anything. Hence, independent of the detail of an axiomatic system, it will never be able to give the full truth.

For mathematicians, this was an important theorem. It took a certain while before the theorem became known and 'appreciated' by mathematicians. Also, though Gödel would probably not be considered a philosopher of science, his discovery has had an impact in that domain too.

In the way Gödel proved his theorem, he used a concept called self-reference to a remarkable degree – an interesting and powerful concept, but also a dangerous one. To simplify somewhat, the concept says that every system can, and has to, create its own reference framework, used by all elements of the system referring to each other, with the aim that the system operates more optimally, but inside rather closed boundaries. Only if one is inside the system does this self-referential framework make sense. Those who are outside (say, for example, clients) no longer understand the system. We could easily make reference here to corporate culture or language, politicians' language, etc. (see Chapter 4 for more detail).

Around 1920–30 a philosophical movement existed called logical positivism (the Vienna Circle). Most of the researcher-members worked in the areas of mathematics, physics and the like. For them the credo was that only what was measurable made sense for science. They based their approach on Descartes' rationalism and Bacon's and Hume's empiricism. Rationality, clarity, measurability and consistence were the keywords. This approach went *ligna recta* against the metaphysical controversy of the previous period. The criterion of verification is central for them. What cannot be verified does not exist for science; it is too speculative. The solution is encompassed in the method. Research should be based on axiomatic systems in concrete, and it should use a language as clear as mathematics. Unfortunately, it was Gödel himself, a member of the Vienna Circle, who proved the limits of this approach.

For them, scientists made the discoveries, and philosophers were there to justify those discoveries. For the first time (probably) we seem to observe a clear-cut separation between philosophers and scientists, though implicitly that divide had already existed for many years. This empiric and positivist approach of science was dominant until the 1960s, but in fact has continued to be mainstream up to the present. Under pressure of the rise of Nazi Germany, many researchers left Austria and Germany in order to settle in the United States. There they joined and reinforced what is known as analytical philosophy. Research in the United States is still very different (more quantitative and positivist) from what is seen in Europe. Certainly in the (applied) social sciences, this difference is very remarkable. But fortunately, also in the United States, we have known some dissonant voices, such as for example John Dewey (whom we shall deal with later).

Popper (1902–94) is no doubt the philosopher (of science) who is most often cited. He continued in that positivist and empirical orientation, but nevertheless developed his theory as a critique on the Vienna Circle. Critical rationalism (as we call his school of thought) is as crucial for a theory as the attempts that have been made to reject it. The aim of science is to falsify existing knowledge, which allows science to progress. Only deduction is acceptable. Induction is too vague for him, and not scientific.

For Popper there exists no context of discovery. Science is a product in itself, and its quality should be guaranteed. Popper's epistemology does not recognize a knowing subject. His epistemology creates or reinforces the division between object and subject that is predominant in most of our scientific work. Science should be something that is outside of the researcher, just as good management should be something outside the manager. Increasingly we see 'alternative' research, however, without questioning whether this is based on a different epistemological choice supporting research in societal problems.

'Until proven to the contrary' is an expression based on Popper's theory. Empirical value of a theory depends on the possibility of falsification. The more you try to falsify a theory (without success), the more it is valid. Every theory is a theory in progress, waiting to be falsified. The moment you falsify a theory, you reduce it to a lesser theory (one valid in fewer cases). To keep the validity of a theory, without changing it, you cannot do anything other than scale it down more and more. Simple theories, therefore, survive longer. The search for causality is therefore a consequence, rather than a goal in itself. The search for causality, already known in logical positivism, was strongly supported by Popper.

For Popper, scientific discovery went from the known to the unknown. Every researcher must use the same methods, including in the social sciences. But Popper was also self-critical. The idea that society should be predictable was unacceptable to him. Predestination was for Popper a serious limit to freedom and democracy. He favoured a democracy which was as much scientific as it was political.

A number of methodological consequences ensued. The mechanism of deduction is the acceptable approach. Everything is contained within a framework of falsification/verification. Something which is falsified cannot be correct. If you have a counter-example, the whole theory is reduced to a simpler theory, or must be revised. For the social sciences, that has serious consequences. You start with hypotheses to test which you try later to falsify, but often rather to validate. In practice, however, you first of all do exploratory research and only at the moment when you know what you can validate do you define the hypotheses. In fact, this on-the-ground approach is a constructive approach. Research is scientific only if it is informed by a theory.

Then Kuhn introduced his paradigm theory from a historical perspective. He examined existing theories through the lens of the history of science. According to Kuhn, the sciences are part of the historical context. In fact, he said that science can even be an 'act': a particular type of research may be more appropriate in a current political context and research institutes which are close to political power receive larger grants. In his view it is not the theory itself which makes the difference, but rather social acceptance of the theory. This takes the form of a comparison. Editors decide whether a paper is worthy of the label 'scientific'. If you have a sufficient number of publications in respected journals, you climb the academic ladder.

For him, the context of discovery and that of justification are not far apart. Methodological rules are never obligatory, but they remain the choice. A consequence is that in the different sciences we use different vocabulary. A truth is therefore only a local truth. It is a known phenomenon in sociology that different groups use the same language differently (compare, for example, the Dutch of Dutch people and that of

Flemish people). This also means that this theory supports a growing diversification of the different sciences. This is not favourable to a holistic approach. The mono-disciplinarian does not exist only in teaching, but also in the world of management.

For Kuhn, scientific groups are more important than paradigms: paradigms are too much a 'self-fulfilling prophecy'. Since they exist, of course they are correct. Outside normal science, theories can degenerate, which eventually leads to a revolutionary epoch in science.

Finally Lakatos tried to regain the equilibrium between Popper's and Kuhn's theories. Lakatos, more liberal than Popper, is an advocate of 'trial-and-error' approaches.

In fact, what we learn is that scientific method, almost by definition, does not really allow innovation in scientific research. This development can only advance in very limited steps and in fact always in the same direction. All research centres adhere to theories of this school of thinking, often without the least dissonant idea. These theories also led to a specific understanding of what is scientific, which we then tried to extend to management and other public functions (law, politics, etc.). The difficulty therefore is to marry an innovative approach with something which is nevertheless well founded and rigorous, always keeping the idea of achieving a goal in mind.

In the social sciences in particular, there were vigorous reactions towards logical positivism. There were principally two types of critical thinking. First of all, there is what we can call pragmatism, or symbolic interactionism, represented by, among others, John Dewey. The Frankfurt School, along with the likes of Marcuse, was very oriented towards the responsibility of the researcher and was, in fact, rather socialist inspired.

Pragmatism is opposed to logical positivism, especially with regard to the fact that rationalism supposes a strict division between the subject and the object. In practice, rationalism means that a number of independent observers all observe the same thing, independently of their feelings, experiences, etc. This way you can justify the possibility of doing research which has general value. But one only needs to consider two people seeing the same car accident and how they report it. Usually the two stories are very different. People colour their observations with their feelings, their own experiences, etc. In fact, many ideas in science and management are based on this separation between subject and object, which in practice does not seem to hold true.

Among the pragmatics, Mead and Dewey played an important role. In classical science, the relationship between cause and effect is explained by understanding, predictions and trials. Pragmatics is based on the use of a criterion to decide the subject of the truth. Something is good if you can use it for something. A process of change in a company is good, since it makes the employees happy or procedures more efficient. Pragmatics accept that there is no research independent of values. Do we really think that Organon is going to put the same effort into finding remedies for diseases in poor countries as in rich ones? There are many treatable diseases for which not enough effort is made. The criterion used is often very straightforward.

According to pragmatics, behaviour is often based on rules which hold true in a social context, and which are seen as symbols (for example, wealth or class).

Another form of critique is given by the Frankfurt School (Adorno, Horkheimer, Marcuse, Habermas), but no doubt their work would take us too far, and is not exactly appropriate to this book. What is important is that the Frankfurt School follows a rather holistic logic. Once we understand someone's point of view, we can better understand their research. Dialogue and communication are much-appreciated research methods for this school. An 'action researcher', someone who takes part in the process of research and even in the process of change, must explicitly show their position for everyone to understand their remarks and research results. This school recognizes conflict as a mode of functioning: in fact, we are speaking about conflict between the real world and the world of theories, or systems. For the Frankfurt School, integrity is important.

Doubtless, Western Europe is very focused – even too focused – on rationalism and positivism, which means that its researchers deny themselves the power to advance more innovative research. In general, we only look a little further along the path of what has already been researched. We look for the method, therefore the certainty, so we already want to be sure of finding what we are looking for. It is convenient to look where we have already looked, since the results are known. The reviews of academic journals confirm that this is the case. However, this mechanism is not a good basis for innovative research. Does research look for the path it is already taking? (I am making reference here to Antonio Machado's famous poem: 'Caminate, no hay camino/Se hace camino al andar'). Is it not chaos and the unknown which create the entropy necessary for discovery instead of 're'-search? Then, notably, we come back to the theory of complexity, which will be very instrumental. Academic research unfortunately has a system of self-referencing, with a common jargon to facilitate the debate that is incomprehensible to outsiders. Is that why companies more and more are organizing their own research, instead of leaning on university research centres? The science of management comes back into conflict with the skill of managing.

Often, the scientific approach is only interesting if it can be labelled 'independent' and therefore 'objective'. That way, scientific choice becomes self-evident. There are, therefore, two separate worlds: the holistic world we live in; and the rational world we use if we need authority and, therefore, distance. This schism in our society, even in our thinking, is not entirely without danger. How does the holistic individual (given that we cannot change) submit to all that? Human beings are looking for a soul and a consciousness of reality, and since they do not find them, they are going to look for them in external factors of daily life. Unfortunately, these are often rather extremist external factors. We see, on the other hand, a movement in quite a few segments of society towards a more holistic approach – for example, in medicine. Western culture is nevertheless too anchored in positivist thinking to be easily able to change.

How can we break this vicious circle? A system based on giving and obeying orders is in strong contrast to a system based on self-organization. 'Orders' and 'organization' thinking are based on very positivist ideas. Later on we will look at the fact that self-realization can only be achieved in self-organization, both at individual and at organizational levels. The strength of an organization remains nevertheless in the hands of individuals. Without individuals, there is no network of agents. This does not at all mean that organizations are without value, or that organizations, finally, cannot learn. It does mean that the strength behind organizations' value and ability to learn is comprised of individuals with their drive, their engagement, their conviction, etc.

It is interesting, at this stage, to dive into 'postmodern' theories again.

## Postmodernism in fact comes from architecture

Postmodernism appeared in the 1950s and 1960s in reaction to aesthetic modernism. Before that, the term was already known but was used more in relation to nihilism, in the style of Nietzsche. As a backlash to modernism in art, postmodernism is an important movement against this modernism. In the 1970s we started to see a movement against architectural modernism. In postmodern literature there are many details but the lack of a general leitmotif running through books. Proust's *A la recherche du temps perdu* is not really appreciated by postmodernists. In the postmodern novel, what is important is the facts (diverse) and the linking of these facts. All of a sudden an action can come and go. The novels are perhaps even realistic. Louis Paul Boon, known for his realist novels, with the theme of social injustice induced by the economic system, also takes particular interest in coincidence, sundry facts, etc.

Because modernism is well implanted in our society, postmodernism is seen in quite a few areas of society. Since the 1980s, philosophers have become interested in postmodernism. It could be said that the beginning, in France, came by way of the post-structuralists. They reacted against rationalism, utopianism and the tendency to base everything on a scientific approach. Well-known names are Derrida, Foucault, Deleuze and Lyotard. The last philosopher we see appearing in books about the philosophy of science, however, is Feyerabend.

Feyerabend said that the practice of science is in strong contrast to the theory. He spoke almost exclusively about the hard sciences. His argument is that all the important scientific discoveries (those of Einstein, Galileo, etc.) could never have been made if the researchers had followed the laws of science. Feyerabend suggests that if we want to find scientific innovation it has to be organized in a non-conventional manner. In fact, one can see the same thing in companies. Those who attack a new market experimentally are those who are still around (for example, in Russia ten years ago). The survivors were those who dared to follow the untrodden paths instead of sticking to existing theories (about management). By following the rules of the theoretical game you would never manage, for example, to do business in Russia.

According to Feyerabend, it is rather the non-experts who find new developments, often going against what is generally accepted in contemporary science. If science is to make sense, it is, in fact, rather anarchistic. The only principle which allows progress is that 'anything goes'. Science, therefore, has to discover, to explore, to go against. This does not mean in any case that it is not necessary to be very precise in a scientific approach. The theories that survive the longest (such as the Sun rotating around the Earth) do so because people continue to think within the existing scientific rules of their time. For the purposes of this book, we can content ourselves with that. Evidently, to understand the modernist–postmodernist debate better, it is necessary to look harder at those who oppose such theories.

Translating Feyerabend's ideas into a methodological approach, we can see here the more constructivist approaches, such as those defended by Le Moigne. Postmodern theory, or constructivist theory, can be translated into a scientific approach by what I like to call the sciences of design, or the 'active' sciences. So, research and management development are activities to carry out with rigour, but they must also be useful for the company which commissions them. Rigour means being accepted in a framework to be defined (for example, the academic world). Useful means that the result must, in fact, deliver something better than what was known before.

A scientific approach in management therefore has the goal of creating useful things. In practice, that takes us back to an approach of building and improving, so we speak about the paradigm of design. We often see the consequences of changes, improvements, etc. in a very precise situation. Often a number of successive cases are resolved in a step-by-step approach.

In parallel with other sciences, complementary developments could be observed. Neuropsychologists develop ideas around the non-existence of the division between an object and a subject. This evidently has consequences in neurobiological developments. The generally accepted rules of neurobiological colonies seem no longer valid. In physics, the theory of complexity is studied, the behaviour of dynamic and non-linear systems. Despite the two twentieth-century revolutions, relativity and quantum mechanics, the thinking of physics is still for the most part Newtonian. We still accept that time and space will be a given which is known and which one can manipulate. Researchers like Ilya Prigogine have developed a completely different approach. In fact, there is a contradiction 'in terminus': it is the rational approaches which illustrate the solid foundations of postmodernism.

The discoveries in neurobiology (that were known as radical constructivism), as well as those in physics give an explanation of the fact that the positivist approaches seem a little artificial in the social sciences. If we try to put together all the observations we have, we could arrive at a new paradigm, one that would allow the manager to act in a fashion more responsible to themselves and their immediate environment. How and why should we be 'learners' in an environment where, manifestly, order leads to chaos?

A paradigm is nothing but a pair of glasses. According to the pair we put on, we see the world through the colour of those glasses. In our case we want to be conscious of what colour the glasses we put on are. This allows us to better understand, relativize and communicate. The problem is that often people are not even conscious of the fact that they are wearing a pair of glasses. The (scientific) culture is not necessarily a known and conscious context.

## An extended taxonomy of the theories of the philosophy of science applied to management

In summary, I would like to propose an extended taxonomy of the theories of the philosophy of science, applied to management (Table 2.1). The table, based on the previous development, contains some approaches which would not classically be taken up in comparable tables. Perhaps one could call it a multidisciplinary taxonomy which, in my opinion, would allow us to progress in management research.

Table 2.1 *My taxonomy of philosophy of science*

| Historical origin | Philosophical theories | Design consequences |
| --- | --- | --- |
| Philosophy | Logical positivism (Vienna Circle) | Deduction |
| | Critical rationalism (Popper) | Induction |
| | Kuhn's paradigm theory | Empiricism |
| | Lakatos theory | Hypothesis testing |
| | Symbolic interactionism | Qualitative research |
| | Critical theories | |
| | Pragmatics (Dewey) | |
| Architecture | Feyerabend's chaos theory | Design paradigm (van Aken) |
| Arts | Postmodern theories (Derrida, | Social construction of reality |
| Usefulness as a criterion | Apostel, Foucault, Deleuze) | Design norms |
| Neurobiology | Radical constructivism (Maturana, Mingers) | Dynamic re-creation |
| | Autopoiesis (Varela) | Emergence of object and subject |
| | Self-reference (Gödel) | Local (contextual) validity |
| Cognitive artificial intelligence | Paradigm of mind (Franklin, Kim) | Adaptive systems |
| | | Implicit learning |

The goal is not to proclaim the least validity for this taxonomy. It is nothing more than a representation of the research of the extent of our thinking. I am consciously searching above and beyond what is accepted today.

## The wider view: a vision of humankind and the holistic world

We have looked at, up until now, a lot of theories, thanks to which the reader can perhaps no longer see the wood for the trees. But these are only a fraction of the ideas which are blossoming in almost all of the sciences and social discussions. In addition, there are numerous religious or esoteric theories which give the impression of holism, or which do not exist, or have a thousand faces. Is there a common notion of holism? Has anyone ever tried to bring all the theories together? Perhaps it is evident there should be all sorts of critiques here. Do not forget that, for me, as long as it progresses things, I am interested.

I willingly make reference here to one of Ken Wilber's concepts which is, to my way of thinking, very handy and usable. He visualizes something which we could call different dimensions of the image of the holistic world. Figure 2.1 gives a summary of Wilber's concept. The top two quadrants make reference to the individual level. The lower two quadrants refer to the collective level. The quadrants on the left have to do with the internalization of the human being (or processes, or things), while the quadrants on the right examine, let us say, the mechanical part (the external). A holistic image is obtained, according to Wilber, if all the quadrants receive sufficient attention. He labels these quadrants the 'I' quadrant, the 'we' quadrant, the 'it' quadrant, the 'its' quadrant. All the quadrants have to live to be able to achieve a life, an observation, a piece of research, a holistic interpretation.

In the top right quadrant we study external phenomena, for example how the brain functions, and so we naturally reduce it to very specific parts, like atoms, the classical reductionism. This partial vision is not completely mistaken, but there is a reaction to it in saying that understanding the functioning of a specific atom does not allow us to understand the functioning of the whole (human consciousness).

What we call, at the heart of science, a global approach, is found in the lower right quadrant; that is, nothing more than one of the four dimensions of holism. Here one can think of the systemic approaches (mechanical), of ecological concepts, sustainable development, etc.

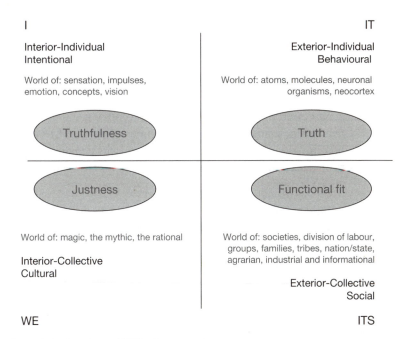

I
Interior-Individual
Intentional

World of: sensation, impulses,
emotion, concepts, vision

Truthfulness

IT
Exterior-Individual
Behavioural

World of: atoms, molecules, neuronal
organisms, neocortex

Truth

Justness

Functional fit

World of: magic, the mythic, the rational

Interior-Collective
Cultural

World of: societies, division of labour,
groups, families, tribes, nation/state,
agrarian, industrial and informational

Exterior-Collective
Social

WE

ITS

Figure 2.1 *Overview of Wilber's concept*

If we really want to understand what the human brain produces, we can only find that in the left-hand part of the diagram. The brain causes emotions, feelings, concepts, etc., and it is these which we use in daily life.

No matter how detailed our understanding of the right-hand part is, it still says nothing about what we think or feel. To get to the dimensions on the left, the classical approaches are insufficient. Communication is the only means of trying to understand how people feel and what emotions they go through. On the left-hand side there is also a collective dimension: one could label it 'culture'.

This has a rapport with what we accept as a group, the norms and values. So a holistic understanding cannot bypass these internal individual and collective dimensions.

Classical science goes completely in search of the 'truth' (identified as on the top right). More and more, we see global approaches to the systemic in science: the functional whole. The true notion of the human being and his or her emotions – which we call, a little paradoxically, a person of 'flesh and blood' – does not give us a real understanding of truth and fairness. Here I want particularly to draw attention to the other three quadrants to thus give a more complete understanding than the dominant thinking that Western culture allows. My goal is to try a more holistic approach in management research and in the understanding of phenomena.

At the heart of each of the four quadrants we once again find a natural evolution from physics, via biology, psychology and theology towards mysticism. Translated into the fundamentals, we go from matter, via life, thinking, the soul towards the spirit. This demands much more explanation, but there Wilber's book (*A Brief History of Everything*, 2000) is an absolute must.

Summarizing this detailed diagram is not only difficult, but does not give full benefit to the diagram. I would nevertheless like to try. Holism consists of an ensemble of 'I', 'we', 'it' and 'its'. This is quickly recognized in certain metaphors of holism, such as 'Art meets science and spirituality', the 'I', 'we' and 'it' of Wilber. Another saying is that the hands, head and heart lead to holism. This can also be attributed to Wilber.

Though the remainder of this book will primarily discuss the 'its' and the 'we' quadrants, it remains evident that we cannot avoid asking ourselves the question for the 'I' quadrant. Though, arguably, some of the chapters could be positioned in the 'it' quadrant, the mainstream of this book aims to go beyond. In fact, the purpose of this book is to give the reader an understanding of (knowledge) management, and illustrate this with a number of examples that lead to a more systemic approach of management (with possibly a focus on knowledge and innovation).

The first part of the book develops a more holistic approach to management, with a focus on innovation and knowledge. It aims to give a broader and deeper understanding of how companies and people interact, and how learning plays an important role in management. But the second part of the book aims to go even further, proposing a quantum interpretation of management. Though I could have decided to deal with the philosophical dimension of the quantum interpretation in this chapter, I have decided to join it with the quantum interpretation itself in Chapter 8, for an improved understanding.

# 3 The underlying theory: a new paradigm

- Does something self-organizing exist?
- Chaos and order: chicken or egg?

## Does something self-organizing exist?

Maturana and Varela are perhaps the best-known representatives of a new pair of glasses to explore the world with, namely self-organization or autopoiesis. The concept of autopoiesis has been applied by several people in different domains and in different ways. A little care is nevertheless necessary if we want to apply this concept very literally. As a metaphor, this concept has very strong characteristics.

The two neurobiologists did not examine the systems from the starting point genes or 'species', but from one of the simplest biological entities, the amoeba. For them, the amoeba has a central role in each living being. They studied how cooperation between these amoebas creates a (complex) behaviour. Each amoeba has individual autonomy at the centre of a particular organism. What appears is that living systems basically function in a mechanical fashion. The behaviour of the system as a whole is generated by its elements and their interaction. Observers find themselves entirely outside the system. Therefore, the observers perceive the unit as well as the environment. The elements of a system react uniquely in interaction with other components. Each declaration of a living system cannot therefore be based on either the idea of the goal or the direction or the final function. In this layout the systems seem to be autopoietic: they are circular, self-productive, self-conservative but also self-referring.

Here we have a few points of reference to see how people collaborate in a company or an organization. Perhaps, effectively, in a company there is no more important objective than profit, or the creation of value for the shareholders. A company cannot be anything other than a collaboration by a number of individuals who are trying to attain their own individual goals and who use a certain number of rules of interaction. If that is the case, then it is remarkable, for such a system creates its own order and maintains itself in a good state (like our body), provided that no artificial order is imposed (something we could call an organization).

By contrast, scientific management does precisely that. We impose an organization and we are then going to control the results attained. It is perhaps the reason for failure (sometimes). At this stage we must advance in the understanding of the process.

What does autopoiesis need in order to be true? What conditions must be satisfied to produce this self-production and self-organization? For that we must go more deeply into the theory. All perceptions, observations and experiences happen to us via our body (our senses) and our nervous system. The body, then, plays the role of the medium of transport. Once observations and perceptions are in the body, therefore, it is impossible for human beings to arrive at a pure description of something, independently of themselves. Each experience is always a reflection of the observer. There is no object outside the field of the observer, but this observation belongs only to them.

What therefore is true in an autopoietic system and how can we face up to knowledge and truth? The truth signifies what? Who supports autopoiesis in maintaining a system in a good state? The survival of the system is therefore a criterion for measuring knowledge and success. Each approach that aims to be scientific can only clearly describe what the observer sees. In effect, the observer plays a crucial role. The comparison with the external world makes no sense. Therefore, the methodology, the manner of leading our investigations, is specific and cannot be detached from the view of the observer. In a company situation, each truth can be just as precious and as important as any other truth. It is not certain that the manager has more reason or a better understanding than someone who is closer to the company process.

There are a few consequences of accepting this. Autopoiesis really says more about the observer than the subject (or should I say object) which is observed. In the case of autopoiesis, at least it is clearly accepted, but where are the other scientific paradigms? An underlying consequence is, of course, that no absolute claim of objectivity can be made, by whatever approach. This was all again confirmed by Gödel's theory. Both belief and theory are pure human constructions which then build a reality instead of being a reflection of an existing reality. For this reason we sometimes speak of a paradigm of radical constructivism. Reality is created and not perceived. Constructivism as a research paradigm is obtaining increasing support in social sciences research, but it is also subject to much more discussion in the more classical sciences. In Maturana's *From Being to Doing: The Origins of the Biology of Cognition* (2004) the observer is presented as the interior system where all the descriptions take place up until the original theory.

Starting from the original theory, there has been subsequent evolution. A key idea which, from a number of points of view, summarizes autopoiesis is 'the more something changes, the more it is the same thing'. At least, this illustrates the practical consequences of a self-productive idea. Systems are often examined as closed systems, such as the immune system, the nervous system, and also a social system. It is the system itself which produces a form of determinism. From the same system comes the structure of the system, which is more than the addition of structures and the elements making them up. Dynamic systems communicate through their structure and interact with their entourage. An individual plays a crucial role in the system, but it is the system which communicates with the external world.

Over the years, self-productive ideas have been successfully applied in the construction of self-generating computer applications. The application manipulates itself to be in an optimal situation at every moment: in this case we are talking about genetic software. A telephone switchboard, for example, must at any moment of the day deal with a volume of swiftly changing traffic. We can easily imagine generating a program which takes account of the multitude of possibilities, but in practice doing so appears rather difficult. We can now develop a software program which manipulates itself in relation to specific volumes of traffic that the switch intercepts. We do not produce a program which specifically resolves the problem, but it is a program which uses ideas of self-reproduction.

I am not expressing a value judgement here, but we see the same thing in, for example, the legal system. The legal system organizes itself as best it can to ensure its survival. To do so, the system is going to reproduce itself and establish its own frame of reference. I have already mentioned the idea of self-reference as a strong but potentially destructive idea. By analogy with the legal system, we can regard each human being (a society, an organization, a meeting, etc.) as an autopoietic system.

People seem to be 'linguistic animals' (and that refers to communication and interaction in a network) who do nothing but play the game that we could call the 'practice of (artificial) living'. Human experience as an observer is crucial, and more important than what really happens in the world. The role of language and communication is very important. All understanding happens through language and its representation, but also all communication with others in a network takes place through language.

The numbers of misunderstandings in the world, in the same group of languages, are symbolic in relation to this central aspect of interaction. Even in the centre of the same group of languages, the Dutch and the Flemish use the same words differently. Sentence structure is different, which leads the same ideas to be gathered in another way. The network of ideas that a speaker tries to transmit is a function of the construction of sentences, even the sequence of sentences. But also on the side of the listener, the construction of phrases determines the message which is received. Communication is no more than a network of agents (people) exchanging a network of thoughts, with the hope of being able to learn something or develop knowledge a little.

With the better objective of producing unity, we can complicate the rules; make communication more difficult, which explains the expression 'he who sows order reaps chaos'. Children who communicate between themselves in different languages, without speaking those languages, may consequently make far fewer mistakes in the formal language and seem able to conceptualize more rapidly.

It seems evident that the messages children want to transmit are simpler than those politicians want to transmit. Here too we immediately fall into the positivist trap: if we can measure something, then we can know. But it would now seem that communication is not at all organized in the same way as thoughts are.

Is non-verbal communication not more efficient and less structured? Does the extreme order help the process of communication, compared to a higher intensity of communication? If everyone in a Spanish café seems to be talking at the same time, and no one seems to be listening, is the communication less significant and less precious? Do similar interlocutions lead to similar decisions?

Contemporary cognitive psychology seems to prove a good number of these ideas. A lot of research is done around language and interlocution, showing that language and action are tightly linked. Language is our 'existence in the world'. Language is really our entire thinking. Even on the subject of language we are still thinking in that language (this is a good example of self-referencing). Knowledge is not linguistic representation, for we distinguish between different things beyond language. Everything that can be said about it is encompassed in our former experiments. Language is, in fact, a social act. Organizations are therefore networks of recurrent interlocution constructed between individuals and groups of individuals. Starting from this thinking, we can also see a certain reorientation in the developments in artificial intelligence.

On the basis of the reigning paradigm of objective observation and the possibility of drawing up optimum rules, we are led to the research on 'machines based on rules', among other things, of expert systems. The acceptance is that all people's decision processes can be captured in rules. These expert systems have known moderate success. The objectivist orientation of artificial intelligence has certainly been overestimated. We can now see interesting developments in two rather different directions. One goes in the direction of research, which we can regard as looking for a self-learning behaviour of systems (emergent behaviour), making use of connectivist structures. This development is especially seen in artificial intelligence. The connectivist structures are structures with which a lot of simple, tightly connected elements and communication make sense out of chaos. In practice, we are thinking here of systems like neural networks, or networks of agents.

The second direction in the research is also dedicated to the self-learning behaviour of systems, but perhaps better translated in this case as constructing behaviour on the basis of 'enacted' technologies. By 'enaction' we mean what Varela calls 'enacted cognition'. An actor 'enacts' a theatre play. If you asked me to play the role of Hamlet, I would try to do so and my efforts would of course not be particularly pleasant to watch. If you ask an actor to play Hamlet, he does not 'play' Hamlet, he becomes Hamlet. Each evening he recreates another Hamlet. Maybe the two find each other in the character of Shakespeare. Managers can no longer 'play' the role of manager, but can simply 'enact' their role. Managers 'are' their role, and it is therefore very difficult to learn this 'behaviour'. You become a manager by experience. You cannot teach someone to become a manager (as I am going to argue later on, we cannot teach something which is based on skills and competence).

For this reason, the personal development path of a manager is so crucial. Only a 'learning' manager will be up to playing the role of the spider in the web, the inspirer and creator of good conditions for others. The manager must and should continually improve themself in this task. Operations or instruments only have a very limited utility and can never play a driving role in dynamic situations. Worse still, they can therefore never have a general validity.

Knowledge is only knowledge if it represents action and creation. Otherwise, we can only speak of information. In this case we therefore find the use and the analysis of communication (conversations), as well as a strong focus on the support of communication (by platforms, for example). To illustrate: 'communities of practice', experimented with by numerous companies, seem to conform well to this preoccupation. This research is not uniquely led by artificial intelligence.

We see the interest in dynamic re-creation in two directions appearing in artificial intelligence research. Things are not fixed, but are produced afresh each time. If I ask someone their age, the information is not stored somewhere particular in the brain. Each time the question is asked, the person is going to produce the reply again. This seems inefficient, from the point of view of a recurrent question, and that is in fact the case. On the other hand, a question is rarely truly repetitive, even if it is asked using the same words, since in the majority of cases it is looking for another signification. The intonation, for example, very often gives a big hint concerning the question and the expected answer. This dynamic re-production as an approach therefore leaves every possibility to reply very quickly to similar or slightly changed questions. For a real conversation this principle is therefore a lot better and more efficient. Furthermore, if the brain needed to store all possible information in order to be able to answer all possible questions, we would need a lot more storage capacity in the brain (and hence a larger head to accommodate that). For a rational and positivist view of the conversation, this seems an aberration and an error of thinking. Language in general plays an important role in this research. The research methods themselves are more self-learning. The general validity of the observations is less declared – something which in classical science is done more quickly.

If we look at the contemporary theories of artificial intelligence for how to think about the subject of reasoning, we get an attitude somewhat distant from the rather positivist approaches of before. Possible interactions between reason and the soul are looked for, which hitherto has been unthinkable in cognitive psychology. Reason (intelligence) is considered as a behaviour: behaviour is what counts. The link between the brain and reason (intelligence) is broken: reason is present not only in the brain, but in the whole body (distributed intelligence). We are speaking here about the concept of 'embodied mind'. Reason, the brain and intelligence are considered less and less to be a sort of computer, which refers to the thinking of the machine behind reasoning. The interpretation, which is generally vigorous, becomes in effect more and more based on shifting sands.

Intelligence is strong in the organization of 'the next step'. It is weaker in the planning of a number of next steps (multiple) and weaker still in the execution of the following multiple steps. Intelligence is the organ of control for an autonomous agent. The structure was formed in a descending manner or by a combination of some elements. The latter appears when we put different people around the table: we get something like a structure resulting from the setting up of a network of different elements (people). Intelligence is something continuous, and not only a sort of metaphor, a machine which functions with zeros and ones. Intelligence does not function with numbers and symbols but with vague notions like tall, taller, smaller, etc.

Intelligence reacts to those sensations which can be translated into sensory perceptions. Then all that is translated into information. It is not the action on the senses themselves which creates information, but the liaison of a specific perception with the existing network of perceptions and information. Sensorial perception, action and knowledge go together to form something that is summarized in the notion of 'enacted cognition'.

Intelligence recombines this old information and experience to produce new actions. Intelligence is positioned in a diffuse way in the whole body, but it seems that even if the modules are independent, they collaborate through their connection between each other. All this represents notions that are completely at odds with what is used most of the time as a basis for our management, especially management that specifically concerns structure and control.

The crucial question is: can a social system be organized from outside? The inquiry into the behaviour of autopoietic systems does not seem to suggest that it can. It seems that each system, even if we want to examine it from the simplest components, can only organize itself, replicate itself and ensure its survival. Although this could be negative at first sight, it represents an undeniable strength. Systems do not necessarily need tight direction with a lot of complicated rules, at least if we dare to give back the control and the direction to the system itself. Intervening in such a system seems therefore to be avoided.

Just as people are often not aware of the self-organization within themselves, the managements of large companies are largely unaware of their companies' internal self-organization. Many subsequent reorganizations directed from 'outside' or 'above' into traditional organizations actually risk destroying the very organizational fabric which has allowed the company to operate as an integrated whole.

But very careful experiments in certain companies seem, however, to indicate that this direction of a more self-organized management could succeed. In practice, related to knowledge management, we ask ourselves how knowledge can be organized in a 'self-searching' and preferably self-finding way (in summary, a self-organizing way) in opposition to the branch structure that we implement in very large databases. The groups responsible for the conception of new products seem to be more creative and efficient if they have more liberty. This does not signify that we cannot learn anything from the past with regard to successes and errors; on the contrary. However, the lessons learned are not translated into the 'ten commandments of innovation', but rather into recipes and stories from which, according to our personal interest, we can extract an advantage. The potential of learning in itself, in companies, is an interesting gift. More and more companies try to provide a more flexible range of training and support which is better linked to the profiles of the posts, providing 'just-in-time, just-enough' learning, based on the development of necessary managerial competencies. Our own research has illustrated (confirming many other publications) that workplace learning is a very effective and efficient way of continuous learning, in particular if related to the development of managerial competencies. E-learning (and I am not speaking of classical e-teaching, or distance or correspondence learning) is a promising development with which a manager, while doing their job, is supported by the learning environment in which those who want to learn will find effective support, adapted to their needs. This also means that there is no classical teacher who teaches classes of pupils how the real world is (or should be). Those who want to learn find what they want and need to learn to then learn by doing (and therefore by learning). All these developments are promising on condition that you have the courage to relax control at all levels.

This must not be translated into saying that everyone does just anything, and then we will see what happens to us. Let me refer here to Alice (in Wonderland). If, effectively, we do not know where we want to go (or where we can go), then each path we can take is good. Which is what we do several times in our Western management; we fix the paths to follow. Not only do these paths change quickly, however, and so we forget to change ourselves, but it is necessary to concentrate on the destination to be reached, instead of the path to follow. The path that goes towards the goal will be made in walking, in the network of employees. As Antonio Machado says, 'Caminante, no hay camino/Se hace camino al andar' (There is no path/The path is made by walking). Management, or the strategy, must be concentrated on the goal to be reached, to then share ideas with the network of employees. In practice that does not often happen. Strategy is often considered secret, and so employees cannot even help management to attain the goal. The agents in the network each have their own preferences and capabilities. In the interaction with other elements of the network they can walk on the path which will lead to the goal by different small steps. If the goal is clear and realistic, the path could be adapted each time adaptation is necessary in practice, and sometimes this could be very often. Knowing the goal, employees can take their responsibility in contributing to this network of walking paths.

Self-organization and self-production are concepts which are strongly embedded in neurobiology – concepts which, when translated into social systems, are receiving more and more attention, but which are radically different from the Western tradition of management. In this tradition, everything must be organized and controlled, based on whichever intellectual tradition is inspiring the manager concerned. But we can well see that in practice such tight control does not work and leads to frustration. Another understanding of the functioning of social systems is possible and can give us other ideas for management if we are able to observe from another paradigm. Is there therefore a paradigm which is scientific (based on scientific discovery) and which gives us another vision of social self-organization?

In our research for foundation, we find inspiration in what is known as the theory of complexity and/or chaos. Scientists effectively starting from a positivist paradigm, but with an open-mindedness which lets them really see, have made remarkable observations. A number of them – for example, Prigogine – have received the Nobel Prize for their research, but very often their knowledge stays essentially within their own circle of researchers in the hard sciences. Only during the past few years have we seen little by little what their theories, especially their application, can mean for social systems. This aspect orients us towards 'the search for an underlying theory'.

## Chaos and order: chicken or egg?

Look at the chaos of everyday life, a point on which I suppose we agree. But how does it work? We have chaos, but fortunately we also regularly have order. Certain things often play out in a well-organized way. The administration is organized, the trains are well organized and planes leave more or less on time. Isn't that order, and how does chaos play a role in that? Is there a theory of chaos? As I have already stated, positivism goes perfectly with our Cartesian attitude. It is, however, in the positivist sciences that the first doubts emerged. As early as 1903, Poincaré made a remarkable observation:

> Sometimes small differences in initial conditions produce very large differences in the final observations. A minor change in the former can cause a tremendous error in the latter. The phenomenon is becoming unpredictable; we have random phenomena.
>
> Henri Poincaré, *Science et Methode*, 1908

He could not prove it, but he could well see remarkable things happening. During certain mathematical simulations, when very small differences in the initial values appear, we notice big differences in the final results. Poincaré could not explain this effect and he had not the least idea that he was making an observation which would lead later to what we know as the theory of chaos and complexity. We must not forget that Poincaré did not have computers at his disposal to experiment rapidly with all sorts of simulations.

We had to wait until 1964 before Edward Lorenz, an American meteorologist, became the first to discover and identify the problem. We have to keep in mind that in the intervening period, in 1931, Gödel's theory had sown confusion. He proved that any axiomatic system, let us say a mathematical system of variables and equations, would not be up to accepting or rejecting all possible statements one day. Therefore, there was no unique, perfect model of the world. This discovery was much more than a huge question mark, making a new turning possible for mathematicians. Among others, Mandelbrot's fractal algebra is one of these new orientations. But Gödel's theory does not give a response to Poincaré's problem.

But now let us turn back to Lorenz. As a meteorologist, he worked with a simple system of three dynamic non-linear equations. 'Dynamic' means, for example, that today's temperature is a function of yesterday's. 'Non-linear' means that somewhere there is a variable with an exhibitor. With his system, Lorenz tried to predict the weather. He made a number of observations and simulations on this subject. Lorenz had a computer, which was not common in 1964. Thanks to this computer, Lorenz could clarify what Poincaré had suspected. The use of computers was indispensable to be able to carry out sufficiently large simulations.

During these simulations, Lorenz had to interrupt his research. In fact, since computers did not yet have screens, they produced a mountain of paper. When he wanted to pick up the simulation later, he wanted to take the last value the computer had produced as the initial value of the rest of the simulation. He had, as a good scientist, a certain doubt. This is why, instead of taking the last value, he took the result of the previous 100 observations and started the simulation with that value. During this new simulation of the hundred last steps, he wanted to be sure that everything would go as well as previously before going further. To his great surprise, Lorenz discovered something which should have frightened everyone. Nothing went as expected. In the first period, he saw small differences appearing, but they were not always the same. They were rather arbitrary. Although the range of discrepancies was at first quite limited, the same values were somewhat random. The biggest and smallest values alternated in a previously unseen pattern. But while the simulation continued, he observed some remarkable occurrences. The new simulation seemed to suddenly react in a strange way. The values showed huge differences in the two directions, and the differences between the first and the second simulation became bigger than the values simulated. Therefore, these values became incoherent. The whole exercise became totally futile.

Lorenz had hit on what we call 'the bug of unpredictability'. In certain systems it seems impossible to predict. From a certain moment, and we do not really know which moment, the system becomes entirely incomprehensible; it displays 'chaos'. Therefore, a prediction can work very well for a certain period, and then suddenly become completely useless.

What had happened? Lorenz had certainly entered the correct number. But although he had used the correct number as printed on the list, it was not really the true number. It was a rounded figure, compared to the one the computer had used in the first series of calculations. It calculated, for example, with precision up to sixteen figures, but only printed eight. Therefore, the number with eight digits after the decimal point was slightly different from the true figure. Do not forget that in real life we often calculate with rounded figures, rather than with the precise number, including several figures after the decimal point.

It appeared to be a question of non-linearity and dynamic characteristics of the system, and so, just like that, Poincaré's worry had a name. Dynamic and non-linear systems cause, by their very structure, unpredictability. A complex system is hereby defined as a non-linear dynamic system.

In company management we are also confronted with complex systems – in other words, non-linear and dynamic systems. Is there a phenomenon in management for which the current value will not be dependent on yesterday's value? The current value is, in part, always a function of yesterday's value. The level of salaries (this year) is without a doubt a function of the previous year's levels. The market share which you can achieve today is without a doubt a function of the market share you could achieve last month. The phenomena of management are, in consequence, dynamic until proven to the contrary.

In addition, each management phenomenon is not only dynamic but also non-linear, except for the processes that are created (built) to be linear (production lines, for example). We have built the latter notably for them to do what we want them to do, and moreover in a way that can be checked and controlled (although we have also had bad experiences of control going off the rails – for example, in nuclear energy centres). But all the interesting phenomena such as market behaviour, competitors' behaviour, employees' collaboration in their daily work, the processes of decision-taking through dialogue, etc., are non-linear and dynamic, and therefore essentially unpredictable and uncontrollable.

So, a paradox of management is: we are trying to direct and control something which cannot be controlled and directed. That would not be so terrible if we were not amazed when it does not work. In fact, it is impossible for management to guarantee success (in markets and/or dynamic companies) through control and prediction. Consequently, we must call into question how we face up to such dynamic systems. What can a manager's role be if everything is unpredictable and uncontrollable? In essence, this is the question that I want to present in this book. What can a manager do if no control approach works? Adopt a learning approach, perhaps?

The cause of chaos, which intervenes in a system for the same reason as order, is even the characteristic of the system. A system does not have a problem with that. It does not have a problem containing order as well as chaos, sometimes demonstrating order, sometimes chaos. We human beings have a problem with trying to consider systems as organized entities which are therefore manageable. Consequently, a problem occurs if we try to deal with a complex system by using control and prediction mechanisms. In practice, the phenomenon is discovered when we try to reach understanding through models. That is what we do all the time as managers independently of the detail of the models, which are, in general, very simple tools that do not need to run on a computer. Certain mental models of managers, like automatic pilot behaviour, are naturally also models.

The phenomena studied in management are continuous (they never stop and constantly change) and not discontinuous. But what measurement can be taken? As precisely as possible, this should always be a point of discontinuous measurement. We therefore continually approach societal processes which are themselves continuous (market behaviour, buying behaviour, human interaction) with variables and decisions based on discontinuous measurement. The point of measurement (of observation) is never really correct. Using the phenomenon Lorenz revealed, which we could call 'dependence on initial values', we know that, since the observation is never correct, the simulation is going to produce chaos.

But there is still something else. In practice, we cannot approach a reality which is by definition continuous, other than by a discontinuous approach (market behaviour). In other words, although we try to do the maximum, and we try as much as possible to be precise, observation and data can never be correct: we can never avoid the virus of unpredictability in managerial applications. To some extent we incorporate this virus in the model. Whichever systematic approach we choose, it will always demonstrate order at certain moments and complete chaos at others.

Now that we know that these observations are not only scientifically important, but also, and especially, that they have consequences for companies (and also for social life, politics and law, etc.), from now on we can look at what we can learn from the theory of complexity. This theory is not new, but in the management of companies or other general social sciences it is still relatively unknown.

Let us go back to Lorenz. Through his research he shed more light on what Poincaré had suggested, and made possible a little more comprehension of the behaviour of complex systems. They are, first, very dependent on the initial value: small differences in the initial value lead to big differences in the subsequent sequence of events. But Lorenz found yet another characteristic of complex systems. Apparently, complex systems can also demonstrate moments of relative calm (stability) in the midst of chaos. Sometimes the simulations turn around points of attraction, let us say points or fields of local stability, then suddenly change and orient themselves towards a more chaotic sequence of events, then calm down again around another point of stability. We call these points of local stability 'attractors', even 'strange attractors', since we do not know when, how or with what strength they attract the phenomenon. Certain complex systems have only two attractors (points of stability), but certain other systems have a much higher number of attractors.

The name Lorenz remains linked to a very remarkable phenomenon in respect to weather forecasting systems. In a certain simple simulation, three equations with three unknowns, Lorenz observed that the phenomenon being studied centred around two attractors. The phenomenon moved around the first attractor one moment and suddenly whizzed off to then settle itself around the second attractor. Next, the phenomenon moved back suddenly to the first and then back towards the second. In fact, in doing that, the phenomenon created a sort of butterfly shape. This therefore became known as Lorenz's butterfly. Someone metaphorically said that if a butterfly flutters its wings in one part of the world this can cause a hurricane at the other end of the world. Although Lorenz did not invent this story himself, people now speak everywhere about the Lorenz butterfly. Now, we would really like to be able to say that all that is impossible – that it does not make any sense. In theory, at least, it is possible, just as simulations show, and in practice the contrary has never been proved.

Despite the formidable progress of science, weather is still totally unpredictable a few days in advance. Do I have to emphasize again that this is also the case in management? We should simply look at the stock market. Do the analysts know why the stocks do what they do? Is there anyone who can do better than the 'random walk' in anything other than the short term? Could it be true that our lack of understanding of stock market behaviour has a relationship with the manner in which we approach the phenomenon, and therefore with the glasses we put on to observe it?

In the 1960s and 1970s we considered the Soviet Union to be the bogeyman, which allowed us to examine the world with a certain perspective, a certain pair of glasses. These glasses are not necessarily non-distorting, but they let us see what they let us see – except that this is also not necessarily true. The Berlin Wall fell, and at that moment the military and economic power of the Soviet Union could really be observed, and we understood that it was really hot air. To represent the Soviet Union as the great danger for the world and development has come to be a little unjustified, at least in retrospect. In the meantime, this vision served all sorts of goals and justified massive investments in, for example, the arms industry and the defence sector. This of course happened to the detriment of other possible expenditure. The point of departure chosen will justify our action. By choosing the glasses we look through, we will see precisely what we want to see.

After the fall of the Berlin Wall, we had to look for another pair of glasses. In the meantime, we perhaps found another pair in Muslim fundamentalism. It is a lot simpler to consider the world in terms of huge aggregates, like the free West, the communist world (although now it is a lot smaller), the Islamic world, the problem states (Iraq, Iran, etc.). Or is the world just a game played by a collection of individuals, organized or not into groups at a local level – groups which are linked in various networks where each individual (or group) can continue to live life in the best possible way, with a minimum of rules of behaviour? Do we not look for an understanding of our theories at too elevated a level of aggregation? The theory of complexity, and notably the work of John Holland, provides interesting points of reference.

We have identified up to this point two characteristics of a complex system: it is strongly dependent on initial values, and it displays local stable moments around what we call strange attractors.

A name which is closely linked with the theory of complexity is that of Ilya Prigogine, a Belgian Nobel Prize-winner, professor emeritus in the Faculty of Science at the University of Brussels (Université Libre de Bruxelles), who unfortunately died a few years ago. His research was oriented towards the dynamics of liquids. At first sight, these theories are a long way from managerial thinking, but very quickly the experiment will lead us to think differently. In fact, Prigogine carried out research on the behaviour of liquids while they were being heated, and he discovered dynamic characteristics of liquids in this phase. From these investigations, he could draw remarkable conclusions.

The best-known conclusion, and the most important for the study of complexity, is the principle of the 'irreversibility of time'. In short, he showed that the future cannot be extrapolated from the past, at least in dynamic systems. The reason is that a dynamic system recreates itself all the time and can branch off at any moment. A dynamic system develops in a non-linear way, and thereby obscures its historic development. The principle makes reference to the concept of the constructive role of time, what Prigogine calls 'time's arrow'. Time plays a constructive role in dynamic processes. Over time, or rather, as time moves gradually on, something new happens in liquids, something with new characteristics; the initial characteristics are never found again if we stop the heating (or if we cool the liquid down). For example, once a cake is cooked it will never again return to being a dough. Coffee, once made, will never go back to being powder and water, and it will also change again if it is warmed up a second time. In the heating process, liquid takes on other irreversible characteristics. Time plays a constructive role. Time contributes to a new creation.

Despite the two great scientific revolutions, the theory of relativity and quantum theory, most of the thinking in physics is still Newtonian: we observe the space–time couple as a fixed one. In Newtonian thinking, time is reversible and we can therefore predict the future from the past, and in theory also vice versa. In fact, we can predict the past from the future, therefore past and future are immutably and deterministically linked. In practice, and here I am referring to practice in companies, that is naturally not the case. In fact, no one has ever succeeded in predicting a market potential, or market shares, or future relationships between competitors. The financial markets are the most eloquent examples, but for other markets too it is equally impossible to forecast other than for the short term, at least in dynamic markets. The more dynamic a market, the more difficult forecasting is, because in this case time plays a 'more' constructive role.

That does not mean that the past is totally insignificant. The past, and more particularly the experiences of the past, are the raw material for human learning (we will come back to this in the next chapter). But the past does not let us predict the future at all (other than for the very short term, or in stable situations where forecasts are therefore not necessary). The characteristics of a liquid, according to Prigogine, are created anew each time. These characteristics are a type of knowledge, and consequently knowledge is created anew each time. It is not enough to mix powdered coffee with water to obtain coffee. We have to go through a process using a coffee machine, and in the course of this process the qualities of coffee are created, by the dynamic behaviour of the system in question.

After Gödel's observations, the principle of the irreversibility of time is the second important phenomenon in the thinking around complexity.

Prigogine also investigated the behaviour of systems far from their balance point, far from equilibrium, in comparison with that of systems close to equilibrium. By way of comparison – and this is in opposition to classical economic thinking – a system in balance is a totally uninteresting system. It contains all information, it is dead, and therefore cannot be moved from its balance point. In terms of information theory, we say that the system understands all the information, or contains all information. There is nothing else to add. A society (or company) in balance is therefore a dead society, and it is extremely difficult to revive it or innovate. Therefore, a system is interesting if it is not in balance, and the same is true for a company. If we go a little further, there is, all the same, a difference between a system close to equilibrium in comparison with one which is further away.

Prigogine introduced the notion of entropy and the production of entropy. Entropy is an indication of the 'amount' of chaos in a system. A system where entropy is equal to zero is dead and in a balanced position. A system far from balance has a high level of entropy. Prigogine observed that systems far from equilibrium are more interesting, because in this state a lot of things happen. It is not, strictly speaking, a question of entropy, but rather the production of entropy, the progression (or diminishing) of entropy. For the purposes of this book, there is no need to go further on this point.

Coming back now to companies, we see also that in mature markets it is much more difficult to increase market share than it is in emerging markets. In dynamic markets (chaotic markets) such as, for example, those in Eastern Europe, market share is won more easily simply because the entropy of these markets is higher. Of course, you can also fall a long way, but this is essentially the risk the entrepreneur takes: those who take risks will be rewarded (won't they?). Companies are therefore well advised to actively look for markets with higher entropy (in fact, rather chaotic markets), but in practice that goes against the thinking which controls and dominates our management practice. We prefer to choose the long and rather difficult path of taking a more stable (and expensive) approach to winning market share. Our tendency to control everything in management is certainly not a stranger to that thinking. 'Controlled growth', with a 'calculated risk', is the credo. But very often we neglect market characteristics. In practice, that does not work as well.

If we speak about new products and new markets, we quickly make the link with the innovatory force of a company. Innovation does not go well with a stable company and a culture of strong control. To explore new possibilities necessitates a rather chaotic company culture, a culture with a lot of entropy, a culture where one can learn and fail. To limit innovation by detailed and defined procedures (as is often the case in practice) is a contradiction in terms: we often call that the 'management' of innovation. To develop these ideas further, we need first of all to introduce new ones.

Another big current of ideas related to the theory of complexity, besides the ideas of Varela and those of Prigogine, is linked to the name of John Holland, the father of genetic algorithms. The development of genetic algorithms cannot be seen separately from research into 'artificial life', with which Chris Langton's name is closely linked. The research into artificial life gave us new ideas to examine. It highlighted remarkable characteristics of systems, notably the functioning of so-called complex systems on the basis of a number of simple rules. It is possible for a system with simple agents (let us say people), in which everyone follows their own simple goal (to survive, for example) and where everyone follows rules of simple interaction, to produce complex behaviour.

Let us take two simple examples: the flight of birds and the game of football. If we observe the flight of birds (in V formation), in general this gives the impression of being well organized, but the individual behaviour of the birds is not very organized. The birds organize themselves so that they do not lose sight of each other but do not touch each other. If we now try to write a programme to simulate this process, based on reductionist ideas, therefore with a classical procedural approach, we will never succeed. We will never manage to understand the birds' behaviour at a sufficiently detailed level. On the other hand, it is perfectly possible to simulate a flight in V formation with the following rule: *always keep a distance of between 15 and 25 centimetres from each other*. If a bird wants to move away, it can do so until it hits the 25 centimetre barrier, when it risks losing its neighbour. The 25 centimetre rule links this bird with its neighbour. When the birds risk touching each other, the 15 centimetre rule maintains a sufficient distance between them. We can immediately see the movement in waves of the entire flight. When a flight approaches a post, first of all the 15 centimetre rule keeps the bird at a sufficient distance and pushes it around the post. The 25 centimetre rule stops them flying off into the distance. At the other side of the post, the 15 centimetre rule again prevents them colliding and the flight continues on the other side.

The game of football has precisely the same qualities. We cannot understand the rules of footballers' decisions. Programming classically, in terms of procedural thinking, does not provide any solution. Once again a few simple rules can provide the solution. They all want to win; there are therefore twenty-two players with the same aim. A few simple rules of interaction are determined between them – for example, not to play the ball with your hand, not to kick each other, etc. These rules are identical for all twenty-two players, only there is one difference. Eleven players play in one direction, the other eleven in the other direction. What happens now is that these twenty-two cooperating agents can develop a very complex game, even though each one of them has a simple aim (in this case the aim is, of course, to score a goal), on the basis of a few simple rules of interaction: this is football.

The coach does not determine the rules or how someone must play. Coaches transmit their understanding of the game and share their experience, after which the players themselves must act.

That is what happens in genetic software, genetic algorithms or 'artificial life'. It appears that a given network of agents (entities, software, people, etc.) with a certain aim in mind, and with a few simple rules of interaction, is capable of very complex acts. It is the underlying principle of agent simulations, a rather recent development in artificial intelligence, for which John Holland is in part responsible. These (artificial) agents appear to be able to learn by themselves and to produce behaviour which is adapted and geared to learning, like the footballer who gradually acquires experience during training. If we now try to create this system, based on simple rules of 'fitness' (the survival of the fittest), then this demonstrates a capacity for learning and for solving complex problems. Agents' systems are therefore an imitation of methods of organizations noticed in human 'colonies' (football players, companies, employees, etc.). The search for rules of decision-making becomes useless. Determining objectives for each individual, linked with rules of interaction, seems to produce the work required. Do we see the parallel with the organization of companies?

Two important developments stem from this: genetic software programs as well as genetic algorithms. A genetic software program is therefore software which self-regulates in such a way as to optimize the execution of the task in relation to the environment at a given moment. Earlier, I referred to the software of a call centre, which genetically self-regulates to be able to manipulate the flow of continually changing communication. Another interesting development is the use of genetic algorithms – algorithms which genetically manipulate chains of 0s and 1s, to provide a multitude of possible solutions. The different possibilities are compared on the basis of their 'strength' (fitness). By constantly manipulating the information, and keeping the better solutions, we finally get to the best solution. This system is remarkable in its simplicity, and strong in its capacity to resolve complex problems.

The basis of these developments, and the interesting applications which stem from them, imply that where the hierarchical and organized structures are not capable of completely understanding this type of system, it is no longer necessary to look in the classical direction: there are a number of alternatives. We can therefore consider companies, or any kind of network or social entity (society, country, international community), as agent networks. These agent networks demonstrate emergent behaviour (or self-creating behaviour) which is produced anew each time by the network (we can compare this with what Prigogine showed us). The role of a manager of such a network is therefore no longer to provide good solutions (if that was indeed the case before), but solely to create the best conditions and circumstances for the network to be able to work in the best way possible in freedom. These networks are self-creating and self-organizing, based on principles we have already found in neurobiology. These networks demonstrate behaviour which is sometimes very complex, but the rules of piloting are very simple. The strength is not even in the links in the network (the agents), but more in the quality of interaction (in the network itself). Effectively, it is the quality of agent interaction in a company, and not the quality of individuals, which will build the quality of the company. Recruiting very intelligent employees brings nothing to the company if they are not prepared to collaborate.

It is clear that the supervision mechanisms for such networks are different from those we classically use in management. What is most important is not what is good or better, but rather how we can speed up the process of learning. It is therefore important to learn from mistakes and successes while each time leaving the network the possibility of creating a new space (with the solution). This network must be held as far as possible away from balance, in order to maintain high entropy and therefore creative potential, but that can only be done with good conditions of basic support. The key word is: learn.

The basis of management is learning; but learning quicker than competitors with the best support of collaborators in their learning. On the other hand, the more order is sown in the network; the more chaos will be harvested. Only a learning human, a human prepared to learn and capable of learning, can play a role in such a network in the best way. The manager is 'only' one element in the network.

Prigogine's work on the one hand and Holland's on the other are accepted by the majority of people in the Anglo-Saxon countries as the theory of complexity. We have also seen in other sciences (such as physics, chemistry or information technology) how evolutions of the same kind are produced, notably with the works of Maturana and Varela in neurobiology.

The autopoietic principle (of self-reproduction and self-organization) conforms perfectly to the character of permanent creation in a system (Prigogine) as well as to the emergent behaviour of agents in a network (Holland). Neurobiological research is a non-negligible fundamental aspect to take into consideration in comparison with what is developed here.

Varela himself made parallels between human organization and the functioning of the human brain (the neural network), which is a very dense network linking billions of 'knots' (neurons). Each neuron is in fact very simple (stupid) and can only execute very simple actions (to pass on or not to pass on energy: yes or no). Connected (in a network), these neurons are capable of marvellous things. The idea of neural networks and their use for understanding organizations has already been studied in my other publications (most of them available on my blog, http://euromed.blogs.com, or see the references to be found in the further literature). This metaphor of the organization as a neural network goes well not only with Varela's theories, but also with the rather metaphorical aspect of Prigogine's and Holland's theories.

A number of more recent theories seem to be found in a new strong paradigm – a paradigm which has rather a lot of consequences for management and managers. If prediction and control become useless, since they are not realistic in dynamic systems, and since we cannot correctly measure them, managing certain parameters or variables (hence the slogan 'we can only manage what we can measure') does not make sense any more. But what is the role of a manager then? What qualities must a manager have to be a good manager? If the manager effectively looked at companies through another pair of glasses (another paradigm), that manager could see other things. The things that we see now, but cannot understand very well in the classical paradigm, could suddenly make sense and we could do something with them today (something different, without a doubt, from what we currently do today). We could understand market behaviour better, even the behaviour of the agents in the network. Everything therefore becomes a question of learning, learning more quickly, learning continuously and inviting others to learn with them: the learning manager as an inspirer in a learning network.

Applying this new paradigm in companies allows us a better understanding, although as yet it is not much applied. A few research centres and even a few companies are following this evolution with interest, but proportionately their number is still very limited. Sometimes small companies manage to organize themselves in an 'organic' manner. These companies seem to give more possibilities for self-creation and self-organization. There are even virtual companies which have succeeded, although in general they are very small.

On the scientific plane, Brian Arthur has been interested for several years in the economic theory of complexity as shown by market behaviour. He therefore observes things completely differently from what we all observe together. Our economic thinking is based on a number of simplifying acceptances, none of which is realized in practice. Human beings are supposed to be entirely rational, possessing all the information, working in a market with a limited number of goods (or services) and a limited number of players. I do not believe that many people think that buyers are rational, or that they possess all the information. In our time, another problem has just been added. Not only is it difficult to possess all the information, to the regret of the Internet, and also thanks to the Internet, but we have rather a continual 'overload' of information. Information is not so very important in itself, but it is its interpretation which makes the difference. All these acceptances which seem to be innocent at first sight are necessary to be able to work with non-dynamic models (or to assume dynamic behaviour to be static). Based on what we know about the faults of a static and linear approach to a non-linear dynamic phenomenon, we cannot hope that these models will give an understanding of real market behaviour (if anyone really still believed that such a thing is possible).

A fourth acceptance of our economic theory is the law of diminishing returns. We need to study this law in a little more depth. Physical goods (or services which are not based on knowledge) are such that if we consume more of one of them, we will obtain less satisfaction for each additional unit (marginal). If we have eaten five tarts, the sixth is not really very enticing. If we have already seen ten films, the eleventh is no longer so attractive. The plus-value in question therefore diminishes. The latest new unit produced less of a plus-value than its predecessors. The same is true in the production sphere. If we have the amount of steel necessary to produce a car, any additional unit of steel will not create any more value.

This economic theory ignores the fact that, in an economy based on knowledge, where the products are principally based on knowledge (even if it is not pure knowledge), this law no longer holds. The characteristics of knowledge are different compared to the raw material of an industrial product. Knowledge increases in applicability the more one shares it. With products based on knowledge, the pre-financing is very important (the research part) even before the product can exist. Let us take medicine as an example, where, at first, investment in research is very important. After this phase 1, medicine can then be marketed and sold, and it will then be necessary to hope that the revenue pays back the investment made. The price of the first copy (of the first product) is very high, but each following copy is very cheap to 'produce' (by copying). Since the sales price remains the same, each additional unit sold can therefore provide an increasing added value per unit (and not decreasing, as suggested in the law of diminishing returns). The first copy of Microsoft Windows costs a fortune. Each following copy costs a few dollars: the time needed to make the copy and a CD.

In knowledge-based markets, something reinforcing appears that is caused by what we call 'positive feedback' – a market strength which does not lead to a balance, but creates a sort of snowball. When video recording first appeared, there were two different standards. VHS and Betamax fought a battle where Betamax was really better in terms of quality and price, but VHS won. What happened is that more videos of the VHS standard invaded the market, then more video equipment manufacturers chose the VHS standard, thanks to which more film-makers produced films to the VHS standard. This snowball led to VHS becoming the market standard. Microsoft DOS (MS-DOS) was not the best operating system for PCs. At the moment when IBM chose MS-DOS as their operating system, DOS was far from being the standard, and far from being regarded as a good-quality product. However, the IBM decision led many developers to create their software programs using the MS-DOS system. The other PC manufacturers (Olivetti, Philips, etc.) then also chose MS-DOS. Windows still works on MS-DOS (though it is well hidden). Another example in the politico-social sector is the pre-election campaigns for the US presidency. Why do all the candidates make such huge efforts to win voices in tiny states such as Iowa and New Hampshire at the beginning of their campaigns when evidently states like Florida or California would give more votes? The reason is very simple: they hope to start out with victories, leading to a snowball in funding to buy more television time, thanks to which they can attract more attention, and then get more financing, etc. Often, in effect, this approach really works.

If we return to the world of business, where Microsoft has clearly won the battle of the PC standards, we need to observe that this phenomenon of positive feedback no longer leads to the usual market share of 15 to 20 per cent in industrial leaders' markets. In the knowledge markets, we observe more like 60 to 80 per cent, and effectively in the Microsoft case we see even higher percentages. Continuing to think in the industrial paradigm is surely due to embezzlement. The justice system that only understands the old paradigm, by which it itself operates, very quickly supports so-called allegations in the knowledge market. If we were to divide Microsoft into several small companies, we would very quickly see another majority player emerging in this market. That is the logic of these types of markets, but if we take a classical approach we have great difficulty understanding that. The theory of complexity gives another vision of this observation.

Western thinking about science and organization in general does not fit easily with the theory of complexity. It is also opposed to Western philosophical and scientific traditions. It is nevertheless evident that these theories not only are interesting, but also could very well contribute to a better understanding of social phenomena. Managers will have difficulty accepting a number of aspects and the consequences of these theories. But very few concepts of Western managerial thinking seem to contribute to finding solutions in a dynamic world. It is systematically difficult to seize on what really happens, and the classical instruments do not always necessarily help towards a better understanding.

How can a manager apply all that? When a controlling manager puts something of a brake on innovation, what should that manager be doing instead? That has a direct relationship with learning: how to keep learning yourself and simultaneously stimulate others to learn? The manager needs to have an attitude favouring creation and innovation.

Further on in the book, I elaborate on the theoretical frame (the quantum interpretation) and some exemplary experiments towards building a new approach to the theory and practice of management. However, we first need some more elements to be able to build this new approach.

# 4 Gödel for beginners: the concept of self-reference

The name has already been mentioned a few times: Gödel. Gödel was a mathematician who was counted among the adherents of the Vienna Circle: the logical positivists. In 1931 he published his now famous theorem, which created tremendous doubt among mathematicians. Not at first, though: it took a while before the full consequences of his theorem became appreciated. He proved something that most like-minded people did not appreciate. In simple terms (which always means putting something a bit wrongly), Gödel proved that one cannot develop an axiomatic system that accepts or rejects all hypotheses. Hence, there will be hypotheses and statements about which the system cannot say anything, or which you have to reject and accept at the same time.

This chapter will be a little more formal than the others. The reader should not be afraid, though. Though Gödel's theorem meant a big turnaround in the mathematical world (and therefore had a huge impact in the other sciences too), that simple fact is not the most relevant for our concerns. It does fit the wider frame, of course, but using Gödel's theorem I want to introduce a new concept, that of self-reference. The reader has to keep in mind that the concept of self-reference, though very instrumental for Gödel's proof, is key in the development of my argument. In order to illustrate self-reference I have to describe at least a bit of the proof.

An axiomatic system, simply stated, is a mathematical system of equations, symbols and numbers. Most readers will probably remember the axioms that formed the basis for geometry. A point has no dimension; two straight lines intersect at a point; two parallel lines intersect at infinity. Occasionally an axiom is added to these, which are hardly controversial, and are easily accepted by everybody as 'true'. On those axioms an entire geometry is built and an almost unlimited set of statements can be proved to hold. A proof precisely aims to accept a statement as true in all cases, and that is what is also understood in daily language as a 'proof': always true, not possible to contradict, and therefore capable of being generalized. If a statement cannot be proven (by mathematicians, of course, and not by high school students), then it is rejected and is no part of mathematics. The reason for developing such kinds of axiomatic systems is to be able to create a number of generally true statements or facts that allow us to have some consistent view on reality. At least, that is what we think on the basis of views belonging to classical Western philosophy of science. Other schools of thought, or philosophical schools, like, say, the Vedic tradition (India), have other ideas about this. On the basis of these other 'truth systems', on the basis of other views about what is generally true, we get a different mathematics.

Let us get back to Gödel now and to the impact of his proof. Gödel's theorem, in fact, goes against the essence of what an axiomatic system should be. Gödel proved that the idea that one could develop an axiomatic system allowing understanding the full truth (of any specific knowledge domain) was out of reach. This does not mean that axiomatic systems or axiomatic thinking would not add value. They still contribute to our desire to organize certain messy situations, but can never give general truth. It is always possible to find a statement on which an axiomatic system cannot decide. It is clear that once this axiom became known among mathematicians, it did create a shock. A number of mathematical certainties were quite abruptly knocked down. It made the necessity clear for completely new developments within mathematics, i.e. fractal algebra (Mandelbrot), but that is a different subject, and one that this book does not deal with.

We can ask ourselves what the importance of Gödel's theorem could be for management. Most probably it will not be much more than a warning finger that says: be attentive. What seems to be impossible in mathematics will no doubt not be possible either in a rational approach to management. When Gödel proved his theorem, things like economic modelling or mathematical modelling in management did not yet exist. Only in the 1950s and 1960s did we start to develop this kind of model, with among others, Jan Tinbergen (who won the Nobel Prize for economics) as one of the founding fathers. Hence, Gödel's theorem only influenced the mathematicians once it was published. It is of course still true that a real innovation in one science seldom has any impact in any other science, which is of course rather strange if sciences are indeed searching for general truth. The reason for this, probably, is that most sciences have no contact with other sciences since they are highly specialized in their field (thanks partly to reductionism).

Seen from a more generally prevailing philosophical culture in the West, Gödel's 'warning' was an important one. Western thinking and Western management (and probably I should say the Anglo-Saxon view on management) is strongly rooted in mathematical and rational thinking. Supporting Western economic theory is the idea that it should be possible to find an axiomatic system that would be generally valid for markets. If you consider the classical supply and demand models, or the equally classical cost models, or the models that attempt to explain monopolistic or duopolistic price behaviour, they claim very strongly that they will be generally valid, yet they are not always recognizable in practice. As a kind of intelligent exercise, there is no problem, as long as we do not claim general validity for them. Along the same lines, we have to ask ourselves how far we need to go in the development of economic models. They will never have general validity (that is what we know from Gödel), but their axiomatic character often suggests much more than they can really show. People who construct such models will say: it is all dependent on the assumptions, and hence clients know what they get. In practice, however, the assumptions are often hidden in the small print at the bottom of the contract. One needs to be a good model technician in order to be able to think along with the model and in order to really understand it.

So far so good for Gödel and his warning finger. What is more interesting about Gödel's theorem is the way he proved it, since this introduces the concept of self-reference, and more specifically the power of this concept. This part becomes, at first sight, a bit more difficult, since we are going to use some symbols. Strictly speaking, using symbols is not really necessary, hence if it scares you too much you could skip this bit and the rest will still make sense. But it does remain interesting to explore how self-reference formally works, and that is something which is important.

The theorem that Gödel proved goes as follows: 'All consistent axiomatic formulations of the number theory contain propositions on which one cannot decide.' Number theory is the theory dealing with numbers, and is not really attractive for non-mathematicians. What Gödel did was to create a self-referring system of numbers – a system in which we talk about numbers, using numbers. Self-reference and self-referential systems are something we know rather well. Language is self-referential. We use language in order to talk about that same language. When one makes a grammatical analysis of a sentence, one uses language, and no other instrument. Using language in order to talk about language is something we are all familiar with, and we do not see a problem with that. A somewhat more remarkable example is the drawings of Escher, the man who can make water run upwards in his drawings. If we look a bit more closely at his drawings, we see that what he does is in fact create a kind of illusion, a self-referencing system, that is not completely valid and that only exists in his drawings. Inside such a self-referencing system, the most impossible things can happen, like water running uphill. The Escher environment is not a real one, but it seems to be very close to reality, which makes it difficult to observe the particularities at first sight. The power of Escher is that he can draw so brilliantly, so close to reality, but nevertheless create his own environment within which he can do the most remarkable things. The same phenomenon is observed in Bach's fugues, but that would lead us too far. In fact, it is this comparison between Gödel, Escher and Bach that inspired Hofstadter (2000) to write the similarly named book, a real bestseller.

Self-reference has to do with loops: phenomena that refer to themselves. Gödel did this with numbers. He used numbers for everything, and in fact he spoke about numbers, using numbers. He spoke in number language. This might seem strange, but let us have a closer look at how this operates. Table 4.1 gives some examples of 'Gödel numbers'.

The sign 'equal to' (=) is represented in Gödel language by the number 5. Five in Gödel language means the same as 'equal to'. The left parenthesis

**Table 4.1** *Examples of Gödel numbers*

| Constant sign | Gödel number | Meaning |
| --- | --- | --- |
| ~ | 1 | not |
| ∨ | 2 | or |
| ⊃ | 3 | If . . . then |
| ∃ | 4 | There is an . . . |
| = | 5 | equal |
| 0 | 6 | zero |
| s | 7 | The immediate successor of |
| ( | 8 | punctuation mark |
| ) | 9 | punctuation mark |
| ` | 10 | punctuation mark |

**Table 4.2** *Examples of expressions with Gödel numbers*

| Numerical variable | Gödel number | A possible substitution instance |
|---|---|---|
| x | 11 | 0 |
| y | 13 | s0 |
| z | 17 | y |

| Sentential variable | Gödel number | A possible substitution instance |
|---|---|---|
| p | $11^2$ | 0 = 0 |
| q | $13^2$ | (∃x) (x = sy) |
| r | $17^2$ | p ⊃ q |

| Predicate variable | Gödel number | A possible substitution instance |
|---|---|---|
| P | $11^3$ | Prime |
| Q | $13^3$ | Composite |
| R | $17^3$ | Greater than |

is represented by '8' and still keeps the meaning of a left parenthesis, e.g. in a mathematical equation. So much for the simpler mathematical signs. But there exist more complicated expressions, of course. Table 4.2 gives a few examples of these.

First of all, we have the normal numerical variables (which represent numbers in mathematics). A $y$ (a variable that can take different numerical values) in a mathematical formula could mean (just as an example): the number that immediately follows 0. The number immediately following 0 is of course also a number itself. Gödel represents that by 13. Sentential variables (which in fact represent sentences) are represented in Gödel language by second powers. A possible expression is 'there exists an $x$ for which it is valid that $x$ follows $y$'. This expression can be represented in Gödel language by $13^2$. As we can see further, we can also construct a full Gödel number for this expression. For a predicate variable he uses third powers. The predicate 'greater than' is represented by $17^3$. As one can observe, the base numbers (11, 13, 17) are prime numbers – numbers that can only be divided by 1 and by themselves.

Then we come to the last step; how does Gödel construct his famous Gödel numbers? A Gödel number is a number that can be deconstructed in a unique manner in order to reconstruct the initial expression. Table 4.3 is such an example. It makes a Gödel number out of the expression 'there

Table 4.3 *Example of a calculation of a Gödel number*

| ($\exists$x) | ($x = sy$) | | | | | | | | |
|---|---|---|---|---|---|---|---|---|---|
| ( | $\exists$ | $x$ | ) | ( | $x$ | = | $s$ | $y$ | ) |
| ↓ | ↓ | ↓ | ↓ | ↓ | ↓ | ↓ | ↓ | ↓ | ↓ |
| 8 | 4 | 11 | 9 | 8 | 11 | 5 | 7 | 13 | 9 |

$$2^8 * \quad 3^4 * \quad 5^{11} * \quad 7^9 * \quad 11^8 * \quad 13^{11} * \quad 17^5 * \quad 19^7 * \quad 23^{13} * \quad 29^9$$

exists an $x$ for which $x$ equals the next number to $y$'. As you can observe, every number or symbol is translated using the first table. Below the second line you see each symbol. These numbers become the exponents of a series of prime numbers. If we eventually calculate this somewhat difficult expression we find the Gödel number for the expression we started from.

Hopefully, despair did not strike fully yet. As has already been suggested, the proof of Gödel's theorem is not really important for managers, but the way it has been proved illustrates the power of the concept of self-reference. And that concept is very crucial in the business world. It is a very powerful concept, with some possibly dangerous side effects.

If we want to illustrate self-reference, we only have to observe corporate culture. Corporate culture is a set of often unwritten rules of what is and is not possible and what is desirable behaviour. The culture is what the company stands for, and clients know what they are buying. Every new employee needs rapidly to become acquainted with that culture, and this is a difficult process, the more so if the rules are not written down. There is nothing wrong with a strong corporate culture. It makes a company into a strong network of people that can easily act very well towards a client who knows precisely what to expect.

But there is also a hidden dimension to corporate culture, and that dimension has everything to do with self-reference. There is a risk that the corporate culture will become fixated on certain rules that make perfect sense for insiders, but have no meaning at all for outsiders. Internally they facilitate and improve communication and efficiency, but externally they do not have added value, other than that the company shares and voices one and the same message. However, the latter is not even necessary. The way a company is organized, and what the shared values and norms are, is not so important for a client as the quality delivered. However, strange things often happen. The rules take over and clients are supposed to behave according to these internal rules which they don't even know. It starts with: 'we should inquire about this'. It continues with: 'in our company we are used to . . . '. And rapidly it becomes: 'our procedures do not allow that'. There is nothing wrong with procedures as long as they do not replace the relationship with the clients. Worse, if the procedures are not known by the client (and that is often the case), then they are not completely understandable for the client.

Governments and civil servants have built a bad reputation through often sticking strictly to rules. This has something to do with political culture and organizational culture. For example, the Netherlands is a country where everything is organized and managed. As a client, one knows what to expect, and Dutch citizens indeed like a strict and strong organization. Unfortunately, this kind of attitude sometimes creates misunderstandings with potential (foreign) partners in mergers. The track record is not really successful: KLM-Iberia, KLM-BA, KPN-Telefonica, KPN-Belgacom, ING-CCF; etc). Only time will tell about KLM-Air France, or should I say Air France-KLM.

Perhaps I could give a small example, taken from my own everyday life, to illustrate the potential damage caused by an overorganized company – which does not mean this could be generalised over that entire company. In the Netherlands, an ISDN connection (rather out of date today) contains three phone lines and a data line. The phone in the living room did not really ever give a good, audible ringing sound when people called us. Since we were able to hear the other phones (on other floors) this was not an issue, and we were not too bothered by it. But of course, it is nice if a phone does ring when one is called. Hence we started thinking to ourselves: maybe the phone is damaged. Replacing it did not provide a solution. Maybe the contact wires were not well connected? But that was not the case either. Then we called client services. For each of the many numbers that I had to go through (it is almost bizarre how one can always find the wrong number), I was given a menu to go through each time. Nice and handy, and probably an efficient way to get a phone call straight through to the right person to help you. But if a client needs to try things (at request of the call centre employee) and each time has to call back, and each time go through the same menu, in order to get each time to a different employee and in general repeat the whole story, it is tedious. And incidentally, each call centre employee starts with the same standard set of questions.

To cut a long story short, one is caught between client services and technical support (it is ISDN, isn't it?). The latter can't do much more than test the line, and if that seems to work, they redirect you to someone else. This is what is known as one-stop shopping; imagine if it were not yet a so-called single front office. Then they give you lots of difficult things to try with lots of numbers and stars, etc. to push, and if that does not work, you can simply call back. Eventually, if you really insist, a technical support person comes to your home. Once that decision is taken, the technician is sent without delay; the system dates from before the rule-based organizational period and the highly efficient call centre procedures (efficient for insiders, of course). And anyway, who wants to go through all the calls and the difficult things to try before the company finally grants you the bonus of a technician? The technician does not follow rules; he loves his job. This is a nice example of strong organization. Without any doubt, this is clear and ordered from the company's perspective, but the client can only observe complete chaos. Within the KPN corporate culture this is a good example of client orientation, and there are plenty of nice and helpful people. But for the client (me in this case), who is no part of the KPN frame, it is impossible to understand why you cannot be helped more quickly and easily. Do you recognize the client services typical of today?

The power and good quality of a well-organized company can tell against the company, if self-reference takes over. For people outside the system, hence clients, it is sometimes completely unclear how things happen the way they happen.

The same can be observed with larger companies that eventually, through size and success, become too internally focused. In the 1980s IBM almost completely missed the shift from the mainframe computer market to the PC market, and barely recovered from that error. Within the organizational learning literature this is labelled the 'boiled frog' phenomenon. If one puts a frog in water and heats the water gradually, the frog will enjoy the increasing temperature, stay in the water and eventually be boiled. If you were to put a frog straight into boiling water, it would jump out immediately. That phenomenon is known. What we have learned from Gödel, and most probably he did not intend to teach this to us, is that self-reference plays a crucial role in this game.

The few examples I have given seem to suggest that this applies more often to larger companies, which have to organize themselves in order to survive. But that is the question. Is this phenomenon only present in companies that issue rules in order to organize themselves? Or is it equally known in self-organizing companies? Autopoiesis (self-organization and self-(re)production) was, as described earlier, a characteristic of networked organizations. Within these systems we saw emergent behaviour. This behaviour, and I now refer to agent-based simulations, is based on simple optimization of one's own goals for each agent and clear communication rules between agents. An autopoietic system is often defined as a closed system. Within the closed borders of the system, it shows learning behaviour, and rules of the games are continuously relearned, learned differently from the starting situation. This is perfectly legitimate and an essential characteristic of such systems. Self-organization is a kind of common denominator, if we keep systems closed – that is, if we do not allow inputs from outside the system that could it give a new élan. IBM was a completely closed system in the 1980s. It did not need the market any more; it *was* the market. Don't jump to the conclusion that this would not be possible in your company. The list of companies that, owing to myopia, were unable to adapt and disappeared is long.

Hence, self-reference is a strong characteristic that apparently appears inside systems. Self-reference allows very powerful and interesting things to happen, and we only need to refer to the proof of Gödel's theorem, which is a masterpiece of analytical 'brain art'. Self-reference is a characteristic of a system that can create a lot of strength inside a system (one could call it solidarity) and by doing so foster a strong power of decision. If we do not recognize self-reference, it can also be the fatal 'attractor' of a system. The interdependence between self-organization, self-(re)production and self-reference is essential, dynamic and not easy to guard against disruption. It could be one of the main assignments of the manager to regularly and voluntarily disrupt this balance. The interaction between these three forces, and not their equilibrium (recall that a system in equilibrium is a dead system), is what drives innovation. In order to keep this going, we continuously need new impulses, if possible from outside, but at least from inside an organization. The interaction between these three forces is ideally facilitated 'at the edge of chaos', at the point where change is easy and new impulses are easy to catch.

Managing a company from a complexity point of view means in fact keeping the company in a kind of orderly state as close as possible to chaos. This means that we should keep the system open to external inputs. Internally, it means that we should give full attention to the creation of the necessary conditions in which people can work optimally in networks.

This implies a limited number of interaction rules, but, above all, good, fast and large communication pathways. In respect to the individuals, one needs to leave space and, preferably, create stimulus to learn – as much for the manager as for the employee. Hierarchical relationships do not really seem to fit into this picture any more. Often, self-reference comes across as a disturbing element for learning. In the chapter about learning (Chapter 5), we return to this issue in more depth.

The issue of self-reference is given even more attention in a specific chapter (Chapter 7) on how, and whether, our society and its legal system are able to learn. It appears that Western society, especially, is characterized as a highly self-referential system. I will illustrate this as an application of the concepts described in this book.

Who preaches order, will spawn chaos: that is why we need a chapter on the learning human.

# 5 Knowledge and learning

● **Can we do anything other than continually learn?**

## Can we do anything other than continually learn?

If it appears that the future is unpredictable and that a management which is 'control oriented' does not address real problems, because the 'better' path does not exist, what is left to us as a manager? If the construction of models (axiomatic systems) is always more and more sophisticated in order to contribute less and less to our understanding, or if more and more frequent use of more complicated rules does not improve our understanding, what is left to us?

The idea that organizations must constantly learn, and therefore become 'learning organizations', is not new. In the 1970s Argyris had already published on the subject of the learning organization, and in the 1990s his ideas had general success, mainly through the success of Peter Senge's book *The Fifth Discipline* (1990). Arie de Geus's famous article in the *Harvard Business Review* (1988) expressed the view that the only real competitive advantage a company could have was to learn faster than its competitors. Lifelong learning is therefore defined as a weapon in the competitive battle, and the transformation of a company into a learning organization is becoming a managerial goal. The conditions should therefore be changed to create a culture in which people can learn and are even encouraged to concentrate on learning from now on. Attention needs to be focused on the group. The literature suggests that groups can learn and that these processes play out differently depending on the bias of a group of learning individuals in a network. It will therefore be possible to improve organizational learning of the group, and all sorts of instruments have been conceived to this end. The centre of interest passed from individual learning (pedagogy and andragogy) to organizational learning.

The question we have to ask ourselves is not so much to know whether groups, after a while, have learned something. Evidently that is possible. The question we have to ask ourselves is: how does that function? What is the mechanism of this organizational learning? And then, if a manager wants to set up a learning organization, how can they do that? Should they look at group processes or rather at individual processes?

The concepts I have dealt with so far suggest that human organizations (companies, for example) develop a form of self-organization. This self-organization is the fruit of a certain number of individual objectives (of each individual, or of each agent as we referred to it before) and of a number of rules of interaction between individuals. Work or learning thus happens by the setting up of the group and by the interaction inside this group, in which each individual has their own objectives, and uses simple rules of interaction. As far as these rules are known and public, their communication is facilitated, but from the point of view of the system, that is not even necessary. If one then applies this to a company, we can see all the actors (employees, managers, shareholders, etc.) have their own (sometimes hidden) agenda.

Each individual follows their own agenda, taking account of a certain number of rules of interaction in a given framework (of limits). This framework, in general, is the company's, which is, from this point of view, a closed system. The framework could be, for example, that the company must survive, or that it stays within the activity of counselling (and does not become a bank, for example). Perhaps the framework could be that the company must make a profit, linked to share value. The fact remains nevertheless that a system cannot be directed towards such an objective, even if it is an objective held by individuals. These objectives are often derived values.

Individuals determine their goals themselves, eventually the derived goals that they want to optimize. In a lot of cases it is, for example, to obtain a higher salary (bonuses, shares), and this can also be in relation to the stock market value. The false reasoning we often make with reference to this is to think that the individual will do their best so that the company attains its goal. But it does not work like that. Now, we could say that it does not matter whether the employee follows their own goal or the company goal, provided that the company goal is attained. Although this thinking is not without interest, it hugely influences the way of directing a company. And then things can turn bad.

Starting from our rational thinking, we not only developed an approach to control, but we have also come to think that groups can have goals to attain and still attain them. We think that groups can learn and change, and we try to direct teams with these ideas in mind. That, by contrast, does not work in practice.

This has nothing to do with the choice of the goals themselves (if they are not already the same in all companies). The goal is to give each individual the liberty to develop themselves by being a link in the network, to create the conditions to support their learning, to give realistic boundaries to the system, and then to facilitate rules of interaction (the communication inside the group). The responsibility can never be elsewhere than with the individual. Communication between people in the same company, or between companies, goes badly as soon as we start to look for the people who are 'responsible'. Responsibility is found on the abstract level, to which neither the manager nor the employee has access. And this is once again an indicator of the possibility that there is something emerging, which is of course important but which we do not find in the purely physical world of processes. Between companies we see the same problem if we speak, for example, about the responsibility in building works. The person who gives the order to build cannot control the quality, and therefore cannot have responsibility for the work. It is rather the company that really does the building, that should manage the quality and that therefore should take the responsibility. The only thing that can be agreed on is the final goal to attain. If a company has to maintain a motorway over a period of five years, you can appoint works supervisors and create obligatory and regular progress measure checks, but the only thing that these measures achieve is to delay the job, create never-ending discussions between parties, and bring about other conditions which are even more uncontrollable. For these problems there is no perfect solution, except, as has already been suggested, to create a contract guaranteeing quality over five years. If during the five-year period the work is failing, the company has to redo the job at its own expense – a simple way to ensure a guarantee through self-control.

The same is true for university students. We cannot judge the quality of the student's learning; it is only the student who can do that. However, the university and the student can agree on the results to be attained (passing an exam, delivering a project, etc.).

Coming back to the example of motorway maintenance, one can get lost trying to make a multitude of rules to define what is to be understood by quality in maintenance. We certainly recognize this type of discussion: we must first of all agree clear definitions before being able to establish whatever else. In practice, that is very counter-productive, even impossible. A concept such as 'a safe motorway' is something that we will never manage to define by common agreement. Safety in the Netherlands, for example, is different from safety in Afghanistan. We have learned to replace communication and the development of shared values by the establishment of rules. Our legal system is a notorious example. This thinking in rules and the idea that rules can replace shared values is so strongly present in Western Europe that it is necessary to look at it more closely.

Rules are most often demotivating for those who already do their work well. I propose to use an example that Professor Kenis gave during his inaugural speech as Professor for Health Management at the University of Tilburg (in the Netherlands). What often happens is as in the following example: 80 per cent of hospitals (and the same is true in all other sectors) offer good services and 20 per cent are mediocre. In general it is simple to see the difference between the two groups. What the government often does is to reinforce the regulations, with the intention of forcing the weaker 20 per cent to become better. In practice, what these additional rules often lead to is that the 80 per cent that are doing well become frustrated by the additional new rules, which are unnecessary for them. The target 20 per cent group works around the rules more easily. In the penal code we always find an article which throws an alternative light on an offence (I am thinking here especially of commercial offences). More rules slow down operations and consequently create, almost by definition, more patients on the waiting list (a huge problem in the Netherlands), or unhappy clients – exactly the opposite of what the aim was. By looking to improve, the best provide worse services, and the mediocre often do not improve, or at least not by following the new rules.

I voluntarily borrow another example given during the inauguration of Professor Kenis. If a child wants to swim at the deep end of a swimming pool in the Netherlands, it must have a (Dutch) swimming licence. It is not enough that the child knows how to swim, since it could demonstrate that to the swimming instructor. No, the system does not work like that. A real licence has to be supplied, and to obtain that, the child has to go through a swimming school, for which there is a waiting list (as there is for everything in the Netherlands). In Belgium (and this is not given as an example to follow, but to illustrate how more chaotic organization can sometimes work more efficiently), the child will be asked to swim, say, 25 metres and can then pick up a licence on leaving the swimming pool. The important question is: can this infant swim, or is it a question of respecting the efficient working of the system? Who sows order will harvest chaos (the title of my book in Dutch, the first edition of which sold out in less than a year).

But the principle of chaos therefore also produces efficiency.

Individuals must consequently be supervised (and I am consciously not using the word 'directed') to coach them to change in the best way for them to attain their own goals more easily. The conditions must be created in a certain way and be continually accompanied in order for the interaction between individuals to proceed to the desired result. It is therefore the manager's role to create the conditions to let them support people in the best way possible and to support them in their development, in the hope that this will lead to a sufficiently good result (goal). A little parenthesis here is that management purely oriented towards 'control and profit' will invariably lead, in developing countries (with very little external protection), to unacceptable and pitiful excesses such as child labour. Until we manage to redefine management and company goals in general as the contribution to the development of employees (managers included), excess is inevitable. The coupling of control (internal) and the pursuit of external goals (profit, stock market value) can only lead to conflict.

What is the role of the manager now? If a control approach does not really work, what is there left to do? What (new) skills and understanding are necessary, but, even more, what (new) tasks must the manager undertake? From what I have said so far, we can distil a certain number of ideas, without wanting to be exhaustive.

- Managers must commit to learning continually themselves. Managers switch to automatic pilot too quickly to find a solution. Thus, a lot of possibilities for renewal and learning are missed. To paraphrase Pirsig (in *Zen and the Art of Motorcycle Maintenance*), it is necessary to put oneself, figuratively, at a little distance from the engine. Listen to the engine and it will tell you itself what the problem is. If it rains, and the engine stops, you immediately think that the rain caused it to stop, but it is necessary to avoid automatic responses and prejudgments. Quick replies seem useful and necessary, but often they interfere with learning and innovation.

- Rather than directing people, I prefer to define the manager's role as to stimulate individuals' learning. This implies, among other things, that you must not be fixed in your ideas from the beginning, but leave space for improvement, learning and, once again, for innovation.
- Who does not like to learn while crossing a street holding his father's or mother's hand? The manager plays the role of the most experienced person, the one who gives confidence to allow others to acquire experience and audacity.
- I am referring here to the role of the coach, of the 'master' in the craftsman sense of the word, but also of the trustworthy person one can go to with failures, without being immediately sanctioned. In short, the manager can facilitate a learning environment with the means which are at their disposal, but always in the context of a coach, of a tutor, and not as a teacher.
- The most important reason for the existence of companies must be to form a network of human beings, as much internal (employees) as external (clients, suppliers, etc.). The company's wealth is the wealth of the network, and especially the rules of interaction between them. The manager can set up the rules of interaction, sometimes pilot them a little, observe them and, especially, try to draw out lessons from them.
- The rules of a network can be stimulated instead of corrected. Management by control often consists of decreeing a lot of detailed rules and controlling to see that they are well respected. The rules become the goal, and not the result any more, which is, however, very important. The tendency should not be to make more and more detailed rules, but rather to look for simple rules of social interaction. The rules only make sense at the moment when they say something about the subject of interaction. Thus, they contribute to a more productive network of learning individuals.
- Finally, management can render the context as rich as possible, but also as wide as possible. A wider context gives more possibilities for renewal and gives space for people who want to learn something. A bigger external network gives more potential for cooperation and therefore more potential for renewal and innovation.

Learning is obviously central in today's management. It is a question not of group learning or organizational learning, but of individual learning. We hope that each human being in a society or company can appropriate the role of learning human being, thereby to contribute to a larger goal. For the manager, learning includes two dimensions: on the one hand, the personal development of the manager, their personal learning; and on the other hand, learning as a 'company process', the stimulation of others' learning.

Trained managers (in business schools) are supplied with the necessary instruments to firefight in companies. In addition, they often have the belief that doing so is the right way: to manage is to control and grow. For that there are some better routes than others, always using the techniques learned. The manager makes use of a series of ready models, models which explain, extrapolate, analyse, etc. They learn how a new case can be resolved. This often resembles a terribly clinical process. It seems that the manager who has just left school thinks that company problems are subdivided into financial cases, marketing cases, organizational cases, etc. On their first day at work, they expect the first case to appear. Evidently this is a little caricatured, but it is basically the common thinking on the subject of managers. To learn (in a business school) is often synonymous with being taught the 'correct' tools. Managers who aim to 'recharge the batteries' will often learn new tools (or refreshed tools); they will indeed 'recharge the batteries' as a process which is somewhat physical. But just as when you fill the car up with petrol, it is soon empty again, the new tools will be quickly eroded.

The learning of the manager has a lot to do with personal development, with the possibility of critical self-analysis and, consequently, showing oneself vulnerable. To become a learning coach, instead of a teacher, calls on other skills. Managers must recognize their strengths and weaknesses and learn to live them. Everyone has emotions and our actions will always be coloured by our emotions. This link between emotions and actions has a connection with personality and emotional development. It is not new ground, but we will refer here to the theories of personal development: the focus is on learning. How can I develop myself so that my personality does not hinder me in my learning, how can I take it actively in hand, and stimulate the learning of those around me? How can I improve my own capacity for learning? How can I continually learn and feel better as a person? This is the main dimension: to manage my own learning.

There is another dimension in which we consider learning as a company process that crucially contributes to its success. This new aspect necessitates a little more attention, and we will focus on it in the rest of this chapter. Machado describes in his magnificent poem ('Caminanto, no hay camino/Se hace camino al andar') a few essential points for learning and knowledge, two inseparable elements in contemporary management. The poet expresses himself on this path which is built anew each time it is walked on. There is no existing path; the path must be made from scratch each time, even if we take the same path. There is therefore no good path, nor correct path; everyone should remake the path each time. In fact, it is also essential in knowledge: knowledge makes the difference only if it permits the creation of something. Knowledge is essentially dynamic: it refers to what someone can do with information. Each street we cross is a new street every time. Experience is certainly important (from the point of view of learning, it is the most important path leading to knowledge), but experience cannot be simply extrapolated. We saw earlier, in the theoretical framework, that prediction in a dynamic context is impossible. So what is left for us is to each time 'rewalk' the path.

Experience is important, but cannot be reproduced. Choosing the direction therefore becomes a pure choice for the manager. Experience can help in effect. Today we are where we are, because we have acquired the experience we have acquired. I can write what I can write because I experienced what I experienced. What we cannot do is formulate the 'best' advice based on the past. On the other hand, we can do it based on experience acquired. It is the same for me too; each time I must remake the path, and in following it I can, and I must, learn anew. From the point of view of an organization we should therefore do something with all these personal and organizational experiences if we do not want to lose all the experience acquired.

Earlier I said that all learning is individual, and here we again find a dilemma. The individual is perfectly capable of learning from experience. In fact, human beings are even sublime at this. Organizations, if they can learn from experience at all, do so with much greater difficulty. Where and how can one access organizational memory and the intelligence of the company? The memory of a company should keep track of all the experiences undergone. The intelligence of a company will then allow something to be done (dynamically something new). What seems to be a human strength seems also to be the weakness of a company (or a group). An important role for management is to promote learning and the sharing of knowledge.

The daily practice of management is to try to explain the best paths for the company. How should we face product innovation? How should the budgets be done? What should be in a marketing plan? How do we broach the question of acquisitions? It is notably the focus on the path, instead of the focus on the goal, which renders management so weak. Remember the story of the swimming licence. There is a procedure for obtaining this licence, and it must be followed. The goal is no longer to discover whether the child can swim. The child who can already swim is evidently demotivated. The employee with good ideas, but who must each time go through the administration mill and hierarchical decision-making processes, must be equally demotivated. In this schematic picture it is the goal rather than the path which is the focus that must be kept hold of. This is very difficult, since the goals are often arbitrary choices based on feelings, vague suspicions, beliefs, devotions, and other feeble or vague concepts which are, in any case, difficult to measure.

The path is very detailed and concrete, and therefore easy to determine and control – except that the path does not necessarily lead to something, or, more precisely, not necessarily to something which is positive for us. A learning manager is therefore a manager who does not explain (as such) the path, but who instead creates the conditions for their colleagues to look for the path themselves, and then to make the path by walking it. As a coach the manager can share a part of their own experience with their colleagues, but they should not at any time prescribe a path. First of all, it is impossible, but also that demotivates the colleagues, and prevents them from being innovative.

In *Alice in Wonderland* this dilemma between the goal and the path was well expressed. When Alice does not know which path she should take, she asks the Cheshire Cat. The cat asks her where she wants to go, and as she does not know, the cat quite rightly says each path is good. Modern Western management is sick with this illness.

Knowledge and learning are inseparably linked. Therefore, an interesting question is: what do we know about learning? We would think that we already have hundreds of years of experience of learning. We have had schools for as long as we can remember, and they are to do with learning, aren't they?

If someone wants to play a musical instrument, they should be prepared to practise a lot. No professor can teach someone how to become a musician. Can we teach someone to become a professional footballer? Only intensive practice can lead to that. To be gifted and not practise incessantly simply does not work. Exercise without being gifted does not work either, of course, but that is another matter. If you want to learn to play an instrument, it is necessary to practise a piece every day. Then you go to the teacher and you play the piece. The teacher shares their experience by highlighting possible mistakes in learning. You go back home to practise some more. Thus, you finally learn to play a musical instrument. It is difficult for a teacher to outline a path beyond one or two lessons. After these two lessons, you have to again see what level you are at and what would be the best next step. A good teacher is an experienced teacher who can share their experience with their pupils and, especially, who can motivate and stimulate them.

Do we learn to drive a car by going to a driving school? No, we learn how to get a driving licence. Driving again is a series of rules which must be learned and then practised, and driving behaviour must be replicated. If the rules are correctly rehearsed and the behaviour replicated, you get the driving licence. Later, you really learn to drive by the experience of doing so over several years. That poses no problem for driving schools, as long as we do not think that we learn to drive a car by going to a driving school. In parallel, if the goal and the means must be clear and the piloting targets the goal, there is no problem with a management based on control, as long as we do not expect the company to be helped by it.

Can we teach a child to cross a street? No, the only thing to do is to take the child by the hand and cross the street with it many times. We try to share with the child our accumulated experience, drawing its attention to cars, traffic lights, etc., and talking about the experiences. Learning is too often confused with teaching. We cannot teach anything to anyone, at least when it is a question of skills (and not rules). We can only try to create the best conditions to stimulate learning. The question is to know whether the final objectives to be attained at the end of the course help the learning. We could even ask ourselves if exams help learning. What is the aim of learning? Is the goal to obtain a certain degree or qualification (with which one makes the path the goal), or is the goal for human beings to develop themselves? If the goal is clear, we can leave people to get there freely and let people train themselves dynamically. So, we can lay down the path in walking it.

Without going into too much detail about the process of learning itself, we can study the examples mentioned in a schema which will illustrate the dimensions of learning (first published in our book *The Hybrid Business School* (Baets and Van der Linden 2004)). This schema illustrates how and where learning takes place in a company, and it lets us understand the role of the learning manager better. As has already been

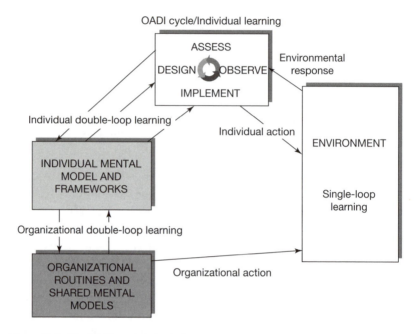

**Figure 5.1** *The OADI cycle, single-loop learning and double-loop learning*

argued, and as the examples show, individual learning is central. From this schema we can explore how we can support organizational learning through individual learning.

At the top of Figure 5.1, Kolb's well-known OADI cycle is represented. Kolb claimed that all learning (that is, individual learning) happens according to the OADI cycle: Observe, Assess, Design and Implement. A child puts its hand on a hot plate and makes an observation; the child has a sensation. The next step is that the child tries 'to appreciate' this sensation, doubtlessly as a painful one. Then it can develop a number of alternative actions, such as leaving its hand where it is, or taking it off. One of these two actions is finally chosen and taken. The child immediately and inevitably makes another observation. If the hand is pulled away, this observation will be perhaps appreciated as less painful. The child can put the hand back on, or abstain from doing so, etc. A child who learns quickly will only need to effect a few necessary cycles to learn about the danger of a hot plate. Other children may need more time to learn (more cycles), so they need more experiences in order to be able to learn.

We could label the children who learn quickly 'smart'; in this case intelligence is measured in relation to the speed of learning. From a dynamic point of view, it is logical: those who learn quickly are smart. In the more classical view of learning, or even of management, the smarter person is the one who is good at solving mathematical problems. We have here another materialization of learning in companies. It concerns personal development, which is crucial in the case of company training, or personal projects. What can we give someone in terms of personal development? How can we measure intelligence, and, more generally, how do we want to treat intelligence inside a company? Is a competency-based approach a solution?

How does a child learn to cross a street? By crossing a street a certain number of times, the child runs through the OADI cycles each time and finally it manages to develop an aptitude (from its own experience) that will let the child organize and evaluate the next action better. By acquiring experiences itself our intelligence creates something we can call a mental model. As Figure 5.1 shows, this mental model will be fed by evaluations and will supply in its turn the possible actions and help the person to choose the best. The more acquired experience there is, the more the mental model is enriched, and the more possible designs can be conceived and then better implemented. The phenomenon by which experiences create individual mental models is often called 'double-loop learning'. What a company wants from its employees is their mental models, but evidently, as they are internalized, it is very difficult to know what they are. That becomes exciting when we try to create learning systems or even (virtual) learning environments which try to reproduce at least a small part of these mental models. We will come back to all this in more detail.

The OADI cycle also explains why all we can teach someone is rules. For learning, the evaluation step (the assessment) is very important. Someone only starts to learn at the moment when they can compare what is said with the mental model they already have in their mind and provided that they want to make this comparison. People learn more easily if they can compare the new thing learned to something that they already know. That is why it is difficult to learn something completely new. In this case, the majority of references to existing frameworks in mental models will be of very little help. We need a long time to find something we can relate the new thing to. A good teacher will try to make it as easy as possible for their pupils to make connections and relationships. In this case, the existing references in our mental model are not much use. So, if we do not give value to an observation, we learn nothing. This is precisely the reason why teaching does not work well.

During teaching, the pupil can listen properly, but we cannot control whether they are going to activate and make use of what they have heard. In other terms, we would like to be able to control whether or not the pupil has been able to make a link between what they have learned and the mental model already in place. Teaching is a form of transfer of information which could invite a pupil to learn, just like other forms of transfer. In any domain, teaching does not guarantee the best result compared to other forms of transfer. Where teaching works best is in terms of organization. Teaching is easier to organize (and to control) than learning, and it is also often better worked. We see here again the manager's dilemma: to learn or to control.

The OADI cycle works partly internally and partly externally in humans. Observation and implementation are done in the external world; evaluation and conception happen internally. The external world, the context, can be seen on the right of Figure 5.1. Action following learning appears only in the external world, when a chosen design is implemented. This individual action will then lead to a reaction in the environment, and a new observation will immediately be made. In order to learn, therefore, an environment is needed even though the forming of a mental model happens internally. This environment is necessary to be able to have experiences because these experiences are the essential source for learning.

As I have already said, individuals learn by creating a rich mental model from experience. In a company, it is an art to be able to share all these rich individual mental models between employees (thanks to which we can multiply experiences). This is what learning in a company (organizational learning) can eventually achieve. So, this is done in the context of actions which support learning. If we want to share this individual learning in one way or another, we need to externalize it. Human learning, for example, is very difficult to share. Only when what is learned re-enters the environment (as the result of an action) can we learn something from someone else.

There is nevertheless another level of learning if we put groups of people together, and that is illustrated in the bottom left of Figure 5.1. Putting people on a project in groups, where they are left to work together, gives rise to shared routines which we call 'shared mental models'. This phenomenon is called 'organizational double-loop learning', and it can be observed when people are going to do something together, provided that they want to exchange mental models with each other. These organizational routines (shared mental models) are very important in a company. They are often self-referring and evident to those who make up part of the system, but incomprehensible externally. They are not a simple summation of individual mental models, and for this reason they are difficult to grasp. As they are shared by a majority, they can sometimes be observed by people on the outside – clients, for example. These routines are, consequently, very important; they are difficult to recognize from the inside, they can be strong, and they can represent a strength but also a weakness.

A metaphorical example of this phenomenon which is used from time to time in several books is that of a cage of monkeys (see, among others, my 1998 book, *Organizational Learning and Knowledge Technologies in a Dynamic Environment*). For those who do not yet know this metaphor, here it is.

You put twenty monkeys in a cage with a bunch of bananas on the ceiling and a little ladder for the monkeys to get to them. What will happen? The smartest monkey (the one that learns the most quickly) will climb the ladder and take a banana. Then it starts to rain, which the monkeys intensely dislike. One monkey in the cage is replaced by a new monkey. The same phenomenon occurs. Another monkey is replaced each time. After a number of replacements, the smart monkeys have learned. These ones no longer climb the ladder; even if the bananas are attractive, they know that rain will follow. For the more stupid monkeys, more experiences are necessary for them to learn the same thing until they understand it. A stupid monkey will climb the ladder and take a banana; it rains. We continue to replace monkeys and invariably the same thing happens. Each new monkey will go towards the bananas while the others already understand that they should not do that. After a number of repetitions of these events, the monkeys have had enough. They will use physical force to prevent the new monkey from going to the bananas. The new monkey does not understand anything of the system, which has in the meantime become a self-referential system, but evidently he cannot do anything other than follow the implicit orders: if everyone thinks like that, then I will do the same.

Twenty successive replacements result in a cage of monkeys who individually all want to go to these bananas but don't as a group, and none of them knows why not. This is what we sometimes call corporate culture. 'Why do we do it like that here?' 'Because we always have.' And so why? We do not understand the culture, however, if we are outsiders. And effectively it often cannot be understood by someone (new) inside either. We know the rule (explicit or implicit) of how to do what, but often we no longer know the reason. That also has a relationship with learning: you must want to change and have the courage to recreate the path each time.

We cannot introduce change at the level of mental models, or at the individual or organizational level. The trajectory of the change must start by a new individual learning, undergoing new experiences (own or shared); then we can hope that these new experiences will lead to new individual mental models which can, in turn, lead, after a lot of collaboration, to new routines and new shared models. These are long and difficult procedures which are almost impossible to pilot. Again we cannot once and for all determine the path to be able to then control it. The trajectories of change which are tracked in this way have often failed. Change is essentially learning, and learning is essentially to make the path in walking it, even if you take the same path. It is clear that a master's role is up for grabs for the learning manager.

We can now try to find a means to support learning, as previously defined. We could make use of support instruments, which should therefore be grafted in their entirety onto the previous diagram. We are looking for systems, in themselves learning, which are capable of learning from others' experiences and taking lessons from them so as to be able, afterwards, to be shared more easily by people. It is these instruments which are mostly found today in the domain of artificial intelligence – although this instrumental side is evidently very important, to my way of thinking, on the organizational side, I do not want to go into it in too much detail here, because the subject is covered in my other books. Notably, we need a lot of contextual references to understand these support tools well and to be able to apply them correctly.

Under the label of virtual learning (or e-learning or workplace learning), we often find virtual platforms which provide the sharing of experience and knowledge, and also which allow working in teams at a distance. On the other hand, in practice we regularly abuse the words 'e-learning' and 'virtual learning' to sell solutions of the collaborative intranet type with the sole goal of distributing a form of teaching. We are clearly not referring to that here. E-learning can be another type of instrument for learner support. Those who are interested as much in the concepts as in the working methods used in e-learning could refer to two of my books with that focus.

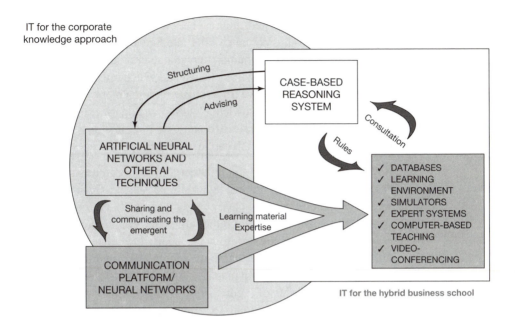

**Figure 5.2** *Learning, knowledge management and information technology*

Figure 5.2 tries to unite the learning systems (complex adaptive systems, CAS) with the virtual learning environments by grafting them onto the diagram of learning, Figure 5.1. Figure 5.2 is an instrumental version of the previous learning diagram, Figure 5.1. Let me try to comment on Figure 5.2 in detail, by identifying the different steps in the learning cycle and the possible supports (instruments). The OADI cycle, and hence the experiences, can be stored in the 'case-based reasoning system'. It is a software program which provides storage of 'stories' and finds them again by means of key words. Now we can create the same idea a lot more easily by putting the stories on XML pages so that we can then find them using a semantic search engine. On the right-hand side, in the outside part, you can see the elements of a virtual learning platform where what one learns can, at any moment, be related to the company experiences. This is a technical support solution which should facilitate 'just-in-time', 'just-enough' learning during the job itself by using everything that has already been learned in the company.

On the left-hand side of Figure 5.2 we try to create artificial intelligence learning systems. With the CAS, we create systems which learn human experiences, case studies, examples in such a way as to transform these experiences into lessons learned, and maybe, eventually, into procedures if possible. These CAS thus contain a little intelligence learned by humans. Without really putting human knowledge into the form of rules (which is classically done in expert systems, and which only work at a very modest level of success), we try to create an instrument which gives the user something of human knowledge without making it explicit. In other words, the question is therefore to know whether it is possible to build simple artificial brains which can learn from experience.

To find whether that is the case, among other things we can use artificial neural networks, genetic algorithms, agent simulation, etc. (techniques which are all based on theories I have already discussed). For certain applications these techniques seem rather efficient. What interests us is their capacity for learning and how they can be used to support human learning. The least we can say is that they seem to learn, and often better than certain people. It would help managers if they understood these tools better. On the left-hand side of Figure 5.1 you can see shared mental models, which remain difficult to dissect, and for which we could use 'communities of practice', for example. In any case, learning systems are only interesting if they bring something to the learning of others. It does not make sense to create a learning system based on the expertise of only one person, or for the use of only one person. The goal will always be to contribute to a learning environment so that others, and preferably as many people as possible, can learn.

There are therefore support techniques for managers who want their employees to learn. We only need now to avoid thinking once again that there is an existing path that we only have to follow. Worse still, this could be the royal road to total failure and disillusion. What the manager could well do is to concentrate on the creation of a favourable context for learning. An infrastructure of knowledge and learning can be very instrumental for helping to attain the goal, especially in medium-sized companies (let's say companies with more than 100 employees) in several localities. The learning platforms will be no better than a relationship of master to learner, but if there are too many people, a real individual learning path is too difficult to realize. This individual learning path remains necessary, and is what we want to support by means of learning platforms, and, if possible, even to imitate it a little. We are not organizing teaching, but a context which provides learning by doing. Employees should be able to make the path themselves in walking it. If we try to sow order too much, we will quickly reap chaos.

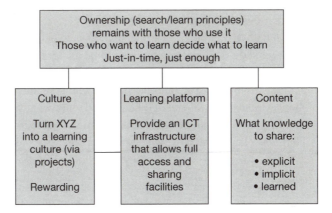

**Figure 5.3** *Your knowledge infrastructure*

On what elements can a manager exercise an influence in order to facilitate learning? Figure 5.3 proposes four elements where managers can have an impact. Of course, the culture is important for developing learning. A learning culture is a culture which encourages learning and which rewards the sharing of knowledge. We could envisage adapting the rewards in consequence. If we want to motivate people to invest in the network, appreciation must be conceived to this end. The piloting of the turnover will lead to individualist behaviour (abstraction made of the network) with the goal of generating revenue as a personal objective. This is completely at odds with an approach in which shared knowledge is appreciated. The reward, certainly in Western Europe, is a strong lever for behavioural change.

Technically, the manager should see to it that people can work easily together, especially in bigger companies. That necessitates the use of information and communication technologies which allow for the effective sharing of knowledge, which in turn allows for cooperation at a distance, but, above all, leaves space for experiment.

Of course, something must be done to put knowledge (which we often refer to as information) at the disposal of employees, if they want to learn. So, we must think about explicit knowledge (rules) and implicit knowledge (experience acquired over the years) and learned knowledge (knowledge obtained after many years of experience in a certain company process). Learned knowledge lies between explicit and implicit knowledge: it is explicit, but experience shows that in practice things do not always happen precisely as the rules would have it.

Above all, nevertheless, employees themselves should remain responsible for their own learning. No one can decide what it is that employees should learn, that will enable them to make their own path in walking it. The manager should allow the employee to be a learning employee. The offer of learning should be oriented not to the offer (often of a course), but uniquely to the demand (and the person who demands it). Management should not decide what should be learned, only what should be offered; deciding what should be learned is the role of the learners themselves. That is the key to success. A learning manager can only work with learning colleagues. Together they can choose to follow an innovative path.

The instruments which have been cited here are, for the most part, support instruments. They target a context which should invite a learning work environment. But there is a lot to do as well in terms of broaching projects (of innovation). Instead of determining in advance how innovation should be done (which works very badly in practice), we should also choose an approach geared towards action. A possible approach is 'soft systems methodology', which comes from the domain of research and design and which lets the manager build and realize projects in a learning way. Soft systems methodology is only one example among a series of 'action research' approaches and tools which try to combine research, project management and change management.

Let us summarize what we have learned up until now in this chapter. At the start, we tried to formalize the learning manager's tasks. Now it is clear how and why the manager's tasks contribute and can be done:

- The main mission of the learning manager is to continually learn him- or herself. Fixed schemas should always be examined.
- Rather than directing people, the learning manager stimulates them in order for them to learn. In practice this means not fixing everything at the outset, but leaving space for improvement, learning and innovation.
- The learning manager is a link in the network of people working together and learning clients. The rules of interaction deserve the manager's attention.
- The rules of interaction in the network should be stimulated so that the network works well. To restrict and correct are not priorities.
- Finally, the learning manager must make the context as rich and as broad as possible.

If managers continue to sow order, they will continue to reap chaos.

Although we can apply these concepts to all sorts of company processes, I want to try to apply the concept of knowledge and learning which is developed here (based on a holistic, rather than reductive, idea) to innovation.

This automatically brings another angle to innovation and argues for a fresh approach. In my recent research projects (see my 2005 publication, *Knowledge Management and Management Learning*) we have looked for another causality in innovation, but it should be clear that this is beyond the classical conceptual framework. In the following chapters I will come back to this in more detail, but let us now try first of all to determine innovation as a learning process in which knowledge, learning and the concept of the holistic individual are united in a conceptual model. Figure 5.4 illustrates this conceptual model. This diagram combines the model of knowledge and learning developed in my research and described here with Ken Wilber's diagram of holism, described earlier. The two of them have been united here, and evidently not by pure coincidence. In this diagram the four quadrants of Wilber's holistic concept are grafted onto my model of knowledge and learning

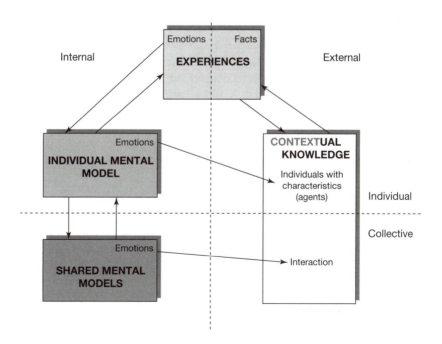

**Figure 5.4** *Innovation as learning*

management. My model is now applied to innovation. By combining it with Wilber's model we introduce another dimension which is entirely new. Although I have already said that the left-hand side of my model happens entirely inside us and the right-hand side outside, Wilber goes into greater detail on the subject of what is behind this type of model. He says that if we speak about our experience, this has two dimensions: a real side and an emotional side. With this real side, we find ourselves in the real world (at least, that seems to be the case). In this real side we acquire experience and learn actions. But these experiences cannot be transformed into a mental model. No change can be effected if we do not put emotion into the experiences.

It is these same emotions which will take care of the filtering for what will finally be shared with the external world. The emotions determine how employees feel in their job but also how and why they want to share, and, more generally, how they want to cooperate.

Meanwhile, we know, through the management literature on the subject of leadership and the emotional quotient, that the emotions are important, and why. As recent research has shown (research concerning leadership but also our own current research), it is precisely this emotional side, this human interaction side, which will create the difference between failed and successful innovation. The emotions are neither easily observable nor measurable. Rational scientists can switch off here. We have rarely managed to effectively integrate the concept of emotions into a conceptual model concerning an aspect of companies (for example, innovation). To introduce this emotional dimension raises a very fundamental question: at what level can we really talk about causality? In economic theory we have become used to talking about economic variables at a very high level of aggregation. We generally rarely consider individual behaviour, and if we do, we consider the individual to be rational. This is also a form of aggregation, which denies the emotional side among other things. If, effectively, this emotional side plays an important role, the aggregation of man into a rational being will contradict the observation. Is causality found at the level of emotions and the exchange of emotions? Or is causality found even outside individuals, as certain theories (those of Sheldrake, Chopra, etc., who are considered in the following chapters) suggest? If this level is not the level of aggregation on which we now carry out research (see the classical theory of innovation), then we are researching on an incorrect level, and therefore we will find things that are of little significance (that is to say, incorrect). Often we content ourselves with a part of the truth or a simplified truth, which then gives partial understanding of a reduced reality. But if we want to effectively consider innovation as a process of knowledge and learning, how can we obtain an understanding of the processes of innovation, how can we pilot them, and how can they grow? How can we render innovation more effective?

The change of paradigm proposed here is really produced in three different domains. For the moment we are no longer examining the reality of the mechanical company, but that of the organic one. Second, I have argued for dumping static and deterministic concepts in favour of considering emergent behaviour. The third ground has a connection with the notion that what is seen from the outside (Wilber's it quadrant) is something entirely different from what is produced inside (the I quadrant). Classical logic is of the style *mechanical – static and determinist – 'objectively' measurable*. It is clear that this paradigm allows the research of causality at a fairly high level of aggregation. We speak about variables on the subject of market sensitivity, the capacity for innovation, a procedure for innovation, etc. Seeing the characteristics of this paradigm, one can theoretically determine, through the aggregates, a causality which allows the directing of reality. In practice it is nevertheless harder. Innovation fails on a large scale in companies.

The paradigm proposed here presents another logic: *organic – emergent – experience and consciousness*. In this paradigm, causality is evidently not found at the level of the variables suggested before. Causality therefore potentially exists at a lower level of aggregation, to be realized in an emergent fashion in the process (over time, giving time a constructive role). This level of aggregation can eventually be the level of 'shared experience'. In any case, we must go to the level of the individual. Cooperation of experiences (of emotions) and the conscience of individuals will create successful innovation (or not).

What our conceptual model introduced as problematic is that we probably look for causality at too high a level of aggregation. The elements built from emergent behaviour are found at a lower level than in the classical macro concepts of innovation – that is, in the emotions of each person individually interested (the most 'micro' possible). The interaction of these emotions (on the right-hand side of the conceptual model) will define an emergent behaviour, using the principles of interaction described before. The emergent technologies are described. What is missing at the moment, and what is necessary, is a coherent theory concerning the possible behaviour at a very detailed level. Where we classically talk of the macro, meso and micro levels of the economy, this micro level remains at a very high level of aggregation, because of the use of generalizations by rational people (clients, employees, etc.). There is no economic theory which considers the individual and emergence at a sufficiently detailed level of aggregation. And this is perhaps why economic theory so often fails in practical application. We must therefore research at an even lower level: let us say at an individual level, even an 'atomic' one. We have found, these past ten to fifteen years, that interesting theories which support the paradigm presented here have been developed and used in all sorts of scientific domains, and can be put into operation in a management context. In these sciences, we call this lower level the 'quantum' level or concept.

On this quantum level, conscience, energy and information melt together. The question to ask is thus: how can we examine this quantum level, or at least start to do so? I shall make proposals (of course, very incomplete ones) on this subject, and will comment on some real-life examples from our own research.

For this reason, I start Chapter 8 with an exploration of recent scientific developments in different domains which, to my way of thinking, give interesting points of reference. In the meantime, and in order to make the proposed paradigm as easy to apply as possible, the next two chapters elaborate on the learning function of both the manager and of society.

# 6 The learning manager

Whoever (for instance, a manager) sows order will rapidly, because of the characteristics of any dynamic system, reap chaos. The principles of why this happens and the mechanisms of how are described in earlier chapters. Does this mean that the manager should create chaos, in order to harvest order? That is what I want to deal with in this chapter. We need to explore the daily practice of the learning manager a bit more.

Theoretically we have already seen that in dynamic systems order does indeed emerge out of chaos. We have labelled this 'emergent behaviour' – an intriguing and constructive phenomenon. It is born almost out of itself; we do not need a manager to pilot it. But the manager can of course support and embrace this process: as described in the previous chapter, it is possible to create an ideal context.

For the rest of the chapter, let us limit ourselves to the learning manager. Not that this means we won't talk about a learning human; a manager is but a human. But the examples I cite all refer to managerial practice. This makes it easier for the reader to draw lessons that can be immediately applied. People active in organizations or associations will, without any doubt, recognize the examples given.

The following chapter deals explicitly with a more societal level (or should we say a more political level): the legal system and the judicial organization. This should illustrate that this new paradigm (or should we say 'other' paradigm?) sheds a completely different light on political and organizational aspects of society. But more about this in the next chapter.

The complexity paradigm, out of which emerges the necessity for a continuously learning human, often suggests a completely different path to be walked, compared to the nicely paved path that we often follow today. We have already seen some examples while dealing with the theoretical concepts. For further illustration let us focus on very practical situations. What should a learning manager do in certain situations? Not that the suggested actions would be the ideal ones; we know that there are no ideal solutions, just examples. The purpose of the examples is not to suggest a better solution, but merely another solution which makes sense both conceptually and theoretically. Without any doubt it will shed a different light on reality. That is often what learning is all about. We should not search for the best solution. We should search for many different solutions and then identify the probability or the degree of reality or wishful thinking regarding some of those solutions.

Of course, it is impossible to give long, detailed examples, since any specific case justifies only its specific lessons. We use repetitive situations that are therefore easy to recognize. In general terms, we are striving towards a new form of network organization in which individuals have a more pronounced input, based on their own experience (or the experience of others). Hierarchical control often appears counter-productive. The support system has as a goal to continually learn and 'un-'learn. Let us just start the exploration and we will automatically see where it brings us.

When, in 1989, the Berlin Wall came down, and we all saw tremendous potential markets in Eastern Europe and Russia, many companies went east. Rapidly it became clear that we lacked a serious understanding of how to do business in Russia (among the many other things that we did not seem to understand in that country). Using our rational, structured and control-driven management, we had the impression of being stuck. The problem was not that Russia did not have any procedures; it probably had more than any other country in the world. But as a result of the visible and, more importantly, the invisible revolution that had taken place, those rules became obsolete. Maybe rules were always differently understood in Russia as compared to countries like the Netherlands (heavily rule based) or France (heavily bureaucratic). Which country manager do you send to Russia? Do you look for the manager with the best results? Or do you go for the manager who learns fast? Or worse, do you look for a manager who is good at solving analytical problems? The fast-learning manager will certainly be of most use. The country manager who is able to learn how to do business in those countries fast, even if it is done in a dramatically different way from what they are used to (or even think is normal) in the home country, will be able to manage your company in what we indeed call 'chaotic' countries. Other than executing sales and marketing plans, this manager will have to lay down their path in walking. While learning fast, they will continually adapt the path, and hence their approach. The faster they learn, the faster they will be able to do business in the new country. Reporting back to the holding company, though, could be completely inadequate. The control mechanisms applicable in headquarters are most probably not adaptable to emergent situations; the country manager's reports might not even be understood by headquarters. In some companies the drive for (immediate) control has got in the way of success in Russia.

Next is the question of whether a company wants to have a presence in such a country. We call this a strategic choice, in which we balance risks against anticipated returns. In this discussion, the control-oriented manager will lean towards risk control: a known country with probably a rather stable market. The battle to gain market share in a stable market will be long, difficult and expensive. In chaotic markets, gaining market share is much easier, but the risks of losing (everything) are higher. The natural tendency of the controlling manager is towards low-entropy markets (with a low degree of chaos). But high-entropy markets, which are continuously moving, are easier to penetrate. Entrepreneurial managers hence need to go to the more chaotic markets, trying to keep their company in a more creative zone far from equilibrium, but also aiming to prevent the company from being pulled into complete chaos. Learning fast from past experience is crucial in such circumstances. The learning manager is able to deal with this; the controlling one most probably isn't.

Let us stay for a while in Eastern Europe, where for years we made fun of the endless queues outside shops. Aside from the fact that neither organization nor motivation in Russia really contributed positively to shopping efficiency and pleasure, another remarkable phenomenon contributed to those waiting lines of people. Once the customer reached the counter, they could ask what was available; the goods were then prepared while the customer went to queue up at the cash desk to pay. After payment the customer could get their goods, again at the first counter. From an efficiency (money handling) and security point of view, this organization is probably not so bad. In reality, however, it was such a slow procedure that, in a badly organized environment, it probably spelled the end. So much for the history; now back to practice. I have already told you the Dutch swimming pool story. If a child does not possess a swimming diploma, it must first go through a procedure that we (experts) have imagined and that seems optimal to us. Afterwards a test is taken and only then, in our opinion, is a child able (and therefore allowed) to swim. One could, of course, simply observe whether the child can swim or not, and that observation decides whether the diploma should be issued. The observation that the child can swim, not the procedure, is what produces the evidence we are looking for, which can then be rewarded with a certificate.

Before you react with shock, thinking that having such a strict procedure does contribute to safety, I of course agree with that. The swimming certificate procedure was invented with the aim of improving security. The safety idea and the necessity to know (via observation) is not the problem. The problem resides in the procedures. Procedures make it easier for humans to take necessary decisions. The real issue or problem is reduced to ticking boxes in the light of certain criteria, and if enough boxes are ticked, the child can swim. If not, the child fails. It is not the desired aim that causes the problem, but the strict procedure needed to get there. After a while the procedure becomes the goal, and the ultimate purpose becomes secondary. This can only be understood by insiders; those who are outside the system look at it and do not understand it. We have built yet another nice self-referential system that does its utmost to survive. It may even marginally contribute to the original goal, but perhaps not enough. Though the example might seem extreme, we observe this phenomenon daily.

We do not need detailed rules for people or companies that really take an assignment seriously. No doubt 80 per cent of companies, people and organizations are successful. Our attention is rightly focused on the remaining 20 per cent. A good question would be: how can we learn from the 80 per cent of successful cases, in order to help the 20 per cent of weak cases? Can we organize ourselves in such a way that the 20 per cent are allowed (not obliged) to learn from the 80 per cent? Can we facilitate and support that learning process? What we often do in practice is different. We try to take lessons from the 80 per cent of good experiences, which we then translate into rules. Those rules become generalized and we oblige all parties to apply them. For the successful 80 per cent, the rules are only a limiting factor without any value added (on the contrary, rules often go with (additional) reporting). The 20 per cent cannot really learn from the rules, are confronted with their weaknesses and will find even more possibilities of circumventing those rules: the more rules are made, the easier it is to get round them. The efficiency of the 80 per cent decreases, without any comparable increase in the efficiency of the 20 per cent. We have lost out, we have demotivated and we have not left any space for renewal and creativity.

Here is perhaps another little idea which would certainly need more detailed thought, hence it is not a real-life example yet; let us call it a thought experiment. Readers will not be surprised to hear that roughly 50 per cent of all planes do not fly within their planned slot-time. By this I mean the planned departure time plus or minus some minutes. I presume that we all think that if we did not plan aviation very strictly, things might go seriously wrong. But apparently this is not the case, since half of the planes fly on a non-planned schedule. Their eventual route may also be different from the planned one. Depending on the eventual departure time and the available free space in the air, a specific route is given. Air traffic control might be a good example of a continuously learning system. Each air controller has a limited set of interaction rules (with colleagues and pilots), and within a certain context the air controller is going to 'enact' (recall action and shaping, creation) their 'control' function. More correctly, one should probably call it a counselling task instead of a controlling task.

Now back to the passengers and how they experience this. Most probably, travellers have had bad experiences with delays, waiting time and missed connections. The official reason is often an overcrowded sky. But how could something that is neatly planned suddenly be affected by overcrowding? That is precisely what a plan takes care of, isn't it? A decision is not suddenly taken to increase the number of flights on a given day from a given airport by, say, 30. Hence overcrowding is most probably not the real reason. Could it be possible that the system simply cannot be planned? Could it be possible that sticking strictly to the plan could be counter-productive? Let us consider for a moment routes that are well connected (as is the case for a significant number of daily flights). Would we need to wait longer if planes stopped flying according to the schedule? The travellers arrive at the airport and check in for their specific destination. Once a plane has a sufficient loading coefficient, it leaves. Would it make any difference for the air traffic controllers? I don't think so. Would it make the waiting time longer? That is worth more investigation. This example might seem somewhat exaggerated, but maybe it is just true (and maybe it is not). It is only an illustration of how we could look differently at a given problem in a more learning approach.

Let us go back for a moment to the Queensday events; these might shed more light on this story too. It is normal for a network to get disturbed. However, a network that is not limited by too many rules can easily deal with a disturbance. Where things go wrong is when somebody chooses the 'security' procedure. Security procedures are often even more drastic and strict than regular procedures. Then a network just stops functioning. Once the security procedure is applied, there is no obvious or easy way to get back to normal. We could have decided to do things differently during the Queensday chaos. We could have decided not to organize things. We could have let any individual in the network (traindrivers, people dealing with the rails, etc.) just do as he or she thought best, using a minimum of interaction rules. If the signal is red, it remains the case that the train should not pass it (that is a minimum communication rule). If the track is not free, a red signal is given (or this decision is automated). If this had been done, we would certainly have had trains, and they would certainly not have followed any schedule. All manned trains would have been able to transport people, rather than just standing still, as actually happened. Of course trains would have gone to 'wrong' places, but what does 'wrong place' mean if nothing is planned any more? A 'wrong' place only makes sense if we think there are also 'correct' places, a place where the train should have been. If we drop the schedule in case of emergency, correct and wrong places no longer exist. Trains go in that situation, and there is no reason to think (statistically) that there would be a priori concentrations where we would have more trains than elsewhere.

With product innovations in companies we roughly see the same process. Innovation is the activity *per se* where we expect there to be most creativity and space for experimentation. But in reality this is seldom the case in companies. Innovation is often studied in detail and a best possible innovation path is identified. Product development teams are obliged to follow these procedures very carefully, and there are regular go or no-go (kill) decisions. Those decisions are extremely difficult to take or to justify, once we accept that there cannot be a best path leading to innovation. What is the basis on which we should decide? Once a product fails on the market, one might deduce that it should never have been made in the first place. But if we stop an innovation process early on, how do we know that it would never have become a good (profitable) product? A human resources manager who seems to be recruiting the right people (and we have to specify criteria for identifying who are the 'right people') will be appreciated for that. But how does a company know that among all those people who have not been recruited, there is not the competitor's future top manager? Isn't measuring success something like looking out through a tiny, narrow window which does not allow us to see what is just under the window? The rules decide what the size of the window should be. Do not be surprised that we only see what the window allows us to see. But there is so much that is interesting going on outside, even just beside the window, but not visible from the window that we have ourselves defined. We often limit our view of reality for ourselves.

Back to innovation management now. The rules themselves do not seem to be sufficient for decisions about continuation or discontinuation to be made. Often such decisions become a question of the management's 'feeling'. In a strictly structured and regulated corporate culture, 'feeling' decides about the future of the company (and its innovations). The better manager has indeed what we may call *Fingerspitzengefühl* (intuition, flair). The paradox (if not the irony) wants the creative procedures in innovation to be restricted, or at least governed as much as possible by rules, while the control function of the process is managed by 'feeling'. It would probably be more logical to turn this around. Allow the creative people to innovate while learning, within a broad area of freedom, and make the aim clear (e.g. a financially viable product in two years' time). This would allow them to apply control themselves, which creates additional learning moments for them. Control can indeed be redefined as learning moments which contribute to the development of the idea itself. That is true for innovation projects, but is equally true if we consider the role of financial controllers and controlling in many companies. Not control but learning should be the purpose. With this insight, controlling would be a nice learning tool.

One could wonder whether it is possible to work with subcontractors without having a very strict controlling mechanism in place. On the basis of my own research, it is clear that control is very often a process that is frustrating for both parties: the controllers and the controlled. It contributes little to the management process. Let us take the specific example of a situation in which control is formally part of the procedures. If a government body subcontracts the construction of roads or large building complexes, many controllers are at work, with a specific set of control mechanisms (and tools). The subcontractors consider the controllers to be undesirable people who always limit their freedom and speed of action. For them, the controller only slows down the process. The controllers often view the subcontractors as something akin to criminals. Would it be possible to see this situation differently? Some learning is desirable here. Maybe we could contractually agree about a bandwidth within which the subcontractor has total freedom. Instead of controlling activities, we move on to managing the bandwidth. If something unforeseen happens (which is often the case), we are not obliged to fall back on rules and procedures, which in irregular situations often do not give a precise answer anyway. Procedures are made for what should have happened normally, but we only need to apply them when something exceptional happens. That is where things go wrong: rules are made for situations where we don't need them. The bandwidth idea allows the subcontractor to learn from the exceptional event (possibly in coordination with the contracting agency). On the basis of their experience, they can propose an alternative solution. The subcontractor's learning gets integrated into the system much faster. If we have to wait until what is learned has been transformed into rules, we will have to wait a long time. Hence there is a choice: between faster learning and integration of learning on the one hand, and the invention of the best possible rules on the other hand. We should choose what we think should be our focus.

Further support for the idea of learning instead of controlling management can be provided by the warranty. Does a consumer control how their car is manufactured? No, a warranty is responsible for the fact that if anything goes wrong during a specific period, the producer repairs the car at no cost. The warranty replaces the customer's control. This forces producers to develop their quality controls and keep them going, for the simple reason that after-sales service is expensive. In this example, control by the customer is in fact physically impossible, but in any case, as is true of other forms of control, it would not contribute to the production process. The warranty, which is agreed up front, takes care of the control and allows freedom and initiative for the producer. What is possible in the area of cars and small electrical goods is of course equally possible in the area of construction.

Control by the customer would become obsolete if we agreed up front about the warranty. A highway that is being constructed needs to be guaranteed for five years, for instance. If the road deteriorates before the five-year period ends, the subcontractor needs to repair it at its own expense. If a computer system is not able to deliver the volumes that are promised, the software company should repair it under the terms of the warranty. The fact that things do not happen like that has everything to do with how we deal with each other in business. Maybe we do not have confidence that the company that gives the warranty will still exist in five years. But even that belief would not change anything about the observation that control doesn't work anyway, that it limits creativity and innovation, and that it could be organized differently. Self-control is again the key concept, and this necessitates an adapted context. The manager could set the context but give control to those being managed.

For clarity, I would like to stress that control is possible, and makes sense, for mechanistic processes (processes that are created in order to produce something following a fixed and predefined number of steps). In the case of a mechanistic process we consider a static and often linear situation with clear causal and deterministic relations. In such a case my theory, of course, does not hold. If I refer to control that will fail or be difficult, I am referring to a system in which the interaction between people is central, not the interaction between machines. This clarification is not unimportant.

Within the debate about corporate strategy we similarly see two schools of thought. The one school thinks that strategy is something normative, and the other group sees strategy more as an emergent process. The 'normative' strategists consider strategy formulation to be the definition of the correct and best path. The execution of that strategy is nothing more than detailing the path to follow, and making sure that everybody then follows it. In this idea, the strategy is identified by a limited number of thinkers who then hand over its execution to the network of employees. Porter is no doubt the best-known figure associated with this idea. Other thinkers, the more organic thinkers, among whom Mintzberg is prominent, see a different form of strategy formulation. For them, strategy is something that emerges out of the company and that is therefore supported by the different layers of the company.

In terms of complexity, Mintzberg refers to the network of employees who continuously, in cooperation with each other, support the emergence of a continually learning strategy. In order to clarify this, but at the expense of some precision, we talk about the search for strategic goals. This contrasts with the more classical vision of strategy that concentrates on fixing the path, after which the goal follows automatically. If the goal is not reached, it is the path that is questioned, not the goal itself. This fixation on the path, which is central in management thinking, is probably one of the most strongly prevailing legacies of our Cartesian, rational thinking in management. This viewpoint would not be wrong *per se*, however, if it did not stand in the way of a more explorative approach.

This normative approach leaves less space for creativity and innovation, and is seldom oriented towards rapid learning from experience. If we consider strategy formulation in a company, but equally its execution and the control of this execution, we can see that the complexity paradigm would shed a different light – that is, a more learning-oriented light. The volatility of a strategy in ever-changing markets is probably better served by a strategy that learns out of itself, based on a broad network of people who, each being responsible, strive for clear aims (within a given context).

The same kind of thinking can be applied to the organization of companies. Most companies are still hierarchically organized. The top decides and the subsequent layers of responsibility have to execute and to control the execution. All middle management layers report back to the top, doing so via different intermediary levels. Reporting does not usually deal much with what could have been learned or what has been learned. For strategy formulation that would be extremely interesting. Often the reporting focuses on the targets that have or have not been reached. It is the person who brings good news (indeed, the Roman messenger still exists in all its beauty) who is appreciated, not the person who is able to create. Creation is seldom rewarded; confirmation and alignment are. The aim of such a company is to limit potential chaos to the minimum, mainly via control. Now we could say: what is wrong with that? Nothing, if we don't worry about the question of whether the path can be identified in the first place. Previous chapters in this book have given arguments to suggest that identifying the path is impossible. The ideal path does not seem to exist.

A more important argument, though, is that companies should not be searching for equilibrium, but rather for chaos. A system that reaches equilibrium is a dead system, one which can no longer change. It cannot receive new information from outside. A living system can never be in equilibrium. A living system is one in which progress is still possible, where we can have higher revenue and we are able to invent new products. Too much structure, order and control seem to lead automatically to chaos. How can we keep a company or an organization at the edge of change? How can we make it possible for a company to continuously innovate and surf on the waves of the ever-changing environment? Probably by structuring it as an optimally learning company. This means a limited top-down structure, a clear context, good interaction rules and clear individual goals.

Virtual organizations try to reach for this ideal. There are successful companies which are almost completely virtual. Most known examples are not really large companies yet, but maybe companies of this kind never grow large. Maybe they split off into different smaller entities, which in turn form a learning network among each other (hence a large company becomes a network of networks). Virtual companies are companies in which the employees (or are they partners?) act on the basis of personal interest. It appears that each one of them is an entrepreneur. The company delivers a context, constituted out of information, a legal structure and a predefined goal. Within this context each individual strives for optimal self-realization. A set of communication rules is agreed on, for internal communication as well as for external communication and even for financial communication (reporting). Often it is supported by an ICT network (an intranet). We see here the practical realization of a network of agents that often produces brilliant results, where both the corporate and the individual goals are easily reached. It appears as if such an approach has sown chaos, out of which order emerges. Indeed, within a dynamic non-linear system – and that is what I am describing here – order emerges out of chaos. One should have the courage to stop controlling and to avoid forcing a predefined organization. Are we moving towards a market (a world) of professionals instead of one of companies?

In (virtual or networked) companies of this kind, but also increasingly in other companies, we observe an interest in sharing experiences on a continuous basis (what we often call best practices). Even the label 'best practices' refers to an optimal path. It appears that there are equally 'bad' paths from which a lot could be learned. Therefore, it would be better to call them 'good' practices, from which employees can choose what they feel is most adequate for them to learn. Only the 'learners' can decide what they need, and this only at the moment they need it. The problem of knowledge is that we do not know what we do not know. If you ask people what they do not know, they are unable to answer. But knowing what it is that you do not know is crucial in learning. You want to learn what you do not know yet, but you cannot identify the latter since you do not know it. You know what you don't know when you need it. If I ask somebody to do an assignment, they then find out what they do not know, but should learn. So, all organized learning comes too late. If the assignment is due tomorrow, it is too late to enrol on a course. That is why just-in-time and just-enough learning, as described earlier on, are so important, and such an interesting alternative.

If we could support a company in such a way that everybody could quickly learn from everybody else, we would support the self-creating qualities of the employee. We are talking about e-learning or knowledge management; in fact, they are two sides of the same coin. Can we support employees in the workplace (of a virtual organization) in their endeavour to learn just in time and just enough? The network paradigm could also give some fresh ideas on this subject.

A learning manager cannot change the company on their own. A learning manager is only one player within a network of many. They contribute as one of the players, but they also have the additional duty of making the network as learning- and sharing-friendly as possible. Knowledge management and virtual learning are going through a tremendous revolution these days. That is described in detail in a few of my books (Baets and Van der Linden, 2000, 2003; Baets, 2005a), and therefore I shall not deal in any detail with it here. The essence of e-learning, though, is based on the principles developed in this book, and therefore we should pay some attention to it.

Talking about learning, we often think immediately in terms of education or teaching (and I refer again to Rabindranath Tagore's poem quoted in Chapter 1). In many languages and cultures in the world, learning and teaching are used almost as synonyms. But they are not. Teaching presumes a teacher, an expert who is able to transfer knowledge to a student (a non-expert). This assumes that knowledge can be transferred, and a main characteristic of most interesting knowledge is that it cannot easily be transferred. Real knowledge can often not be transferred at all. What we, in general, call knowledge is nothing more than transferable information. Out of that information, an individual, a human, can make knowledge: the potential to 'enact' (action and creation) something out of that information. Teaching, as is unfortunately still often the case in schools (at all levels), focuses on that information transfer. Learning, however, refers to the fact that learners (we do not even have a good word for it) adapt their mental model, their way of thinking, on the basis of fresh experiences. A coach could play a role in this process, but learning can only be undertaken by a learner. Learning is therefore individual and cannot easily be controlled.

There are two plausible ways to measure learning. The first is to ask the learner to carry out certain activities (assignments) and observe whether they have developed this creative capacity. Another way might be to 'draw' somebody's mental map and see whether it has changed after the presumed learning. In our research we have used consecutive neural networks in order to simulate that approach, with encouraging results. Translated into a corporate context, and then in the first place the first possibility to measure learning, we identify here the space that we should give people to start 'undertaking' (being an entrepreneur) in the company, which might show whether somebody has indeed learned something.

E-learning, or knowledge support, is therefore not oriented towards the creation of good and exhaustive content *per se*, but rather on exploring and discovering, using a sufficiently rich content that is inviting for learning. We talk about a learning environment (a learning lab?) in which the learner can acquire new experiences by doing, within a framework in which questions get answered. The environment should, in the first place, not fix the learning path, but rather agree on what the learner is supposed to learn, leaving them totally free to fix their own learning path, via trial and error. Often we could coach a learner, specifically in their first steps, in order to get them acquainted with the environment and in order to motivate them during their exploration. The learner themself will have to lay down their path in walking.

Within the education world we see almost daily new so-called e-learning products, which are almost exclusively e-teaching oriented. Again we see the prevailing Western mode of rational thinking materializing into control. The possibility of controlling the learning path becomes more important than learning itself. We no longer wonder whether somebody can swim, but are only interested in seeing whether they fulfil all the criteria that we defined beforehand. Sometimes those criteria match the target; often they don't. When high school final exams are set (they are centrally organized in many European countries), are we measuring the capacity to handle information (and maybe even a bit of knowledge), or do we really test whether we have young people who are able to develop their creative power during their university studies in order to really contribute either to research or to creative action (management)? Or don't we even look for that at university level any more?

Would that be the reason that most companies feel it necessary to restart the training of fresh academics in-house (via trainee programmes)? Why would it be necessary for somebody who has just finished a four- to five-year university study to immediately restart studying (and often I really mean restart, and not continue learning)? And again we observe the omnipresence of our reductionist thinking, since many companies create their own 'corporate universities', which are often almost identical copies of the existing universities. This seemingly closes the circle. We have made a full round trip. Does no one question the fundamental philosophical choices (explicit or implicit) on which our educational model is constructed, if we observe a rather high failure rate? Yes, philosophical questions are probably rather too metaphysical and, in business, what we are after is measurable results: what cannot be measured cannot be managed! Therefore we prefer to deliver measurable teaching, instead of unmeasurable learning.

Is it indeed true that what cannot be measured cannot be managed? Or is this again a manifestation of our Cartesian prejudgement? Is somebody who has a fever sick, and somebody without fever not sick? If we observe a high body temperature, what do we observe, other than that the body temperature is high? Measurement is in fact the reduction of reality to a tiny part of that reality. Eventually we can measure that small part, but we no longer have any idea at all about the larger entity that initially interested us. Nevertheless, that is what we do all the time. We measure small parts and draw conclusions about the larger whole. We observe a stock value and we give an opinion about the viability of a company. Imagine a group of boys who want to wash an elephant. They feel it is a big and difficult (even complicated) task. Hence, one of them proposes dividing the elephant into smaller pieces. Each of them washes one smaller piece, and afterwards they try to put it all together again. Fortunately, they rapidly understand that they end up not with a clean elephant, but a dead elephant. The different pieces, taken separately, do not reconstruct the whole any more. One cannot reduce the elephant to the simple addition of a number of composing elements.

Organizing management education into different subdisciplines that we can all measure, and hence manage, very often does not lead to the desired result once we reassemble the pieces. No longer is the whole created. A business problem is not an addition of a marketing problem, a finance problem and a logistics problem, for instance. All those different aspects continuously interact with each other and in doing so, create, via emergence, the issue or problem being considered. Reducing a problem to one aspect of it does not give due regard to the problem, and eventually it will hinder the management of it. Hence, measuring and managing are not one-to-one related with each other, as we so often hope. This idea, however, perfectly fits Western thinking. For other (managerial) cultures, our way of thinking is not always equally clear, and even sometimes not understandable. We should at least be aware of that.

We could continue for a while with examples, but, I have already said, these are merely illustrations of ideas that have been developed earlier in the book. The arguments are not in the examples, but in the developed concepts. These illustrations have, I hope, brought the concepts more to life for the reader. In practice, on the basis of the complexity paradigm, using brainstorming sessions and workshops (the network should be activated), we could consider corporate cases or problems differently. These sessions and workshops could be managed or coached by outsiders, but managing or coaching them could equally be an interesting role for the learning managers themselves.

Therefore, I would like to zoom in on something that would make lots of sense for a learning manager within their network, by which the manager supports learning and initiates the continuous learning and change process. If a manager does not want to impose their ideas, but rather would like to allow learning via action, then something like 'action research' could be an interesting support instrument for the manager. The word 'research' refers to the act of learning, not to what we understand as academic research. In any action a learning component is included. We only undertake action in order to allow learning, or at least to be able to learn. But learning in itself is not sufficient either. Learning, in turn, should lead to action. The cohabitation of action (management) and learning (research) eventually allows both learning by doing and doing by learning. How does it work out?

There are many action research methods and techniques, and this book has no ambition to list them all, or to discuss them in detail. It is interesting for the learning manager, though, to gain a basic understanding of action research, and the interested reader can explore the topic further in the relevant literature. The method I would like to illustrate here is called soft systems methodology (SSM), but I intend it only as an illustration of one of the many existing methods. It was designed by Peter Checkland of Lancaster University. He, and after him many adepts, have described his method in detail, starting with his first book, *Systems Thinking, Systems Practice*, first published in 1981. There has been much positive experience with this method, mainly in Britain, and therefore there are many publications that precisely highlight the practical use of the method. In continental Europe the method is less well known and apparently less popular.

SSM is based on the idea that whatever question one might have, this question is never finished or final, and while one is searching for a solution, the question itself changes. If we want to build systems – and SSM is mainly used for building information systems – the different stakeholders should have a shared concept of the problem area (the 'problematique', as the method calls it) that the system aims to address. This seems evident, and a software developer will call that the user's analysis. However, questioning people, potential users, does not seem to be sufficient. In fact, people do not know what they do not know, and hence they know even less what they need in order to be able to give the 'correct' answers to the questions posed by the user analysis. If we knew all the answers, organizing would become extremely easy. However in practice, we do not know that much, not even what we do not know.

Therefore, the problem definition phase itself contributes largely to the comprehension and the clarification of the problem. This cycle, in fact, continues endlessly. The learning manager should keep this cycle going continually, in order to keep the entropy in the company as high as possible, but also in order to feed and support the continuous change and learning trajectory in the company. SSM attempts to structure a complex problem, but expressed in actions: things that can be undertaken. SSM considers a system as a whole: it is a holistic and process-oriented approach. That is one of the reasons that this action research methodology is appropriate for this book. Eventually, the manager wants to use the structuring of ideas in order to come to real applications of change processes, using a change method like this one. This method allows learning about the ideas themselves, the method and the applications. Theoretical concepts are usually only oriented to the understanding of either the underlying ideas, or the implementation methods in certain applications. The method itself (how we come to a certain understanding) is seldom critically argued in companies. The quality of the method, however, is crucial for the quality of the results obtained. SSM does not search for a problem (and a solution), but for a problematique (a problem area). This holistic perspective is a large part of its value added. The inherent change process that is an essential part of the method gives it its eternal dynamic character. That is a second strong point of the method.

SSM considers a 'problematique' as existing in two different worlds. In the real world there is a problem area that is considered as problematic. This problem area can be represented by 'rich pictures': in fact, drawings of what people experience and think of doing. Disagreement is drawn by crossed swords, ideas are represented by light bulbs, etc. The actual symbols used are not important, but the attempt is to make as rich as possible a picture of the problem area, with the aim of being able to communicate it later. One could also use 'stories' or any other means of transferable 'easygoing' representation. All this takes place in the real world, in the company, between the people working. Next, the target is to sidestep into the world of 'systems thinking about the real world', which I describe a little later, in order to be able to compare these thought models with the reality. If one compares those thought models with the real world, change trajectories appear, consisting of those changes that are desirable from a systems point of view and that are culturally reachable. Those choices cause consequential actions. Though the steps appear to be rather sequential, the ultimate aim is to create and manage a continuous adaptive process. Continuous interaction is crucial; the process is highly interactive, and the purpose is that inside people, internalized models eventually emerge. In order to start the method, a more sequential approach is probably rather easier.

Now let us go to the systems world in which we think about the real world. In that systems world there are two interesting exercises aiming to create clarity in action. Based on the rich pictures that are still describing the real world, we attempt to create 'root definitions'. We could have a generalized root definition that dissolves in a multitude of more detailed root definitions. In general, and based on experience, taking five root definitions in order to describe a problem area seems very workable. A root definition is a long sentence containing the following elements: the clients, the beneficiaries or victims, the actors, the transformation process, the *Weltanschauung* (the way of seeing the world, or higher reasons), the problem owner, the environmental constraints. SSM uses a mnemonic for these six elements: CATWOE (clients, actors, transformation, *Weltanschauung*, owner, environmental constraints). The creation of these root definitions is a process that generates a lot of learning, and it is a clarifying way of dealing with problems.

Once the root definitions are agreed on, they are transformed into conceptual models. This step explicitly introduces the change trajectory (the dynamic element) into the analysis. Conceptual models are expressed in verbs. They translate root definitions into 'human activity systems'. To a certain extent, they can be compared to process models, though in general they are richer, given the holistic perspective within which they are used. In practice, just as with the root definitions, this stage proves to be very difficult and will often go against our implicitly reductionist way of thinking. Exercising action research approaches, with some coaching at the beginning, will be a necessity for most managers who want to use them. Of course, SSM lets us make and compare different scenarios, which intensifies the learning moments.

Eventually, those human activity systems are compared with the real world again, in order to identify desirable and realistic change goals. Despite the fact that this method is attractive and has proved its usability in systems design, in particular in information systems design, it has even more potential within a learning management approach as an action research methodology. For the learning manager, SSM (or comparable methods) is an intervention technique that both fits the holistic perspective and is based on the power of the network. SSM is an example of a methodology that managers can use not only in order to support their own dynamic learning, but also in order to encourage the learning of many others. Control is no part of this methodology any more. Indeed, we can talk about a paradigm shift.

# 7 Does our society ever learn?

We would expect that society would learn. In previous chapters I gave examples of how we could consider the world differently, from a more holistic point of view; that is essentially the subject of this book. I gave examples of how people (managers) and systems can learn, what the limits of learning are and what good experiences exist. We cannot avoid, at the same time, asking whether our society, the economic environment in which we work, for instance, is able to learn, and if it is unable to learn, why is that? If we considered society and, still more so, geopolitical organization from a holistic perspective, would we see other things? In the first chapter I gave an example taken from a pseudo-public company: chaos on the Dutch railways. What we saw in that example is that a drive for more order most probably led to chaos. If, however, we consider all the specific processes the employees executed, they did their best, and did what they were expected to do very well. But that does not seem to be enough any more. The whole is more than the sum of the parts. In dynamic systems, emergent behaviour appears, as already explained. We may want to call it a snowball effect. This behaviour has its own rationale and follows its own logic. We can of course have an impact on this behaviour, but we do not know the outcome.

I also mentioned the Enschede disaster (the explosion of the fireworks factory). As soon as possible after this disaster, investigators searched for errors and guilty parties in order to identify who and what to blame. Errors that are made on purpose or that are based on significant malfunctioning or lack of reactivity fall under the juridical domain and should be considered as such. This is not what I am referring to here. Often an error, or a guilty person, is not easy to identify. What happens in reality is a chain of small actions that could each have been different, in which case the disaster would not have happened. In the aftermath of such a disaster we often concentrate on guilt, revenge and a refinement of the rules. But do we also try to learn something from such an event? Or is it enough to have identified guilt and provided compensation? Is it indeed bin Laden who is responsible for the World Trade Center attacks (which still may need to be proved), or is it a system in which he has played an important role, but in which the United States has played a role too? Is Iraq the only country responsible for the US war against it, or is there a kind of system which has a clear shared responsibility among all the players? If the latter is true, then a condemnation of bin Laden and/or even an execution would not solve anything. Isn't that what we observe today in Iraq?

It is highly reductive to think that one single person is responsible for this kind of disaster. Isn't it a bit simplistic to think that a group of roughly twenty people creates a disaster of the World Trade Center kind? Also, in this view of world politics we see the extent to which reductionism is an integral part of our culture. George W. Bush likes to speak about an attack on the entire Western world: how does this manifest itself? Bush forces people to choose between United States or terrorism: isn't there anything else in the world? In a very short period of time somebody responsible is found (or should I say is appointed?); in an even shorter period of time it is decided that we should bomb an entire country (Afghanistan) with many more casualties than those lost in the twin towers disaster. If this doesn't prove to be satisfactory (to whom? what is satisfaction?), we continue with another country; and so what next? Do victims in countries like Afghanistan and Iraq have a lower 'value' than those in the United States?

If we want to study our society and its functioning, we cannot avoid the two most important pillars of that society: the judicial system and the political system. And in both of those pillars, we rapidly encounter self-reference within a self-organizing system. We see that our political system lives its own life based on its own functioning rules. It has developed, and continues to develop further, its own reference frame. For those inside the system, this facilitates exchange and action, but for those outside the system (the citizens) it is not understandable at all. We expect the legal system to be driven by a societal consensus: the legal system exists by request of the society and with the aim of protecting that society against excesses, and keeping it viable. In practice, however, it appears that the legal system – or, better, the judicial system – develops its own self-referring frame and that it decides and operates on the basis of this self-referential system. The system no longer seeks justice and fairness, but rather it attempts to keep itself manageable and it serves the cohesion inside the system. The system itself becomes the purpose to serve, instead of the search for justice.

In politics we see this movement even more clearly. The language and reference frame of politicians are often miles away from the concerns of society and its citizens, which should be their main concern. At the end of 2001 we were talking about a new kind of war against terrorism that was nevertheless fought with very classical weapons (now weapons of mass destruction). Citizens' general feeling as regards justice will no doubt be agreement that terrorism needs to be prevented and isolated as far as possible, and that it is an unacceptable act, and the prime aim of the judicial system should be to protect society and its citizens. It becomes very reductionist if that aim only seems to concern a particular part of the world. If it becomes accepted that within that limited reference frame, it is permissible to (freely) bomb other countries, then I seriously miss the systemic dimension of our reality. In fact, most probably it is no systemic approach at all. One 'agent' in the network feels under attack and wants to reaffirm his or her supremacy. But any action undertaken in the network (of world politics) contributes to the self-organizing capacity of this network in order to create a new situation. There is no causal relationship between the action and its effect in the network. But it is propagated through the network. From a reductionist point of view one could presume that there would be simple causal relationships, with maybe some disturbing emitters in the ether. From a holistic point of view there are no 'disturbing' emitters, but only emitters that, all together, make music. In the chapter on quantum economics (Chapter 9) I shall give an example of an alternative understanding of organizational dynamics (in the case of conflict creation).

The geopolitical system seeks its own survival. That became very apparent after the few terrorist attacks in the West. Hence, something needs to be done; that much is clear. Are we now searching for reductionist solutions for a subpart of the problem, mainly serving the interests of a particular part (or group) of the system and its population? Or should we be looking for solutions that would make the geopolitical system a more learning system? Could we consider what we have learned from the experiences we have shared in the past (in the entire world, hence)? Couldn't we finally understand and create our thoughts on the basis of the network structure of the world and all the self-organizing and self-creating forces of these networks, in which case we would be able to create a real breakthrough? But it would go against our reductionist and causal thinking culture.

Today, each political system is focused internally, thinking from within its own context, and this is as true of the Iraq of Saddam Hussein as it is of the United States of Bush, as true of the Palestinians as of the Israel of the Likud party. Even Osama bin Laden has most probably a fully legitimate reason for his behaviour, seen from his context and perspective – let us say, seen from his legitimacy. Iraq invaded Kuwait and had its own right to do so, according to Iraq's worldview; the coalition chased Iraq out of Kuwait again, according to them, on the basis of its own legitimacy. But maybe they are both right, each from their perspective and context. They all legitimize (which has to do with their respective legal systems) their actions on the basis of their view of law and legal systems and on what is fair and just. We can only understand any party if we are willing to accept their respective reference frames (their context, as we discussed earlier). What we observe in a conflict is not the addition of systems and actions, but rather the interaction of different systems in a larger system (that is again holistic on a higher level of integration). Holistic systems integrate in an even larger holistic system (we often call these 'subsystems' holons). This is difficult to observe and to understand if we continue to base everything on our own system of values, if we continue to search for causal relationships between 'non-correlated' events.

Judging (be it positive or negative) therefore does not make much sense if we do not know the contexts of the different parties, or if we are not willing to accept different contexts. Judgement maybe has little meaning at all, and would probably be better replaced by understanding and learning. How can we do better next time, and not always make the same kind of errors? Can we reinforce the network, and don't we need to change the interaction rules to do so? These are interesting questions that could contribute to an improved world order. This, however, does not exclude the problem of a specific 'agent' who voluntarily puts him- or herself outside the system and hence becomes a threat. The network, with its aim of surviving, could protect itself by isolating this one element and taking it out of the network. The reason for doing so should, however, be supported by the network.

It is not about judgement; rather it is all about an observation about how to deal with the world. The question to raise and answer is, therefore, how can we make a political system a learning system? Maybe there is even a question before this one, namely what can we learn from how the system has operated? What we discover is again self-reference within self-organization. I am going to illustrate how powerful the concept of self-reference is in our legal system and how it stands in the way of a holistic learning view.

A brilliant, but somewhat abstract, book gives an intriguing view of our legal practice: Teubner's *Law as an Autopoietic System* (1993). I am going to use the essential ideas of that book and illustrate them with some practical examples. Though I may sound sometimes like a bit of a know-all, the idea is to generate ideas that contribute to a deeper and, even more importantly, a wider understanding of how our society operates and how it could work better.

The legal system is not, as one would expect, driven by world powers, politicians, nature, or even God's will. Law seems to emerge out of the random nature of its own system. This idea is what I want to develop further, but also to illustrate with examples.

The self-referential quality of the legal system resides in fact in the nested structure of that system: legal actions result in other legal actions; in fact, they are highly networked. Everything is expressed in the same 'units'. Language talks about itself in the same language as someone who talks about language. Remember the Gödel story in which Gödel uses numbers in order to talk about numbers. He could have chosen language in order to talk about numbers, but he didn't. The fact that he chose to use numbers (and hence self-reference) is precisely what allowed him to prove his theorem. This is also a choice for the legal system – and, of course, it is a choice that has its advantages (for the system, as in Gödel's proof) – but it is a choice that does not make the system accessible for outsiders. In such a system, only the system (say, the laws) can create validity, and not, for instance, social or moral evaluation.

The legal system has a second important quality: since it is continuously created by people, it is self-organizing and autopoietic. Not every self-referential system is self-organizing, by the way, but that doesn't matter too much in this context. If we now consider the legal system as a self-producing, self-referential system, we can consider it as a non-trivial machine that is determined artificially, that cannot be determined analytically, that is dependent on the past but, of course, that cannot be anticipated in the future. A more classical definition of the legal system (the one we most often have today) will rapidly lead to paradoxes. And indeed, for most people it is difficult to understand how the legal system operates. Criminals are released owing to errors in the procedures; proof that is obtained in an illegal manner cannot be used, however important the crime. Those who infiltrate criminal networks, sometimes risking their life, are later attacked by the system for using illegal approaches, and in the end they end up being the accused. Outsiders, like parliamentary commissions or citizens, don't understand anything any more. However, inside the legal system all is understandable, correct and can be explained.

If we are looking for an autopoietic perspective, there is some logic in the system, but that does not mean it is socially acceptable. Poetically speaking, the legal system is an eternal dance of dancers inside a closed network of interacting elements. Though this description thus far explains a lot of behaviour in the legal system, which makes it an elegant description, it remains incomprehensible for society and for citizens, for whom the legal system was created and exists.

What we observe in the legal system is that, precisely because of its self-referential quality, the autopoietic character can be maintained. The reproduction of elements in the legal system continues, completely independently of its (social) environment. The justification is not sought via an embedding in the social system, but rather internally, through self-reference. As already indicated, self-reference is not automatically linked to self-production or self-organization. If, however, they coincide, one gets a spontaneous creation of an order that continuously reinforces itself and that is internally oriented. An interesting question is whether a system could also become self-reflective. Is it possible for a system to develop its own set of values and norms? If that were possible, it would be clearer whether the legal system is still embedded in society or not, or whether it has its own set of values and norms.

While we would expect the legal system to have been strongly influenced by societal and social evolution, in practice that does not really appear to be the case. The legal system is a closed system. It communicates with its environment via the decisions that are taken (independently of the grounds on which those decisions are taken). Those decisions provoke reactions. For instance, a certain decision could provoke societal reaction such as violence (just think about the riots in Los Angeles when a policeman was found not guilty of the maltreatment of a black man), which is a societal reaction against the legal system. Indirectly this is feedback on the legal system, but feedback that can only get into the legal system via the legal system's treatment of new illegal actions (hence new court cases). The feedback can only be of a derived order. There is no immediate impact. Society cannot take an active role inside the legal system; not only was the legal system set up in such a way in West

European democracies, but we, the system, have wholeheartedly embraced that reality. Eventually the system is locked in a strong self-referential, self-organizing situation. Outsiders barely understand the system's relevance to society.

An important tool in this movement is communication. We could choose to speak about the legal system using ordinary language that would be understood by everybody and that would allow everybody to take part in that legal system. However, the choice has been made to use a legal language, a more formal language that is only understood by (insider) specialists. The fact that this legal language is disconnected from regular social communication, hence not understood by society, will only lead to more self-reflection on the part of the legal system and its language. The consequence is that actors in the legal system need to be experts, and that citizens who seek justice cannot take part in it any more. Furthermore, those experts, let us say lawyers, are in turn also part of the system. In a perfectly autopoietic system they are only part of a larger network, and they can only contribute to the survival of the system, hence not necessarily to the optimal conduct of any particular case. The citizen who seeks justice seldom finds it, but instead encounters a self-referential system with players who contribute to the system, who are part of it and who keep it going. Those players, on the other hand, do not have any choice in the matter, since if they decide to distance themselves from the system, the system is no longer willing or able to work with them. The lawyers' trade union is an organization that should be able to have an impact on the system if lawyers desire it to do so.

The legal system selects itself, with the aim of becoming better (of surviving). That happens via a large number of different players in the system: judges, lawyers, the public attorney, people who take the minutes of court cases, etc. Those players use a common self-referential language. Because they do so, there is no guarantee that a court will take a decision that is socially relevant, let alone socially optimal. An optimal legal system does not equal an optimal society.

Let us look at some examples. First of all I would like to exclude here crime that has an ethical dimension: murder, or comparable crimes that involve life or death. In such a case a legal system cannot help a lot; personally I believe more in jury cases. A number of countries do indeed have such a system for life and death crime, and it would be worth studying this in more detail. That is not the aim of this book. I am talking here about the many cases (in fact, the vast majority of court cases) that deal with fairness and justice: divorce, illegal competition, quarrels between neighbours, etc. These are minor cases that nevertheless take up a lot of the legal system's resources. The reason for this is that the procedures are very complicated. In many of these cases the legal procedure itself becomes the subject of discussion, instead of the process of identifying 'justice'. Personally I do not think at all that in order to be able to judge fairness or justice, it is necessary to be a professional judge – at least, not if the aim is to find justice rather than to correctly apply the law (a set of rules). In other words: not if it is not the aim to keep the legal system going, but rather to give citizens justice in line with their rights.

Let us take the example of a divorce. Lawyers for both parties raise the stakes and exaggerate the facts (sometimes even make up facts) in order to raise their clients' claims as high as possible. Truth and honesty are aspects that do not really appear much in this process. Remaining honest yourself does not always pay off, since the system itself assumes that the claims are artificially raised, even if they are not. The aim is not to identify what is correct and honest. Lawyers are part of the system and therefore play their part in the game. The official case starts with an artificial setting, instead of a reconstruction of the truth. Both parties can say whatever they like; there is no attempt to find out what is true at all. Even a flagrant lie does not become a fact any more; it is just a *fait divers*. From the point of view of the legal system, indeed that is not important. For the survival of the system, neither truth nor rights are important. Central to the matter is the self-reproducing system that continuously needs to create new rules (laws) in order to survive. Eventually a decision is taken, which is not so much a decision based on rights, but rather one that refers to one or other article in the civil code. Basing its judgment on article such and such of the civil code, the court decides on whatever that article allows, independent of the real dimensions of the case. In the final written decision there is seldom reference to any kind of societal justification, but only to the embedding of the decision in the system and its rules (the civil code).

Indeed, in order to play this game the players need to be experts. They have to know all the rules (the law), and there are many; they continually increase in number (and sometimes they also die out). Furthermore, the players need to know the rules of what we call the legal procedures (how the game is organized). These are not always evident, though the game is not much more than a set of rules. It is not so much the archaic setting (court of justice, gowns, etc.) that keeps the citizens at a distance; rather, it is the complete alienation of the citizen from the legal procedures and, later on, from the irrelevance of the court decision. For the insiders, the decision is clear, but for the people concerned (both victim and possible offender) it is often difficult to understand. But who do legal procedures exist for? Aren't legal procedures there to protect the victims? No problem, the system will say, since we also know the appeals procedure. One always has a second chance, though under exactly the same rules. And eventually the legal procedure becomes the aim, rather than the process of seeking justice.

Would it be possible to do things differently? If we did not feel the necessity to follow a particular procedure, we could organize matters differently. Then we could return to the sources of our legal system and our legal thinking – already a few centuries old. If I go back to the example of a divorce, the parties could tell their stories to a 'wise' man or woman. After having heard both parties, the wise man or woman could take a decision referring to, and based on, reason (and not based on articles of the civil code); the logical follow-up would then be a division of the couple's goods. Of course, both parties would argue about whether the final decision was correct, but at least they would have a better feeling that justice had played a role. A possible appeal case would argue less about the procedure and more about the argument of the case itself.

We could now start arguing about what we understand by a wise man or woman, and we could even fix some rules in order to be able to identify such a person. In practice, that is not the most difficult problem to solve. One could compare it with the annual appraisal of your employees. We make a lot of effort to invent a procedure, related criteria and a questionnaire in order to be able to identify who does or does not satisfy and to what degree. The manager who is responsible needs to fill out the form and eventually come to a common evaluation with the employee him- or herself. These meetings are very often difficult and tense, and not always very productive. If, however, somebody asked you 'off the record' who does and does not perform in your department, it would probably take you just a few seconds to make that list. You are even able to rapidly suggest some actions to improve performance. The problem is not the appraisal in itself; the problem is created by the procedure that is put in place in order to carry out that appraisal. Again, often the procedure seems to be more important than the aim of appraisal. But rules and regulations, in this case too, stand in the way of a straightforward evaluation. Using the rules, we attempt to arrive at an 'objective' decision which does not really have anything to do with reality any more. The procedure survives, the evaluation fails. The idea behind all this is that the more detailed we can make the rules, the better the eventual decision. Is it easier to judge on the basis of a constitution of, say, twenty-five rules, or on the basis of a civil code of several thousand articles? Are those thousands of articles adding anything to the essence of the constitution, or do they only detail it in order to make judgment easier? Do the many laws contribute to a better understanding of our constitution (which we all feel is right anyway), or do they only exist for the organization of the legal system and, in doing so, start to take on a life of their own? Often that life of their own goes further than the initial aim for which we have created the code in the first place.

Exactly the same thing happens in the legal system. The legal system is second-order autopoietic: it is not only self-reproducing, but also self-contained and auto-descriptive. That opens the door for what we often see in our modern society: rules start to take on lives of their own. Since the system is self-contained, rules will lead increasingly to more rules. The rules keep themselves alive and continue to reproduce. The rules become the drivers of the system. The rules become the system. Nobody cares whether we still have, behind the rules, a holistic idea of what is really happening. Reductionism creates its own reality instead of making an attempt to understand reality as it is. That is what we observe in companies, the legal system and probably all social systems that are based on a reductionist view.

What role does the learning human play? In the legal system as described in this chapter, the answer seems to be no role at all. The system is piloted by the rules, and not by a learning human. As with companies, having more rules kills the initiative of the learning individual. A minimum of rules is useful (a kind of a constitution), and then we only need a network of players who interact on the basis of that minimum set of rules. Except for ethical dilemmas, where only a representation of society (a jury, for instance) could make a judgment, every wise individual would be able to do justice if the system were conceived in such a way for that to be possible. In the present system there is little space for a learning lawyer or a learning judge, other than one who learns how to contribute to the survival of the system. If we accept for a moment that the aim of the system is to survive, then the lawyer and the judge are going to learn how to contribute best to the continuation of the system. Client, be warned.

The legal system, as it exists, only creates noise for the social system, and vice versa. Whereas the two should be inseparable, they live completely apart, each with the same aim: to survive. The realization of this aim, however, is sometimes different for the citizens. The feeling of uncertainty and the feeling of not having adequate legal protection increase. Actions like the bombing of the World Trade Center do not contribute positively to this fear. But is it surprising that terrorist groups readily appear and grow?

If we take the legal system as an example of wider societal organization and its responsibility, we often see the same kind of phenomena in the political world. Autopoiesis and self-reference are two strong concepts. They can create beautiful realizations, but they can also be very destructive. Holistic systems – and all social systems are holistic systems – cannot be reduced to rule-based systems. Autopoiesis and self-reference will kick back furiously. The distance between people and systems will invariably increase. The more that expert rules play a role, the more the network is neutralized, which will lead to a system with its own rules which eventually keeps itself alive. People and mechanistic systems become alienated, and no amount of optimization will help. Knowledge, learning and experience are crucial for a good working social system. The translation and reduction of learning into rules, and the self-regulation and self-reference inherent to those rules, will cause the rule-based system to start to take on a life of its own, which will eventually lead it away from the original goal. The instrument becomes the goal.

In the world's political thinking of today, such a process is easy to observe. Political regimes and politicians have reduced the world to their reality, often the reality of one particular country. In order to keep their own system (country, political union or religion) alive, they define rules and laws. The legal system falls into the trap of becoming what I have described as an autopoietic and a self-referential system. The legal system becomes the aim and no longer the means to a larger purpose. The economic principle behind the society, or the religion, or any other ideology, doesn't make any difference. Both Western societies and Islamic societies (like Afghanistan and Iraq) share this characteristic. The world is reduced to 'their' world, with its own rules and laws that in turn reinforce themselves. Inside each respective society the social organization has no influence on the laws. Within each system actions are confirmed and supported. They cannot be understood by outsiders. The United States has the 'right' to attack Iraq, at least according to its system, but Iraq does not understand why. Iraq had 'right' on its side in the Kuwaiti war, at least again according to the Iraqi system, but it did not find any understanding outside that system. Both are right, within their respective systems. The world is not improved by all this. The system that is called the world is deconstructed and the different parts start taking on lives of their own. The pieces of the body are cut off and fortunately they can even continue to survive, but the body is dying.

The only country which has ever been condemned by an international court for terrorism is the United States, which might surprise some people. The International Court of Justice did indeed condemn the United States for its invasion of Nicaragua, which was labelled a terrorist attack. Immediately the United States refused to recognize the International Court (and at the same time it lessened its cooperation with the entire UN). Although the International Court has a clear role to play according to Western thinking about democracy and freedom, this role seems to cease when one's own acts are brought into question. This makes the world order a kind of caricature. Each country falls back on its own ideas about right, order and terrorism. Dialogue and progress stop.

Learning stops if we cannot think outside our own frames; if we know beforehand the answer to any question. Learning is also daring to admit that one doesn't know and that one should investigate what could be learned, before being able to take action. Planning action and executing it is simple, according to rules that are defined beforehand. Learning and having the courage to do differently is much more difficult. The political system is not one that gives much evidence of learning. The legal structure that supports it is certainly partly responsible. The choice to accept the functioning of the legal system as we know it, and its 'stubborn' actions, is in fact a choice that society, represented by its politicians, makes.

The power of our society and the strength of humankind will again and again have to come from the learning potential of humans. Discovering this power, and learning how to work with it, could become a major challenge for managers in the decade to come. Therefore, we need an understanding of, and insight into, how systems operate and how creative potential emerges out of networks. That is what this book has been dealing with. Understanding and significance receive a lot of attention in this book.

Despite all the understanding and significance that we can give, the learning human will have to give form to his or her actions. The final chapter aims to suggest a few ways of doing so. The aim is not to define the correct path. We know that no such thing exists, and even if it did exist, it would not really help. The final chapter aims to give some ideas for creatively taking action. It aims to illustrate how learning managers can find their inner self in order to use this for responsible action within a network society. This search for one's inner self cannot be learned from books. Eventually, the learning manager will need to explore and experiment in their own personal development, possibly supported by a coach.

Before that, in the two next chapters, I will develop an alternative understanding of managerial and societal interaction, based on a quantum interpretation of that same reality.

# 8 The quantum interpretation

- The new key concepts in science
- The paradigmatic proposal
- The research agenda

Given the insight into complexity that we have developed and its consequences for management the way we have discussed it, we are now ready to explore an alternative interpretation of the managerial reality that would allow us a different managerial approach. In this chapter we explore the quantum interpretation of reality in general, before, in Chapter 9, applying this quantum interpretation to economic theory and reality.

What Prigogine and complexity theory in general discussed fundamentally was the existence of any causal relationship. In fact, he was surprised that despite the two fundamental revolutions in physics in the twentieth century, relativity theory and quantum mechanics, physics is still mainly Newtonian. It presumes a fixed time and space concept, in which the future is causally related to the past. Complexity theory shows the impossibility of this assumption, and so do relativity and quantum mechanics. But still we ignore it. Why would economics and management not follow the same reality as the physical world? Isn't management related to physical processes?

Most of the introduction to this chapter is based on Cushing's marvellous work on the philosophy of physics.

In both the special and the general theory of relativity, the notion of causality, in which a cause precedes its effect, remains intact in the relativistic formulations of electrodynamics and mechanics and of gravitation. In quantum theory the usual meaning of causal connection between one event and another is therefore called into question.

More than just pure logic and empirical evidence were at play in the exemplary discoveries of Maxwell, Planck and Bohr. Similarly, other factors are often relevant in theory construction and theory choice, as was the case too for quantum mechanical thinkers. Examples of such criteria are fertility, beauty and coherence.

The discontinuity versus continuity dichotomy can be seen as contingently rooted in philosophical commitments and in the physical phenomena studied.

By the late nineteenth century there were already significant, even if not overwhelming, philosophical precedents for the concept of indeterminism (including the possibility of inherent chance) in nature, as opposed to the straightforward determinism often associated with classical physics. Sören Kierkegaard believed that objective uncertainty can force one to make a leap into the unknown, so that decisions cannot always 'even in principle' be based on a continuous chain of logic. For example, one of Hoffding's tenets was that in life, decisive events proceed through sudden 'jerks' or discontinuities, an idea incorporated into Bohr's view of atomic phenomena.

Schrödinger concluded: this means that there is no alternative but to take seriously the de Broglie–Einstein wave theory of moving particles, according to which the particles are nothing more than a kind of 'wave crest' on a background of waves (Klein, 1964). Einstein, de Broglie and Schrödinger shared a commitment to a continuous wave as a basic physical entity subject to a causal description.

There was a split in philosophical outlook along generational lines: the 'older', essentially classical worldview of people like Einstein, Schrödinger and de Broglie versus a radically different, ultimately *indeterministic* conception of physical processes engendered by a generally younger generation (Bohr and Born being exceptions here), including Heisenberg, Pauli, Jordan and a new member of the group, Dirac from Cambridge University.

In 1927, at the Solvay Congress, de Broglie proposed a 'principle of the double solution', in which he suggested a synthesis of the wave and particle nature of matter. At that Fifth Solvay Congress he presented some of these ideas in a form he termed the pilot-wave theory. Here a physical particle was pictured as being guided by its pilot wave. Neither Einstein nor Schrödinger gave positive support to de Broglie's ideas: Einstein because he did not like the non-local (to be understood as apparently instantaneous action at a distance) nature of the theory, and Schrödinger because he wanted a theory based only on waves (and not on waves and particles). People including Heisenberg and Born, who also spoke at the 1927 Solvay Congress, strongly favoured the indeterministic or non-causal picture.

On the standard, or so-called Copenhagen, interpretation of quantum mechanics and, in particular, the Schrödinger equation, we no longer have event-by-event causality and particles do not follow well-defined trajectories in a space–time background. The theory predicts, in general, probabilities, not specific events.

Dirac argues that an intrinsic distinction between large and small is related to the effects produced on an object when it is observed. The act of observing the system (the cat, in Schrödinger's famous thought experiment) has forced the system into a given state (Dirac, 1958).

We now come to one of the most profound issues in the interpretation of quantum mechanics: that of causality (in the sense of a specific, identifiable cause for each individual effect). Dirac (1958) observes: causality applies only to a system which is left undisturbed. If a system is small, we cannot observe it without producing a serious disturbance and hence we cannot expect to find any causal connection between the results of our observations.

In this same spirit, Heisenberg too felt that, since the mathematical structure of quantum mechanics is so different from that of classical mechanics, it is not possible to interpret quantum mechanics in terms of our commonly understood notions of space and time with classical causality (Heisenberg, 1927).

This sudden and discontinuous change of the state of a quantum-mechanical system upon observation or measurement is an example of one of the central and long-standing conceptual difficulties of the standard interpretation. It is termed the 'measurement problem'.

The Heisenberg uncertainty principle and the lack of absolute predictive power are an inherent feature of quantum mechanics. In principle, there is no deterministic scheme to predict the exact future trajectory of an electron. Bohr developed this idea further. Today we refer to this dependence of the outcome of a measurement upon the means used to effect it as *contextuality*.

In 1935, Schrödinger formulated his famous 'cat paradox' (Schrödinger, 1935). Consider an initially live cat placed in a steel box that is then sealed. With the cat is a sample of a radioactive element whose probability of random decay in one hour is exactly 0.5. Things are so arranged that if an atom of the element does decay, then a device will shatter a vial of hydrocyanic acid and kill the cat. Otherwise, the cat continues to live. When the problem begins, the wave function for this combined system (cat + atom) necessarily corresponds to that of a live cat. However, as time passes, there is some finite probability that the atom has decayed, so that the cat is dead. Suppose that, at the end of one hour, the wave function for the system is an equal mixture or superposition of the state for a live cat and that for a dead cat. In this case a macrosystem, the cat, would be thrown into one state or another by our mere act of observation, provided that the wave function gives a complete, objective description of reality. Schrödinger did not believe this to be reasonable. Einstein wrote in response to this (in 1939): 'I am as convinced as ever that the wave representation of matter is an incomplete representation of the state of affairs, no matter how practically useful it has proved itself to be.'

An obvious rhetorical question now presents itself. What does the wave function represent – our state of knowledge of the system (in which case quantum mechanics is incomplete), or the actual physical state of the system (in which case there must be a sudden change of the system upon our observation of it)? Although the system may appear in either of two states (or 'components') before the measurement, nature has (in the image suggested by Dirac) been forced to 'make a choice' when observed. Since the system is thereafter in a definite component, no subsequent interference with the other component is possible. The 'collapse' of the wave function has taken place.

In 1935, Einstein, Boris Podolsky and Nathan Rosen (generally referred to as EPR) published a paper titled 'Can quantum-mechanical description of physical reality be considered complete?'. It is important to point out that EPR assume that action at a distance does not exist. This assumption is often referred to as the *locality* assumption: no instantaneous action at a distance. Bohr responded to the article, perhaps even more explicitly than EPR had done, denying the possibility of any actual physical action at a distance (non-locality).

Heisenberg summarized Einstein's view on quantum mechanics as follows. The conviction that the world could be completely divided into an objective and a subjective sphere, and the hypothesis that one should be able to make precise statements about the objective side of it, formed a part of his basic philosophical attitude. But quantum mechanics could not satisfy these claims, and it does not seem likely that science will ever find its way back to Einstein's postulate.

EPR introduced the deterministic hidden variables theories. It assumes that there is a set of variables, or as yet undiscovered properties, of a system and that the exact space–time behaviour of the system is causally determined by the values of these 'hidden' variables. The introduction of such a large number of hidden variables may seem a high price to pay to maintain locality and realism. John Bell proved a remarkable theorem in 1965. Simply put, no determinate, local hidden variables theory can agree with all of the predictions of quantum mechanics. Consequently, it can now be asserted with reasonable confidence that either the thesis of realism or that of locality must be abandoned. Either choice will drastically change our concepts of reality and of space–time (Clauser and Shimony, 1978).

It is generally believed that a causal interpretation of quantum mechanics is impossible, although no proof of this exists.

We characterized the standard, or Copenhagen, view of quantum mechanics as requiring complementarity (say, wave–particle duality), inherent indeterminism at the most fundamental level of quantum phenomena, and the impossibility of an event-by-event causal representation in a continuous space–time background. So, on the Copenhagen interpretation of quantum mechanics, physical processes are, at the most fundamental level, both inherently indeterministic and non-local. The ontology of classical physics is dead. The heart of the problem is the entanglement (or non-separability) of quantum states that gives rise to the measurement problem. This entanglement makes it impossible to assign independent properties to an arbitrary isolated physical system once it has interacted with another system in the past – even though these two systems are no longer interacting. The non-separability characteristic of quantum systems can be seen as an indication of the 'holistic' character of such systems. Some claim that we need a new concept of causality, but it is not clear what that would be. Heisenberg long ago suggested introducing a new class of physical entity, *potentia*, into our theory (and into our ontology).

Quantum mechanics is the blackest of black-box theories: a marvellous predictor but an incompetent explainer (Cushing, 1998).

A Bell-type theorem is proved and taken as convincing evidence that non-locality is present in quantum phenomena. Quantum mechanics has undeniably introduced us to non-locality, entanglement and synchronicity – concepts that thus far have not been applied in business or economics.

What we have done in the preceding chapters, on a slightly more metaphysical plane, is to explore the right-hand quadrants of Ken Wilber's diagram and also the bottom left-hand quadrant a little. What a knowledge and learning approach envisages is, in fact, being able to go into the left-hand quadrants, especially the bottom one. This is the important thing for an approach to knowledge, but it is also the principal difficulty. We have already suggested that the solution will be, in effect, to go as low as possible on the aggregation level (human emotions, team members) to allow innovation to produce itself through the emergence of processes. In fact, we want to explore the quantum reality of management. The real remaining question then becomes clear, and it is a question for the top left-hand quadrant in Wilber's diagram. It is a double question: can, and how can, you make the concept of innovation holistic, and so encapsulate the personal emotional side? but on a deeper level we can ask ourselves this question with reference to conscience and causality, and the 'seat' of consciousness.

The more down-to-earth question is: on what level can we find consciousness? Is there something like a collective consciousness (for example, in a company, on the subject of innovation)? And does everyone have a sort of essential element of incorporated consciousness with the possibility of connection with others (at the level of consciousness)? Translated to companies: do consciousness, engagement, emotions make a difference for a company? does a company have a 'soul', a consciousness? Is there a link between this 'consciousness', if it exists, and the success of a company? Are vision, emotions and consciousness linked? More concretely, who determines the choice of a client who has a preference for one company rather than another? What lets potential clients make a distinction between two companies which in fact offer the same services (for example, two big banks such as BNP and Crédit du Nord, or two consultant companies such as PricewaterhouseCoopers and Accenture)? And finally, can we arrive at an approach, accepted as scientific, that gives at least the beginning of a response to these questions? Although these questions are, of course, a little metaphysical, this does not prevent them from remaining important questions. We will now see who the most famous scientists are, most often from the hard sciences, who are asking themselves these inevitable questions.

Dr Mitchell (astronaut on Apollo 14 and 'man on the Moon') notably asked himself this question on the role and the understanding of consciousness during his trip back from the Moon. He was convinced, after having doubtless experienced a marvel of science, that if we cannot manage to understand and study consciousness in a scientific manner, we can never get the world to progress. Departing from this objective, he created a foundation (the Noetic Society; www.noetic.org) which works on the research of consciousness. The Noetic Society sponsors research by people like Rupert Sheldrake among others, whom I will say more about soon. But, to take another example, Pauli, a founder of quantum physics, was, like some of his colleagues (as argued before), equally interested in these types of questions (as I will illustrate later).

Once we accept holism, constructivism and emergence as fundaments of a new paradigm, we cannot avoid touching upon a paradox, perhaps the most important paradox in science. Despite the two great revolutions of the previous century – the theory of relativity and quantum mechanics – almost the whole scientific community is still focused on Newtonian principles, that is to say, fixed space and time. If we know what happened yesterday, then we also know what will happen tomorrow (and also what happened the day before yesterday). Science still does very little with the space–time continuum that these revolutions have offered us. In the hard sciences, at least, there are groups of researchers working on this subject. In economy and managerial sciences this revolution seems to have been completely sidestepped. Our thinking is still Marshallian, the economic thinking of the nineteenth century (Arthur, 1998).

To illustrate this inevitable question, I want to give a few facts and thoughts which reflect the subsequent work of Pauli (van Meijgaard, 2002). At the end of his scientific career, Wolfgang Pauli asked himself how we can know whether human cultures can live with a clear distinction between knowledge and belief (an idea, moreover, of Max Planck). For this reason, according to him, societies are in difficulty if new knowledge arrives and puts accepted spiritual values into question. The complete separation between the two can only be a solution in the short term, and one of facility. Pauli had predicted (was he right?) that there will be a moment in the near future when all the images and metaphors of classical religions will lose their strength of conviction for the average citizen. So, we will get to a situation where classical ethical values explode and we have a period of hitherto unknown barbarism. He was touched and very interested by what he himself called 'background physics': the spontaneous appearance of quantitative concepts and images concerning the physical in fantasies and dreams. He said he also had them himself. Their character was very dependent on the dreamer himself. Background physics has an archetypal origin and that leads (always, according to him) to a natural science which will work just as well with matter as with consciousness. He was also enough of a realist to say that if a researcher in physics has observed a subsystem, the observations are as much dependent on the observer as on the instruments.

According to Pauli, the physical concept of 'complementarity' physics (van Meijgaard, 2002) illustrated a profound analogy with concepts such as conscience and the unconscious. Two extreme cases which can never be attained in practice are someone with a 'perfect conscience' (Eastern philosophy suggests that this can be attained uniquely in death, also called nirvana) and something like a 'bigger spirit' which will never be influenced by a subjective consciousness. This 'bigger spirit' is what Eastern philosophy calls 'the consciousness' and Western psychology calls 'the collective unconscious'. Pauli accepted that physical values, as much as archetypes, change in the eyes of the observer. Observation is the result of human consciousness.

Pauli wrote a book with Jung on this issue. Where Jung talks about defined archetypes as primordial structural elements of the human psyche, Pauli introduced the notion of the 'collective unconscious'. They both believed that we are moving towards a joining of the psyche and the physical.

The introduction of the interesting notion of 'synchronicity' in this co-authored work is one that we will find again later in this chapter in the work of other authors, some of them in other disciplines. Synchronicity may be a key to the understanding of what causality is and, for this reason, I am devoting a little more time to this concept here.

Synchronicity (being united in time), according to Pauli, appears in all the sciences and the techniques in which simultaneity plays a role. We must take into account that we are not speaking about a *causal* coherence (from cause to effect) but about a *coincidence* (= being together in time) which must be considered useful even if we cannot explain the deep cause of this simultaneity. We must remember that we always speak about synchronicity if the events concerned occur in the same time period. The concepts of statistics or the theory of probability are of another order. Probability can be calculated using mathematical methods, which is impossible when speaking about synchronicity.

Synchronicity (according to van Meijgaard) may be considered to be the basis of numerous phenomena which are difficult to explain and which are often called non-scientific. This book will not go into these aspects. The way to understand van Meijgaard's ideas better is that the widening of consciousness and the dissolving of borders are only possible when we keep, in addition to our energetic causal thinking (classical), a space for *synchronicity and information*. It is to Pauli's great credit that he indicated the necessity to create space for the concept of synchronicity in scientific thinking. Jung speaks about this as the 'a-causal' link. Sheldrake (more on this to follow) later confirmed these ideas with his theory of morph(ogenet)ic fields.

Is the 'causality' looked for in the science of management more a 'synchronicity' as defined here?

Pauli and Jung proposed that the classic triad of physics (space, time and causality) be extended to include synchronicity, thereby forming a tetrad. This fourth element works in an a-causal manner, and it is, in effect, the polar opposite of causality. Pauli and Jung believed that these oppositions were orthogonal in time and space.

The idea of an a-causal link, or non-locality, is a new concept which should contribute effectively to the science of management (and specifically to the management of innovation) by making it more concrete. The term 'non-local' comes, in fact, from Einstein's opposition to his own grandchild, quantum mechanics. Einstein, along with two of his colleagues, Boris Podolsky and Nathan Rosen (as already mentioned), illustrated that quantum mechanics has long-term implications, not yet well thought out, particularly for the behaviour of two separated particles. I shall refer to this by using the term 'EPR' thinking (Polkinghorne, 1990). According to Einstein, classical quantum theory is not complete. This theory does not allow us to measure the two separated elements at the same time (let us say x and y), since there is an uncertain relationship between the two. If, by contrast, we can measure the behaviour of two particles and observe a relationship, this relationship was already there independently of the measure (according to EPR). The majority view (of researchers) concludes that the observation of one particle produces a direct and immediate effect on the second. In effect, there must be a 'togetherness-in-separation' against the intuitive (a theory which Einstein refused to accept, calling it 'spooky action at a distance'). It is this effect which is often called the EPR effect. Later, Bell illustrated that if there were a strict locality, there would be relationships between the observable quantities (Bell 'inequalities') expected by quantum mechanics which would not be respected in certain circumstances. Alain Aspect did research based on measured observations, finally confirming non-locality. There is an amount of non-locality which is no longer 'reducible' in our physical world. Quantum entities which have interacted remain mutually connected ('entangled'), independently of the distance between the two quantities. Even nature seems to attack pure and simple reductionism (Polkinghorne, 1990). The subatomic world can no longer be treated in a purely atomic way.

The implication of these observations is that the phenomenon of 'entanglement' (non-locality) includes a real remote activity, not simply epistemological but in fact ontological in nature.

Recently, the Bogdanov brothers have published an interesting book that summarizes their PhD work (in theoretical physics and mathematics): *Avant le Big Bang*. In their book they attempt to take the understanding of the quantum interpretation a step further. Interesting as it is, it has of course been discussed by many others who still seem to stick to more classical theories. In their theoretical work, and hence in the book, they make an attempt to explore what could happen beyond Planck's wall ($<10^{-43}$). Not only do they find non-locality, synchronicity and entanglement, but they also find a possible explanation for non-locality. As is well known, we currently accept four dimensions: three of space and one of time. The Bogdanovs, however, theoretically observe a fifth dimension that would be a fourth dimension of space, expressed though in 'imaginary' time. Explaining the concept of imaginary time would take us too far, and it is extremely mathematical, but it has to do with the famous $i$ in mathematics (the square root of a negative number). If they theoretically observe this fifth dimension beyond Planck's wall, it of course also exists before that 'wall', which would mean that there is something like an interwovenness between time and space. Time has a space dimension and space has a time dimension. Though their proof is rather convincing, and their PhD examiners were mainly Nobel Prize winners, the least one can say is that even if some scientist wants to dispute their conclusions, their observations and proof are elegant, whether or not they turn out to be true.

This development should not be misunderstood as an extension of the search in physics for the string theory. The latter is not concerned with the (Bogdanov) singularity, but accepts Planck's wall as a fact of life.

All these developments in physics bring us to define what I call 'a quantum structure'. To illustrate this quantum concept, and with the goal of doing a thought experiment, I would like to explain Mitchell's 'dyadic model' as he describes it in his book (Mitchell and Williams, 1996). Stated simply, the concept of non-locality is derived from quantum physics (as explained before). In fact, in the experiments he demonstrated that particles (photons) stay attached in a 'mysterious' manner, even if they are displaced in directions contrary to the speed of light.

The dyadic model is built on the idea that everything is energy. This basic energy is linked to information, what Mitchell calls structures of energy. The energy and the information form a dyad. The information, in this context, is the basis of the capacity of matter to 'know' (and so has nothing to do with information as treated in information systems). By way of analogy, in the science of management this dyad could typically reside in people, and then be transformed, through interaction with others, into more knowledge, new knowledge, and/or more innovative knowledge.

All matter contains a sort of 'awareness', or, in other terms, a capacity to 'know'. If it did not, how could molecules 'know' that they must join up with others to form cells? In a subsequent state (a more complex state), it could be that in the human body and brain, matter evolves such that it knows what it knows. It is therefore capable of self-reflection.

Another dyad in his model is 'awareness' and intention, which equally make up part of the evolutionary process that leads to consciousness. Consciousness and innovation, accepted elements of the energy information scheme, are the basis of self-reflective consciousness. There is also a little evidence that matter 'knows'. For that, Mitchell refers to a subatomic level with the non-locality attributes 'quantum entanglement' and coherence, although we never know with certainty what form this 'knowing' will have. So, Mitchell uses the notion of non-locality.

The non-locality is illustrated by the famous connection proved and explained in more detail before ('entanglement') between partner photons which are sent in opposite directions. However, they remain able to immediately ('instantaneously') communicate between each other over large distances. This is related to the 'knowledge' of these particles. Human beings are equally made up of these sorts of particles.

So how does such communication function, according to Mitchell? The groups of particles seem to have special characteristics of resonance and coherence which are evoked by the groups themselves. This resonance includes historical knowledge about universal matter. This idea strongly corresponds to Rupert Sheldrake's observations. The body/brain can receive holographic information in the form of virtual long-wave signals. Mitchell's dyad suggests that the particles 'know' by their inherent qualities of conscience and intention. The groups of particles communicate between themselves on the basis of quantum holograms (what Sheldrake calls the morphogenetic fields), which include information about the universe. As our body/brain also works in a holographic way, it can recover this information. Apparently nature does not lose its memory concerning its own evolution. Mitchell believes that it is our intention or directional attention which links us holographically with the signals or non-local long waves.

The greater the experience of satisfaction, the more the consciousness of each cell in the body will resonate with the holographic information engraved in the 'quantum zero point' (the lowest possible state of energy, in an almost, but not quite, resting situation; Polkinghorne, 1990) of the energy field. This phenomenon refers to what we know as to be 'carried along'. If a person lives in harmony with their biological rhythms (all sorts of rhythms), the body is in balance and they will fall ill less readily. In the material world we can witness a phenomenon of 'being carried along' if we put two pendulums beside one another. Although the movement of the pendulums in the two clocks seems at first to be totally arbitrary, after a certain time the movements adapt to each other and the pendulums move in harmony. The two clocks are 'carried along' with each other. In the world of medicine, many of these ideas are found in Ayurvedic (holistic) medicine.

This quantum approach of energy, information and communication allows us to suggest causality at a much lower level of aggregation; that is to say, at a quantum level (to be defined in detail further on concerning the economy and management). In effect, we should really speak about synchronicity or coincidence rather than causality. It is important that it is this structure which allows people to realize what they want to realize; that could be, for example, to protect themselves against viruses, to simply survive or innovate as in companies. It is therefore a question of elementary particles (let us say the characteristics of people if we translate them into economic behaviour), which are linked in solid networks with all sorts of matter (the context), which, in turn, interact with this matter and, in doing so, become part of the wider energetic field (morphogenetics) which contains knowledge and information. When more members of a team (or a company) are 'carried along', their actions will have more success – for example, in teams working on product innovation. In the experiments and research which we will come back to later on (Chapter 9), we will be able to illustrate the innovation processes in a huge multinational. We used agent simulations, among other things. The understanding of innovation should therefore be based on 'being carried along', quantum structures, synchronicity, morphogenetic fields and individual space for self-organization.

Others (Caro and Murphy, 2002) have applied the quantum concept to art and aesthetics. And although this is not the subject of this chapter either, it is interesting to see how the same principles of synchronicity, non-locality and quantum structure can be applied in art. The cradle of this quantum movement in arts is in Spain. Caro and Murphy's book includes chapters on quantum art, quantum literature, quantum anthropology and quantum politics. Towards the end of the book, the authors suggest that the quantum principle makes more profound sense and they integrate it with the understanding of societal phenomena.

Dalla Chiara and Giuntini (1999) tried to apply the quantum logic to the concept of truth and interpretation in art. They first of all dedicate themselves to the subject of poetic force and ask themselves if truth in poetry is less 'true' than observed truth. Where quantum theory and orthodox quantum logic deal uniquely with problems of absolute clarity, leaving no place for different interpretations, problems linked to language are evidently vaguer. But true humans are not clear and absolute notions either. What is it to be 'honourable'? What is 'important'? Quantum logic does not only work with well-defined, unambiguous concepts. With these problems, semantic uncertainties are only the result of the fact that the problem is not completely defined in detail. The authors plead for a vague quantum theory (perhaps even to be compared with fuzzy logic). They use music as an analogy. A piece of music does not consist only of a score, but of a mass of different possible combinations between the same score and different musicians' interpretations. It is therefore a combination of senses (emotions) and symbols, but although every combination is possible, not all are necessarily good.

After these illustrations concerning the use of quantum concepts, non-locality and synchronicity, as much in physical science as in the science of language and music, I want now to come back again to Sheldrake's theory, which is founded on biology. Sheldrake, who is a well-known Cambridge biologist, is now an affiliated Research Fellow at the Noetic

Society (which we talked about above). Although his theory is controversial (as is often the case with a new paradigm), it has been validated by quite a lot of research, as his many publications witness. As ideas, these theories are entirely in accord with the scientific ideas developed so far. But Sheldrake's research is also an example of the way in which I want to give form to my own research.

In a paper that Sheldrake wrote with Bohm (1982), they broach the subject of 'implicit order'. Implicit order is something like a ground below time, a tonality, of which each movement is projected in explicit order (what we know). For everything we see here, there is something in implicit order which is at the origin of this projection. If an event is repeated a lot, that event has a constant built component behind it. A sort of (fixed) link is born. Via this process, the forms of the past can continue to live in the present. This is more or less what Sheldrake calls morphogenetic fields, created by morphogenetic resonance. If something climbs into 'totality', where neither time nor space is fixed, it could be that things of the same nature will attach themselves to one another, or resonate. Because neither time nor space exists in this totality, things which happen at a particular place could therefore also happen elsewhere, or at least have an influence.

These ideas are very much in line with what I have introduced as the Bogdanov singularity and the Bogdanovs' observation that a fifth dimension could exist, being a fourth dimension of space expressed in imaginary time. Comparing the different 'quantum' interpretations in the different sciences seems to converge on what can be understood as an emergent understanding of this quantum world and its consequences.

Although Sheldrake and Bohm's theory, mentioned above, is the scientific topic that Sheldrake is vigorously researching these days, his theory of proved morphogenetic fields could be very useful for us. The hypothetical characteristics that Sheldrake attributes to morphogenetic fields are the following:

- They are self-organized 'collections' or 'collectivities'.
- They have a time and space aspect and they organize from time/space schemas of vibrations (energy) (and therefore from interaction).
- They attract the systems under their influence towards characteristic forms or models. They organize the realization of these activities and preserve the integrity of these activities. The goals or the places where these activities are attracted are called the attractors.

- The morphic fields are put into relationship with holons (units which are themselves entire). The morphic fields therefore include other morphic fields in a climbing hierarchy (nested hierarchy) or holarchy. These holarchies are created in an emergent fashion.
- They are structures of probability and also their organizing activity is probabilistic.
- They include a so-called closed memory, formed by self-resonance with its own past and morphic resonance with comparable anterior systems. This memory is cumulative. As more models repeat themselves, they become more normal.

Sheldrake's idea of morphogenetic fields complements the latest ideas that Varela was able to work on (before he died), dealing with how something like resonance could be responsible as the organizing principle in networks. Varela's suggestion became illustrated by Sheldrake's research.

In fact, these characteristics identified from morphogenetic fields are completely in parallel with the paradigm developed in the previous chapters. They could just as well be the characteristics of an economic system, a market, a company.

A last science where holistic concepts are more and more popular is, without doubt, medical science. Although various important thinkers are active in this subject, Ayurveda (the ancient Indian medical science) and, more particularly, somebody like Dr Chopra (1990), with his research and experiments, are doing more and more research into quantum concepts of healing. In these experiments also, we find a basis for the approach I am proposing.

Ayurveda is a proven medical science, originally from India, which examines the holistic individual in a different way as compared with Western medical science. Unless medical care is urgently needed, in which case it is immediately necessary to act locally, Ayurveda looks for a natural balance in the human being. It will be clear that Ayurveda is a preventive medicine: the best doctor does not have any patients. The carrier of all this is energy, which is not entirely astonishing and is in line with other theories presented in this chapter. The human body has its own system of regeneration, its own defence mechanisms, and the art must then be to reinforce these. The heart, for instance, is seen as an important regulator of those energy flows. Certain illnesses, such as stomach problems or migraines, are always caused by an imbalance. To remove the symptom therefore does not often help (unless the condition is urgent or acute, as has already been said). To put back the balance is the message. Seeing that the body is a very complex network with all sorts of cells which know exactly what they should know to be able to cooperate with the others (knowing perfectly with which others), it is necessary to disturb this network as little as possible. For many reasons, the World Health Organization (WHO) has identified Ayurveda as the medical solution for developing populations.

I would not say it too loudly, but certain of these ideas are becoming increasingly popular in Western medicine. Healthy living and good nutrition are now also credos in the West. Nevertheless, the 'why' of this advice is of a different nature. Ayurveda considers the human body to be a self-organizing system composed of a lot of simple elements which, taken independently, are very stupid but which together form a formidable distributed intelligence. Entirely in parallel, we can consider a company as a network of 'simple' elements which each 'know' what they need to know in order to be able to manage to form correct networks with others. The knowledge of a system is found in the community, not in a local element.

The interesting thing is that these theories reconfirm the concepts proposed before. In particular, Chopra's theories concerning synchronicity and non-locality are interesting for the arguments already developed here. I do not want to go into detail, but his theory and his approach confirm the theories already broached. Even if we do not want to go so far into the topic of medical science, since we are, and remain, interested in managerial theory, it is clear that there are already quite a few scientific concepts, proved in other sciences, which could be useful for us.

To summarize the essentials of all these theories, we can say that quantum reality, which is expressed in non-locality, synchronicity and entanglement, is promising for offering new understanding for a more efficient harmony of the concept of causality in management and the economy. Instead of talking about causality, we would do better to talk about synchronicity (coincidence). These concepts are therefore the underlying theory for the experiments and the research agenda which I am going to propose further on.

In line with the research already cited, we can ask ourselves a number of important questions. Certain scientists would inevitably say that the ideas expressed here are perhaps a little metaphysical and therefore difficult to deal with. This is evidently not a good reason not to try. By definition, innovative research never follows paths already well marked out. I have already dealt with that in detail when we spoke about the philosophies of science. But understandably the question arises of whether we can talk here about a paradigm shift. In any case, that is what I want to suggest.

My feeling is that the classical paradigm does not allow us to advance in understanding problems of management and the economy in general. We are limiting ourselves here to innovation, but of course there are a number of other imponderable questions to deal with in economics, such that classical economics is increasingly referred to as a lost science. The 'random walk' does better than a portfolio manager. Markets collapse and create themselves with such irregularity that experts can only research these changes afterwards for explanations. Enormous companies (Arthur Andersen, Lernout & Hauspie) disappear from the scene just like that in a period of a few months.

Where is the intelligence in a system, where is the coherence, and, finally, where is the causality? How can we subsequently do something? Does intelligence reside in the network and, if so, what are the constructive elements in our economic and social systems? What are the organizing principles?

The restrictions which the economy faces are sufficiently well known. Arthur (of the Santa Fe Institute of Complexity) has been researching them and publishing on this subject for years (Arthur, 1998). Others have also already indicated where classical economics has known its limits (for example Martens, 1999). Arthur correctly remarked that our economic thinking is still based on Marshall's theory, which dates from the nineteenth century. This economic theory described a society mainly based on industrial production, in which limited resources should be shared between alternative uses. Something – a resource – that is used in one product cannot be used in another product. So, one obtains the so-called law of diminishing returns. The more a specific product is available, the lower its added value becomes. After we have eaten five pieces of pie, the sixth piece seems much less attractive. If enough raw materials necessary for production are available, any new unit of raw material has a lower added value. But what was accepted wisdom concerning an industrial economy no longer holds water in a knowledge-based economy. The most important assumptions that cast doubt on its applicability are that human beings are rational, that in a market all the necessary information is available (and the players on these markets are perfectly informed), and that only a restricted number of goods and services are possible. If we take only the acceptance of human rationality, I believe that I have illustrated well enough that rationality can never be considered without the emotional side.

But economic science also ignores today's reality, which is that we live in a knowledge economy. Production costs, in the narrowest sense of the word, today make up quite a small part of the total cost of a knowledge-based product (look at the R&D and marketing share of the costs, for example). If we look at knowledge-based products, economic logic is completely different. The production of the first copy of a product costs a lot of money (because of the necessary research up front), but each subsequent copy costs very little, and therefore returns become much higher per copy sold. The first copy of Windows cost several billions; it was therefore sold at a big loss. However, each subsequent copy costs the time needed to copy it and the price of a CD, or, even cheaper, the cost of downloading. The real costs of knowledge-based products occur in their development. Knowledge does not lose its value when it is used several times. Sharing knowledge does not lead to the loss of resources. In this case, within a knowledge economy and/or with knowledge-based products, we observe something which we may call a law of increasing returns on the economic markets. Dealing with these concepts in more detail here would take us off the subject, but it is clear to Arthur (1998) that we need a redefinition of economic theory.

Martens (1999) equally pleads along the same lines. He concludes that neo-classical thinking in economics is not in a position to create an economic system which will be 'self-maintaining', or to give an understanding of the self-creating capacity of such a system. According to him, innovation is incompatible with classical economic thinking, which thinks in terms of balance and competition. He also makes a plea for the creation of a new economic theory, taking into account the fact that it is necessary to be able to incorporate consciousness in such a theory. Unfortunately, he does not really suggest how to do it.

Because causality is considered at too high a level of aggregation, economic models provide little understanding of the dynamic behaviour of markets and companies. Research must be refocused. For the moment, we have to discover the level at which causality or synchronicity play a role. In other words, we have to develop an understanding of the importance of the quantum structure for management. Part of that research is oriented towards the way in which we can visualize and understand the organizational principle of that quantum world. If we accept the quantum structure, then are 'complex adaptive systems' going to allow us to understand economic reality?

## The new key concepts in science

In order to be able to clearly formulate a new paradigm in management, and develop an adequate research agenda, I would like to summarize here a few fundamental concepts, often developed in sciences other than economics or management. Once these concepts are defined, I will make propositions about the methods which will allow us to transfer them to economics and management. Such a transfer is not a self-evident process, and is in itself already an interpretation. Each topic defined is automatically a research issue. Part of the research to be undertaken is to find evidence for the existence and validity of most of the concepts. At the moment the concepts, and their translation from physics to management, remain largely metaphysical.

- Although it is not really the concept of another science, it is worth repeating that the approach developed and proposed here is inscribed in the holistic paradigm. Holism, as I want to understand it, makes reference to Ken Wilber's theories. He defines *holism* as an eternal dynamic interaction between four 'spheres': the mechanical (external) and individual sphere; the mechanical (external) collective sphere; the internal collective sphere (common values); and the internal individual sphere (emotions and consciousness). Clearly, in the rather reductionist and rational approaches it is the external individual sphere which receives most attention. 'Classical' ecological scientific movements are especially interested in the collective, but always external, sphere. My scientific topic tries to go beyond that, by including more values, emotions – that is to say, consciousness. Holism, as defined by Wilber, is evidently founded on a *constructivist* approach.
- My proposed approach fits clearly into the *sciences of complexity* as Prigogine defined them. Prigogine defined the sciences of complexity as the study of dynamic non-linear systems. In particular, he was always very interested in two important aspects: the role of time, and behaviour far from equilibrium. He illustrated the constructive role of time in complex processes, expressed in the principle of the irreversibility of time. This principle says that an important

consequence is that in complex systems you cannot extrapolate the future from the past. Complex systems are extremely sensitive to the initial conditions; minimal changes in these conditions can have major effects in the further development of the process. Finally, Prigogine defines the most productive state of a (complex) system as one that is far from equilibrium: 'order at the edge of chaos'.

- John Holland, a pioneer in artificial life and agent systems, has developed a complex adaptive approach (CAS) called *agent simulations*. This approach simulates the interaction between different agents and, consequently, simulates *emergent behaviour* in those kinds of systems. An agent, according to him, is a mini software program. Each agent has characteristics. It is necessary to define the field of action (the limits of the system) and to identify a minimum of interaction rules (and exchange rules). Then it is necessary to make the system iterate, and simulate the dynamic interaction between those agents. The agents meet each other, interact, exchange (and so learn) and, step by step, we get to a global behaviour with qualities which emerge from the interaction itself.

- *Synchronicity* (being together in time), according to Pauli, appears in all the sciences and the techniques in which simultaneity plays a role. It is necessary to take into account that we are speaking not about a causal coherence (from cause to effect), but about *coincidence* (= occurring together in time) which must be considered as useful, even if we cannot explain the more profound cause of this simultaneity. We must remember that we always speak of a synchronicity if the events concerned happen during the same period of time. The relationships therefore become *a-causal* (in Jung's words).

- Max Planck proposed (and this is contrary to classical physics) that from time to time radiation is emitted and absorbed in energy pockets of a specific size. Such a pocket is called a *quantum*, and this is in fact considered as the unit of quantum mechanics. The amount of energy is proportional to the frequency of the quanta: low frequency therefore equals low energy. Einstein considered a ray of light to be a collection of quanta. These light quanta are called *photons*.

- The implication of these observations is that the phenomenon of *entanglement* (*non-locality*), including a real activity at a distance, is not simply epistemological, but in effect ontological by nature. And here we have just defined what I call a '*quantum structure*'. In view of its ontological nature (Polkinghorne), it cannot be ignored.

- A work by Sheldrake and Bohm (1982) broached the subject of *implicit order*. Implicit order is something like a ground underneath time, a totality, from which each movement is projected in explicit order (order that we know). For everything we see here, there is something in implicit order which is at the origin of this projection. If an event keeps repeating itself, there is a built constant component behind the repetitions. A sort of (fixed) link is born. Via this process, forms from the past can continue to live in the present. This is more or less what Sheldrake calls *morphogenetic fields*, created by *morphogenetic resonance*.

- Ayurveda considers the human being to be a self-organizing system composed of a lot of simple elements which are, when taken independently, very stupid, but which together form a formidable *distributed intelligence*. In parallel, one can consider a company as a network of 'simple' elements which each 'know' what they must know in order to be able to form correct networks with others.
- The ontological nature of this quantum structure forces us to look again at our approach to innovation, and on a wider scale at our economic theory. *The understanding of innovation must therefore be based on the 'carrying along' of quantum structures, synchronicity, morphogenetic fields and individual space for self-organization.*
- In their recent work, the Bogdanovs, in search for what they define as the Bogdanov singularity, suggest the existence of a fifth dimension. This dimension would be a *fourth dimension of space, expressed in imaginary time*. This theoretical development suggests a formal system in which time and space indeed become closer to each other; in fact, they share a dimension. Their proposed theoretical framework could be the beginning of an explanation of most of the concepts illuminated here.

## The paradigmatic proposal

To summarize a few words, the paradigmatic proposal I would like to make here consists of the translation of elements defined above into the framework of the economy and management, in the first place with a focus on innovation, for the very simple reason that this is a main managerial concern. The ontological nature of this quantum structure makes it, in my opinion, a kind of scientific obligation to research this structure further. In fact, in the first place it is necessary to translate a number of the scientific concepts suggested above into the framework of innovation (or management in general). Of course, the propositions made are still subjects of research, therefore they cannot be other than only propositions – research hypotheses to be confirmed (or rejected) after empirical research. In this section I am therefore going to try to define a few elements of this translation. In any case, the following chapter makes a connection with a few research projects undertaken in which the working hypotheses I have established seem to be confirmed. This constitutes a first kind of evidence, a suggested understanding, which we will deal with in the next chapter.

The concept of quanta, the simplest element in the interaction, should be researched most profoundly in the agents who are people. Therefore, the idea 'basic energy' can be translated as human qualities which are as much intellectual as emotional (and eventually they are also translated into energy). Everything like these quanta plays a role inside humans (in interaction with other quanta), for the concept of non-locality is also linked to other quanta (qualities) of other people (in the market, the company, etc.; reference can be made here to morphogenetic fields). It is clear that this hypothesis is in effect partly a pragmatic hypothesis, since in the final analysis it is also necessary to be able to do simulations. Thus, it is not impossible that we may find that the level of (energetic) quanta is even more detailed. If not, we will inevitably fall on the theories of non-locality, which certain people still consider non-scientific.

Supposing that the quanta are as defined here, clearly there are also rather explicit and measurable elements (level of experience, education) as well as implicit elements, like vision or goodwill (towards working in a group). The choice of these more measurable and less measurable elements as possible quanta is partly a pragmatic choice that has to do with a need to couple the interacting quanta idea with the pragmatic necessity to later interpret evolving behaviour within its holistic concept.

Every 'collection' of humans, such as companies, markets, project groups, etc., is considered as an agent, in the sense defined here (making reference to Holland). Whenever I refer to 'agency theories', I am thinking of a-causal relationships and self-organization. Humans and even, in effect, the quanta as defined in the previous paragraph interact with their qualities as agents. The rules of interaction are, in fact, often rules of exchange of experiences, knowledge or simply learning of respective agents. The underlying theory of non-locality and synchronicity allows us to theoretically justify the reason for the agent simulation results. Since, theoretically, there is synchronicity, a network of quantas and agents can create emergence. Synchronicity justifies the rationality of the emergence of processes and also explains why, in effect, entire markets can co-evolve, as we can see daily.

The theory of synchronicity, of non-locality and 'entanglement' is the justification (ontological of course, but also epistemological) of the functioning of simulations. This theory gives us a basis from which to be able to understand the emergent phenomena that the simulations produce. Without this underlying theory there is still doubt about what an agent simulation really shows. Although I make reference in the first place to agent simulations, the same thing can be said for artificial neural networks (ANNs).

The concept of entanglement will be responsible for most of the interactions that can be observed in the simulations (comparable to the interactions in reality). Finally, emergence, or the emergent phenomena, is the result of dynamic network behaviour (of agents, of quanta).

All this leads to the theme of my current research, which is based on the theories explained here: can we obtain another understanding of the 'logic' of economic behaviour which is closer to observed reality? Is this logic a quantum logic and how does that then present itself? For practical reasons, we shall limit ourselves first of all to the issue of innovation, but we could, of course, ask the same questions regarding the working of the whole economy. What are the basics, the principles of construction and the role of (non-local) consciousness? At what level is causality found, or is it better to talk of synchronicity? How does the organizing principle work? How do we place the idea of causality in relation to non-locality and synchronicity? If we can reach an understanding of economic and management behaviour, will this let us develop a new economic theory, or at least a theory of innovation? Can we develop a quantum theory of management?

Of course, a few of these questions may not have an answer, and certainly we cannot find an answer to all of them through a research agenda. But the general theme of research has, in any case, been set.

The scientific proposition which I would propose to research is the following: to be able to understand the phenomena of management better, we must research the quantum structure of the economy. Synchronicity, non-locality and entanglement create emergent behaviour via a network of individual interaction. With 'complex adaptive systems' it should be possible to create the start of an understanding of these phenomena. In today's company this emergent behaviour especially makes the difference in the strategic triangle of knowledge, learning and innovation.

# The research agenda

The research agenda, as defined here, needs to be understood as a number of steps that we should answer in order to get to a real understanding of what I have labelled a quantum interpretation of management. This set of steps should indeed lead an academic research agenda into that quantum interpretation, but it is an equally important set of questions that a practising manager cannot avoid taking a stance on. These steps are the materialization of the newly proposed paradigm that is developed in this book.

Some of the key elements of this research agenda therefore become the following:

- Is there a quantum structure (or at least interpretation) of management phenomena and what is this structure (what is the role of the consciousness, synchronicity, morphogenetic fields, etc.)?
- Can one create empirical evidence on the emergent character of management phenomena, in particular of innovation?
- Can 'complex adaptive systems' (CAS) help to visualize emergence, synchronicity and morphogenetic fields?
- Can one understand better the crucial role of knowledge, learning and innovation for companies, and, by responding to the previous questions, also render them useful from now on? I therefore suggest that the proposed research domain be limited at first to knowledge, learning and innovation.

In the following chapter I shall report on a more formal economic interpretation of all this, based on research undertaken, that illustrates this research agenda to some degree. The evidence of the next chapter suggests a first proposal for that quantum interpretation of management. Evidently, the following chapter is an illustration of the potential of CAS (since CAS is the research tool used). As the entire text suggests, probably the most crucial issue for companies where a quantum interpretation could really make a difference is, to my way of thinking, the junction between knowledge management, continuous learning and innovation. For this reason, the applied research agenda (applied to real day-to-day management problems) will therefore be geared towards:

- knowledge management;
- learning;
- innovation;

but also, and especially, on the interaction between the three.

These three subjects should not be examined separately (as is often done in classical research) but, on the contrary, as an inseparable collection, a holon. My research over the years has made that very clear. Each attempt to separate knowledge, learning and innovation from the other two leads us inevitably into a mechanical approach to each of the concepts separately. Science notably meets problems and limits in its reductionist approach.

On the other hand, a research agenda should not be considered a strict and restrictive framework. Although I have tried here to determine an agenda, clearly it is only a very short distillation of all that is done and could be done within the frame of this new paradigm for management. This agenda can therefore not be considered independently of its epistemological and theoretical framework. My own learning and experience have led me to this point in my career as a researcher. The agenda cannot be considered independently of its context (the reality of corporate life) either.

In this context, and in the given scientific framework, all research which contributes to the agenda is welcome. It cannot be otherwise. The agenda, as with all matters one studies, is in itself also emergent. This emergence will inevitably go together with an attitude of research and exploration of everything that could be important in contributing to the enriching of the paradigm described here. In a number of PhD and Master's theses which I have been able to supervise (see the list at the end of the bibliography), this width of field of investigation and opening to innovation appears. A constant in the research agenda is the discovery of transversality, by which I mean going across multiple disciplines or functions. One should not think always in terms of marketing, finance, human resources, etc.: the transversal nature of management means that it cuts through different functionalities. In general, research has tried to go into depth too quickly, in my opinion. Research is often interested in a tiny little detail instead of understanding the global picture. So, it is not surprising that it is difficult to learn something more global. I want to break this vicious circle with this proposed research agenda.

NOTION, the Nyenrode Institute for Knowledge Management and Virtual Education, was a first attempt to create a research centre with such an agenda. NOTION has contributed a lot to what I write here, notably in giving more content, richness and understanding. NOTION is thus part of a first attempt to realize this agenda, but it is also in itself an important contribution to that agenda. This type of positive feedback is evidently typical for this type of research.

NOTION was sponsored by five companies: Achmea, Sara Lee/DE, Philips, Atos/Origin and Microsoft. For four years they have financed ten people to research full time on the feasibility of this research agenda. Of course, there was, on the part of these companies, a philanthropic aspect, and also an effective interest in the results of the research projects. What the companies have in common is that they measure the importance of knowledge, learning and innovation, that they know the practical problems in their domains and that they want to improve their activities concerning these issues. All the theses examine a very practical issue for the company concerned. The theses at the heart of NOTION have a strong characteristic of theoretical innovation, but also a strong empirical element usable by the sponsors. The book *Knowledge Management and Management Learning: Extending the horizons of knowledge-based management* (Baets, 2005a) makes a scientific connection between this research and the observations of the NOTION researchers.

This combination of theoretical work on innovation, which also proves that it is applicable and that it creates more value in its applications, is, I believe, the path to follow in management research. I want to contribute willingly to that. My mission now is to build a subsequent experiment at a research centre. The E^cKM (the Euromed Centre for Knowledge Management) will follow this path, which is already partly trodden.

# 9 Quantum economics, or the quantum interpretation of management

- **Classical business economics in the light of a quantum interpretation**
- **The basic idea of the quantum interpretation and its visualization tools**
- **Market behaviour**
- **Management learning**
- **Human interaction**
- **Conclusions**

## Classical business economics in the light of a quantum interpretation

It is clear that what we know as business economics, the theory that forms the basis of our managerial thinking, cannot hold any more within a quantum interpretation of the world, other than as an exception to, or a specific case of, a more general rule. In this chapter I suggest the framework of a new kind of economic thinking that fits the quantum interpretation and that allows us to gain a deeper insight.into business practice. In the first part of the chapter I will critically summarize what we know as business economics, in order to illustrate, in the second part of the chapter, with some examples, how a quantum interpretation sheds new light on our experienced reality.

Standard business economics is based on four main assumptions. The first is that all economic agents show rational behaviour. Though this is certainly partly true, it is obvious that, for instance in buying behaviour, there is not always a lot of rationality. Worse, marketing in fact aims to influence so-called rational behaviour with mostly emotional elements. The acceptance itself of marketing as a valid activity and even a managerial discipline contradicts this assumption fundamentally. As argued in this book, no observation, no measurement and, even more so, no interpretation can be objective, therefore the assumption of full rationality cannot hold in reality.

The second assumption is that the different economic players are fully informed (which is necessary in order for them to be able to act rationally). Specifically in this Internet era, this assumption seems highly theoretical. Not only is it virtually impossible to have all information, but, even more so, the interpretation of all available information brings us again to the non-rationality of information. Indeed, information can only be transformed into knowledge by individuals – knowledge that allows the user to enact behaviour (action and shaping). Being fully informed, independent of the knowing subject, is not reasonable.

The next assumption is the alternative use of resources. In practice this means that once a resource has been used in one product, it can no longer be used in another product. This is clearly an industrial point of view, in which it is mainly material products that are produced. In the knowledge economy, things are different. Information and knowledge have multiple uses and, what is more, the more they are shared, the more their value rises. As argued earlier, that is what causes the law of increasing returns (see my remarks about Brian Arthur in Chapter 8). The law of diminishing returns, a basic one in classical economics, does not hold in the knowledge economy and does not hold in today's economy.

The fourth assumption, which is made for convenience and is the one that probably causes least harm, is that there are a limited number of goods and services. It is clear that, certainly in the knowledge economy, services are often used for different purposes. Any service might therefore become a set of different services, according to the use that the clients make of it.

Mandelbrot, particularly in respect to financial markets, finds a rather similar set of assumptions that modern financial theory makes in order to justify its financial models. In his most recent book (Mandelbrot and Hudson, 2004), Mandelbrot illustrates the catastrophic consequences of those assumptions on day-to-day financial portfolio management, destroying both the theoretical basis of those models and their financial performance. The assumptions he identifies behind classical financial theory are the following:

- People are rational and only aim to get rich.
- All investors are alike.

- Price change is practically continuous.
- Price changes follow a Brownian motion (independence of consecutive observations; statistical stagnation of price changes; the normality (bell-shaped curve) of changes).

In general, the strong assumption behind most financial processes, but equally behind many managerial processes, is the normality of phenomena (99 per cent of the observations fall between the mean, plus or minus three times its standard deviation). Observational reality certainly does not confirm this assumption in most volatile markets, however.

Clearly, these assumptions all fit within a reductionist framework, limiting reality to a theoretically viable environment. But the consequence is that observations in such a limited framework do not allow extrapolation into a real world that does not obey the assumptions. *The Economist* (17 April 1999) commented, in 'Quarks and coaches':

> The one group of people to whom most businessmen rarely turn is economists. Big firms ask economists to predict the ups and downs of national economies, but when it comes to finding ways to run their own company better, many managers would sooner consult an astrologer.

Furthermore, there are a number of concepts defined that do not really matter, that are acceptable but not really relevant, or do not add any value to the understanding of a particular problem. An example of such a concept is 'the circular flows of income and spending between business and households', where banks and governments play the role of 'multiplier' or 'catalyst'. Multiplier and catalyst are concepts based on different assumptions. Multipliers indeed fit equations and causal relationships. A catalyst is not always determined as suggested. A catalyst brings a situation into acceleration, without always precisely knowing where it is moving to. The use of the word 'catalyst' in fact suggests a different kind of reaction, where what is meant, when analysed in more depth, is really a multiplier. Reality has shown that tax policy, possibly based on these theories, does not always seem to work. In fact, it became a political debate, and hence a political choice, whether one *believes* in a more important role for the government (always via taxes) or not. Independent of whether economic theory works, tax policies are political choices, where all the different parties assume or invent possible side effects that would make all the difference.

The claimed aims of macroeconomic policy, again a set of political choices, are full employment, stable prices, economic growth and a balance of payments equilibrium. So-called macroeconomic models prove unable in particular to catch the dynamics of those markets, and therefore become completely irrelevant if a country finds itself in a highly dynamic environment (hyperinflation, political treaties, threat of a revolution, etc.). In the case of a stable situation, of course, those models would work, but are not necessary then.

The essence of monetary theory is based on the equation $MV = PQ$ (quantity of money × velocity = price × quantity). Neither untrue nor wrong, but it is not particularly helpful for the manager – and that sums up the essential 'axioms' of business economics.

Next I would like to summarize what is known as business economics by briefly going over the structure of a standard business economics textbook. A textbook will typically start by describing the 'international economic environment', concentrating on high-level aggregations like average wage level, labour cost per unit, trading price, competitiveness and efficiency that would *not* be discounted in any other variable. Such a chapter will finish by explaining the role governments play in business practice, referring to legislation, taxes, trade zones, etc. This kind of chapter is an example of what I argued earlier, namely that economics in general reasons at a level of aggregation that is entirely too high for one to be able to find any useful relationship at all (apart from a causal one).

Most textbooks contain a chapter on macroeconomics; that is interesting but not really part of business economics. In a chapter on the organization of firms and markets, where we expect to see some organizing principles, mechanism on how processes emerge, etc., we mainly find legal issues: a summary of a business law course.

The chapter on business objectives is the one that builds foremost on the assumptions and axioms (stated or hidden) of business economics mentioned earlier in this chapter. The chapter starts with a discussion about mission statements, carefully avoiding identifying whether it is talking about a goal or a path. The earlier chapters of this book have made this difference clear, as well as its consequences. In reference to the 'rational behaviour' assumption, a company is claimed to pursue the profit maximization principle. This maximization is based on a number of equally impossible assumptions that in fact limit reality to an artificial (unrealistic) but, above all, linear and stable situation. Those assumptions are the following:

- There is no division between ownership and control (which in practice is, of course, years out of date for any larger company). The ownership (the shareholdership) is represented in a general assembly of shareholders, but the daily management (the control) is done by professional managers. An interesting discussion here is whether we observe a different kind of management in SMEs (where ownership and control are often either in the same hands, or close to each other) and larger companies. Most research does indeed suggest a difference.
- Full knowledge is available of costs and revenues (economic theory assumes full information), which is often not the case, and cannot be the case. An additional problem is that even if we could identify a fully correct picture at any moment, we would fail to capture the dynamics of this process (certainly on the revenue side).
- There is no problem with fixed cost allocation (since there is theoretically only one product). In most companies this is far from the case.
- The management shows rational behaviour and has only one objective, which are weak assumptions, as already argued.

The difference between ownership and control (not to mention other stakeholders, who are dramatically ignored in business economics) also opens the debate between sales revenue optimization, growth maximization or sustainable development. Simon (http://www.juliansimon.com) talks in this context about 'satisfiers' instead of maximizers.

The classical mistake, or should I say weakness, resides in the process description of how to get to the corporate goal. The mistake is due to oversimplified assumptions *and* presumed static, linear behaviour. Business economics focuses on fixing the path, instead of explaining the emergence in networked systems. Next the fixed path should be realized, and management reduces itself to a control mechanism for the realization of the path (not even always of the goals any more). The law of increasing returns (described earlier) in a knowledge economy is only one of the examples of how disastrous the classical law of diminishing returns is when discussing the knowledge economy. The illustration of this type of mistake can be found in the classical aspects of business economics: demand analysis; cost theory; pricing theory.

Demand analysis is often done using linear regressions (in best cases, as described in textbooks), denying the dynamic behaviour of markets. Apart from the basic assumptions already mentioned, a number of technical assumptions (often hidden) need to be fulfilled in order to be able to apply linear regression. Homoscedasticity (normal distribution of the error term) and the absence of multicollinearity (collinearity between explanatory variables) are only two of them. Non-fulfilment of these assumptions causes numerical deficiencies in the results that cannot be observed in the classical statistics of the regression analysis. *In quasi-stable, quasi-linear markets, all those models work, which only illustrates that this situation is a special case (a simplified form) of a more generally valid quantum interpretation.* In fact, regular business economics theory is a special case of the more general quantum economics theory, only applicable to quasi-stable and quasi-linear situations.

The fixed and variable cost theory, based on oversimplified assumptions of no cross-relationships and full information, is again a special case of a more general cost behaviour structure. Once we accept cross-relationships between products (services) and human production actions, we automatically fall into the network paradigm.

Other than in oligopolistic markets, which are again a special case of fully interacting markets, pricing in non-linear dynamic markets becomes a question of strategizing. The best example of strategizing games can indeed be found in game theory. The best-known case is no doubt the prisoner's dilemma, in which two 'players' play against each other, each having two possible strategies. (Reality, of course, is infinitely more complicated, with a huge number of possible strategies for each player.) The unknown in the game is that each of the players ignores what the other plays. Game theory knows zero-sum games or non-zero-sum games. Game theory has been used to illustrate pricing games. As the law of increasing returns suggests, strategizing of prices goes much further. According to Arthur's theory, the aim is to get a snowball effect going at the right moment. If a company strategizes a market correctly, it should be able not only to price correctly, but to do so at the correct moment. That kicks off the dynamic process of market penetration, often leading to important market shares. A wrong strategy (price or timing) causes the product to die out. The law of increasing returns explains why demand analysis and pricing cannot be considered differently. In dynamic situations (knowledge markets), market behaviour and price interact in continuous feedback loops and can therefore only be studied jointly. It is clear that this market behaviour, incorporating pricing issues, will become the backbone of the quantum interpretation of business economics.

Most classical textbooks have two more chapters. There is a chapter on investment analysis, concentrating on investment appraisal that is highly dependent on a lucrative anticipation of the future expected returns. A final chapter needs to discuss corporate strategy formulation, discussing goals, but most often fixing paths. Porter's chain of value analysis, and/or his five forces model, has survived the major quantum revolution. It still identifies a number of generic strategies – cost leadership, differentiation and focus – that, if all assumptions indeed worked, would lead automatically to a fully transparent market with all players having all information. This would reduce strategy to the one and only really plausible strategy in such a situation of fully informed markets and players, which is a pricing strategy (hopefully based on cost leadership). Again, in the event that the assumptions were true and the model worked, the remaining players would be pushed into having minimal profits and eventually losses, which we can indeed observe in certain markets. The airline market is just one illustrative example. As much as markets are emergent and pricing is one of the many loop variables in such markets, strategy cannot be identified, but emerges out of the interaction of market players.

In this chapter I would like to propose a new approach to business economics (in practice) which I would like to call a quantum interpretation of business economics. It is clear that stable and linear markets are a special case of this quantum interpretation, as simulations could easily visualize. The laws on which this economic interpretation is based are the ones described in this book. The remainder of this chapter will illustrate a few cases of this quantum interpretation.

## The basic idea of the quantum interpretation and its visualization tools

When we describe companies and markets, we are actually describing the continuous non-linear and dynamic interaction of agents within a holistic concept. Business behaviour is the outcome of such interaction. Business economics is the theory describing the reasons why this quantum interpretation should work, but equally how it works, as is done in the principal chapters of this book. The issue now becomes to find a correct visualization tool.

The quantum interpretation of business economics has three complementary foci: one on the environment, one on the company itself and one on people's interaction. In order to label them more in line with current business practice, we could say: market behaviour, management learning and human interaction.

*Market behaviour* describes the environment of the company, the context, the interaction that takes place in what we call markets. Markets are not necessarily physical markets. Even what we call physical markets are composed of numerous so-called virtual components. All players and influences are of course never physically present on such a market. Policy is made and has an impact, without really being always very explicit. In fact, under market behaviour we talk about market and pricing interactions, out of which strategies emerge.

*Management learning* considers the company in its most essential processes (as described in this book): innovation and knowledge considered as learning processes. Instead of a control-oriented model, we need to develop and apply a learning-oriented process, in particular around innovation and knowledge. Both are essential for the longer-term development of the company. Both innovation and knowledge management may need some supporting technical tools (such as financial reporting and logistics). However, the latter are necessary but not sufficient elements of management. Those elements are easy to copy, can be described and easily optimized, and can therefore never become a real source of sustainable (profitable) development. It does not make them useless, but just as with the architect's profession, it is not the tools that the architect uses that make the difference.

*Human interaction* of people (inside and outside a company) is probably the one complex resource that needs to be understood and carefully monitored. Human interaction needs to be understood as the potentiality of the interaction of people (agents) producing either individuals who co-create out of emergence (at the one extreme) or agents who cause a really disastrous conflict (at the other extreme). The situation obtained is not what is important; rather, what is important is the process of potentiality and its evolution. Human interaction, just like management learning, might need some supporting techniques, which are, however, never of a nature to replace the necessity to understand the interaction itself.

Up until now there have been few publications about the process of business economics as a learning and emergent concept. Likewise, there have not been many publications about emergent behaviour and the methods of studying it either. However, three exceptions have greatly inspired me with agent simulations and neural networks, with, to my way of thinking, satisfactory results.

Epstein and Axtell describe in their book *Growing Artificial Societies* (1996) how artificial societies can emerge, how they self-organize, how they grow, how they learn and even how they enter into conflict (and how they resolve these conflicts). The book comes with a CD with simulations whereby one can correctly see what is described in the book. This book is absolutely to be recommended as a first initiation into the domain of emergent behaviour. In different steps, the 'societies' learn things which are successively more difficult. The purpose of the book is not especially to show that simulations will effectively be a copy of the reality. It shows that agent simulations can be a path for visualizing emergent behaviour. In addition, the book shows that we can obtain a form of 'self-organization' in these learning 'societies'. To tell the truth, the book creates a sort of learning laboratory for those who are interested in the emergence of artificial social systems. This book was certainly, for me, a motivation to research agent-based simulations. It visualizes the types of processes on which I wish to obtain more depth.

Another remarkable book is Wolfram's *A New Kind of Science* (2002). This long and impressive book gives minutely detailed examples of emerging behaviour, in the sense of an organization suddenly finding itself in disorder. It is a hugely detailed piece of research towards a scientific approach which is constructivist – which builds from very minuscule particles. The book compares simulation diagrams in search of structure, similarity, order and chaos. It is a plea for a new scientific approach. In the light of the large quantity of evidence in the book, it seems to me difficult to still seriously doubt the feasibility of agent simulations after reading it. The book supports very clearly the scientific concept according to which multiple different elements, each very simple in itself, by following simple rules of interaction can create complex behaviour. This approach entirely fits the theoretical framework which is developed here. It supplies the fundamental empirical dreams for many of the theoretical concepts which are commented on here.

Mandelbrot has developed what is known as fractal algebra. Fractal algebra is based on the concept of self-similarity: a combined repetition of simple structures can give a complex form, and therefore a complex form can be easily approximated by an iterative combination of such simple structures. The basic figure of such structure is a fractal. Artificial life research is in fact based on a similar kind of assumption. In line with Wolfram's study, Mandelbrot creates complex geometric figures that seem to approximate (financial) market behaviour rather adequately. Wolfram's and Mandelbrot's proposals are pure geometric approximations of the same kind of reality that we attempt to approximate in this book using either neural networks or agent simulations. The advantage of the latter, for use in management and business, is that the structure of interacting agents (or interacting knots) comes closer to a corporate reality and it is easier to identify within a social reality. Mandelbrot's books, however, illustrate that his fractal geometric approach has huge potential for understanding market behaviour in particular, and most probably management issues more generally.

For the remainder of the chapter, I would like to report on a number of real-life projects researched in existing companies and markets that form a first layer of experimental evidence for the quantum interpretation given in this book. The projects are organized according to the three subdivisions under which the quantum interpretation of business economics may be considered.

## Market behaviour

The first project (van den Broek, 2004) deals with innovation and attempts to investigate the structure of innovation itself. Once this structure is revealed, the next question becomes: can governments stimulate innovation (which has been a very popular discussion topic in the Netherlands in recent years) and, if so, how? The chosen concept of innovation was grafted onto the model developed here in the previous chapters, although we are not explicitly examining in this project how innovation works at the company level. In this study we look at innovation more generally, at a sector level, even a national one. The main question is to investigate whether innovation can be subsidized (by the government, for example). In the study, on the one hand, neural networks were used (in order to visualize an emergent structure) and on the other hand, brainstorming sessions were used as a control tool.

Through the neural networks we tried to establish the real structure of innovation as an emergent approach in small and medium-sized companies (SMEs). Questionnaires were distributed among all kinds of stakeholders: entrepreneurs, financiers, government. These questionnaires sounded out the interest in and visibility of a number of factors which could play a role during innovation. Depending on the structure found, we can see whether the variables which are effectively important can be influenced by, for example, the government. Such variables were not found, and, as it happens, the government cannot play an active role in the promotion of the innovation process in the economy. To then validate the result of these neural networks we organized focus groups as a control tool. In the brainstorming session, we also tried to obtain an implicit structure for innovation processes, to map them and then to check whether they coincide with the results of the neural networks. This combination of methods worked rather well. In this project the use of CAS allowed the emergence of a new structure, and not the imposition of an existing (desirable) structure, but rather the harvesting of a self-creating and self-organizing structure. The actors in the process created the result, without taking account of the theoretical models that would exist.

As I have already said, the results give a new understanding, and are, again, encouraging. With neither of the two methods (which seemed to confirm each other) was evidence found of the subsidiarity of innovation in the economy. The strength of innovation of the SMEs is uniquely found in their own hands. The research then suggests how entrepreneurs can organize innovation effectively.

A second project examined the dynamic character of the market for applications in telemedicine (Braaksma and van Liere, 2004). To give an account of an innovative company in the telemedicine market (remote medical care and monitoring), the market and its evolution were studied, always with particular attention to its dynamic character. The question was to know whether it was possible to simulate the dynamic behaviour of this market, which would then allow the company in question to position itself on the wave of potential market innovations. Such a form of innovation approach would be grafted, almost in real time, onto market behaviour. The factors and actors which influenced the successful introduction of innovation in telemedicine were, in the dissertation, the research subject. For the research, agent simulations were used, where the agents were different actors in the market. Also in this research, we created a control group with interviewed experts.

The mechanism of this specific market was characterized by the phenomenon of increasing returns and positive feedback. In practice, that means that the company which gets ahead of the others, in a specific product, will very often stay ahead of the crowd and retain a large share of the market. The exploration of this market is possible only through an approach of discovery and continual learning, hence the agent simulations. More than ever, this market seems to show emergent behaviour. This study suggests that the important elements in the strategy of the introduction of telemedicine applications are the following.

The networks and the structures of cooperation lead to a favourable structure for the telemedicine products. The perception of the notion of telemedicine is very variable, which could seriously encumber the positioning of the innovation itself. High-potential telemedicine solutions are found essentially in the 'care' segment of the market. The acceptance of these telemedicine products can be improved by developing 'business cases' in which attention is paid, on the financial side, to the aspects of care and added value of this care. As a consequence of this study, the company will adapt its strategy. Instead of the company concentrating on product development at the top end of the market, the choice now made is to organize the network of partners rather in the 'care' segment of the market (in contrast to the 'treatment' segment).

These results could seem self-evident, a posteriori. Nevertheless, as in every other case, this approach at least allowed the justification (in a theoretical way as well as based on evidence) of these conclusions.

## Management learning

The next project (Harkema, 2004, 2005) corresponds precisely to the subject of innovation as a learning concept. This research was based on the conceptual model which was commented on earlier in this book, where innovation was determined on the basis of a model of knowledge and learning. To make the model operational we chose agent simulations. The research was done on real case studies for Sara Lee/DE. This company has a rather classical approach to innovation management, in which they manage a strict project protocol, with a number of go/no go decisions to be taken. Little is learned in each project and still less of what is learned is passed on from one project to another. Furthermore, very strict procedures to be followed by the new product development teams are set out. There is therefore, in our definition, little room for innovation. The monitoring of the procedure is more important than putting a successful product on the market. At the end of the project, the debriefing concentrates solely on knowing whether the procedures were followed well or whether what was planned was obtained effectively.

Senseo (the new-style coffee machine, with coffee pastilles, co-developed with Philips) was evaluated as a failed project, although it was economically without doubt one of the spectacular successes of the past few years. Other products which have followed the procedure correctly have been evaluated as good examples of innovation, although they have largely flopped on the market in financial terms.

I want to explain the part of the research where agent simulations intervened, and present a few results. The rules of the game in a multi-agent simulation are the following: the agents control their own actions; they are autonomous; they have the strength to attain their goals and the possibility of doing so. In this application, six different types of agents were chosen: marketers, R&D people, project managers, technical developers, production staff and senior management. The field of action inside which the simulations took place was divided into four regions, the manager's office, a local project and a hall (where everyone could meet up). Certain regions were limited to certain categories of agents. The agents moved around in a random way (they could speak together during a meeting in the corridor). Individual and group thresholds were decided. This value had to be attained (by information exchange) to be able to get to learning. All the agents of a group had to have attained their individual threshold for a 'group' to be able to learn. The characteristics were given to all the agents at different levels. They had the following characteristics: three sorts of functional knowledge, three sorts of expertise, experience, hierarchical order, control, motivation and confidence. Each agent therefore received eleven characteristics just as a threshold value to obtain to be able to learn.

A series of interaction rules is determined. This has a relationship with how the agents learn between themselves. In fact, there are several matrices which determine how the different agents could learn from each other. The parameters allow for adjustment of the simulation to be as close as possible to reality. A sort of clock is established which rules the number of repetitions. In theory, it is therefore possible to do a simulation in parallel with a (green) field project and so see whether what the simulation shows is effectively what we can see in reality. In this case, the simulation did not particularly show what could be seen (for that, we have eyes), but rather was able to show the underlying structure. It visualized the dynamic character of the process.

In the research a number of scenarios were simulated, with different teams, different weightings, etc. We tried to stay as close as possible to real cases. In the last step we tried to map a number of scenarios onto real cases. Although this was not the objective at the start, it was nevertheless rather a success. It would have been interesting to do a simulation in parallel with a greenfield project, as stated before. The existing agent simulations can do this, if Sara Lee/DE wants to make use of it.

I do not want go into detail here about the simulation results. For that, it is necessary to refer to the relevant publications or to the thesis itself. The first observation to make is that the simulations in fact show emergence and learning. As a consequence of the qualities of the different agents and the scenarios chosen, learning flowed effectively in different ways. The roles of senior management and the project managers seem to be important factors in the facilitation of learning. The more these people stayed in the background, the more, and the more quickly, the team learned. Learning seems to show a relationship with the quality of the innovated product. The question is therefore to know whether this effectively suggests that a key to success is the team's motivation, which will use, at the right moment and in the right way, the knowledge accessible by synchronicity. The simulations show that self-organization is important for learning, and also intervenes, in fact, if we leave a margin for it. The fact that confidence plays a key role in a whole clutch of simulations confirms this.

I do not want to deprive you of a few conclusions. Control seems to be an important factor in the failure of innovation. It is produced in the following way:

- Senior management almost exclusively uses financial factors to measure success, whereas the project participants use other variables.
- The rigidity of processes gives people very little possibility for correction.
- Management takes decisions without dialogue (team changes, go/no go decisions).
- All the communication goes through the project manager, which renders the team very dependent.
- The teams are united on the basis of their knowledge, although the team members themselves value confidence, motivation, commitment and solidarity more.

A few additional conclusions:

- Interaction is important, so harmony between people is crucial.
- Confidence and control are two contrary variables.

- Confidence and motivation have a strong influence on exchange and the creation of knowledge.
- Confidence must always be built. The level at the start, if there is one, is never enough.
- Interaction without knowledge does not allow learning.
- Interaction without confidence and motivation does not allow learning.
- Interaction is always necessary for the construction of confidence.
- Motivation and organization seem to interact positively.
- If there are agents at group level who do not cooperate, the learning of the group stops.

Although certain observations are doubtless known, I want to underline two things. The classical theory of innovation does not allow us to lean on these observations. They are observations of practice, to which the classical theory has no theoretical response. The theory developed here, on the other hand, frames perfectly what is observed.

Other than observing these facts in practice, I should like to draw attention to the fact that they are the results of simulations. That means that they manifestly show a real image of innovation, as readers (and managers of innovation in general) will recognize. The theoretical ideas developed here, linked to CAS simulations, are not negligible in contributing to the suggested research agenda.

This has been an important mission for these research projects in general. It is a first little piece of evidence which supports the quantum interpretation and its research agenda; it illustrates, but also gives an idea of the potential for success. The least we can say is that the results are encouraging.

A further project tries to draw a knowledge map of an R&D centre of a large chemical multinational (van Diessen and Gommers, 2004, 2005). The project identifies the most important variables which contribute to the capacity for knowledge creation in the company. Once the structure became apparent, we could study how this creation of knowledge and innovation (since, in fact, the goal of management of knowledge, as in quite a few companies, is to improve the capacity for innovation) can be supported. In this study we consider something we call 'actionable knowledge', which means new knowledge about new phenomena. In the framework that we are studying here, we speak clearly about the dynamic aspect of knowledge.

The research will call again on adapted methods which specifically observe the dynamic nature of knowledge in its context. This study uses neural networks and looks for the main variables in the actionable knowledge field. In the company, researchers clearly identified two different groups of employees, differing in the speed and the quality of the creation of knowledge. The policy to follow therefore consisted of training the 'followers' by supporting them in becoming more gifted. Here too the researchers used CAS in support of this change process.

In this study we broadly identify a number of more or less important driving forces. In dynamic interaction these variables influence the potential for the creation of knowledge. These variables are united under the following headings: human characteristics; organizational context; learning culture; process phases; process complexity; the availability of information; and technology. At a high level of aggregation – or rather, in a subsequent stage of 'networking' – we obtain the following subsystems: social subsystem; process subsystem; technology subsystem.

It is interesting that in this approach we used CAS to generate the dynamic structure and the map of knowledge in an emergent fashion. The goal of this mapping is, among other things, to support the character of dynamic creation of knowledge, always with a view to improving the capacity for innovation. Let me also underline that we do not see how the results could be obtained by more classical methods and concepts.

A last project within this section on management learning deals with a major multinational glue company. The company's present business model shows that production of its products is not where its competitive advantage lies. Instead, it is new and valuable ideas, solutions and services to consumers that are the distinctive factors. To sustain the competitive advantages, the continuous creation of new knowledge and new combinations of existing knowledge is of great importance. In that way, distinctive competencies are created and can be sustained in the future.

'A solution for every job', 'easy application features', 'user information' and 'high product quality' are all competitive advantages which can only be accomplished if the company has competencies such as creativity, innovation and adaptation to the changing environment. These competencies are supported by knowledge of the environment, of products and applications, of consumer behaviour, etc. Acquiring, creating and transferring that knowledge is what is understood here as learning. Knowledge, learning and the ability to innovate are related to each other and crucial for the company's business.

The company's change in strategy from a production- and R&D-oriented company to a marketing-oriented company has led to changed requirements concerning knowledge, innovation and learning. The knowledge infrastructure has not adapted to that situation, and product knowledge still almost exclusively rests with three people who started the company more than twenty-five years ago. Consequently, the company is becoming dependent on knowledge from suppliers, and this negatively affects creativity as regards new products, applications and packaging. The question is: *How should this problem be transformed into a proper knowledge infrastructure?*

Summarizing the above and combining it with the research questions, it becomes clear that knowledge processes at this company will be investigated from the complexity perspective. Knowledge, learning and innovation cannot be looked at separately, but the focus will be on interactions between agents and their environment concerning knowledge. The conceptual model shown in Figure 9.1 has been made.

As can be seen from the conceptual model, agents interact with each other, influenced by many different parameters. Eventually all interactions lead to the same output: new products and product applications. The new products and product applications, the way employees interact with each other and how the company communicates with the outside world all lead to its competitive advantages. These competitive advantages in turn

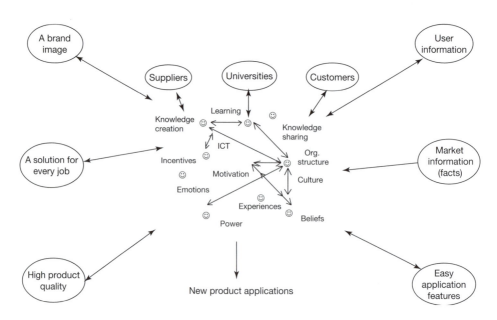

**Figure 9.1** *Dynamic conceptual model*

influence the behaviour of the complex system. The complex system will constantly adapt to the environment.

A case study has been performed on three real cases at the company. The case studies support the multi-agent simulation by providing a practical set of parameters and valuable insight into the problems that appear in the company's new product development projects.

Agents are often deployed in environments where they interact with other agents who possibly have conflicting aims. In this research, Netlogo was used, a programmable modelling environment for simulating natural and social phenomena (free download from http://ccl.northwestern.edu/netlogo/).

The multi-agent simulation is designed to explore the behaviours of the complex system, the company, in new product development projects. It will help in gaining insight into how complex phenomena can arise from relatively simple interactions between the people involved in those projects. The main research questions which are considered are:

- How does the interaction between the key players in the innovation process work?
- What factors influence the way the people share their knowledge with other key players?
- What factors influence the way people create knowledge?

The multi-agent simulation model concerns knowledge creation and knowledge sharing of agents in a complex adaptive system, eventually leading to successful new product development (NPD) projects. Agents simulate the people involved in NPD projects. No distinction has been made in the model between tacit and explicit knowledge.

The model is based on the assumptions that knowledge sharing and creation lead to an increase in the knowledge value of agents and that exceeding a certain threshold value of knowledge per agent (individual) and at the same time per department (collective) eventually leads to a successful project. It is recognized that factors other than knowledge play a role in the success of an NPD project, but these are left aside (as they were in the case studies).

The dynamics of the model are simulated by autonomous agents. They move freely (randomly), but the real-life openness between departments at the company was put into the model as a probability that agents of a certain department move to agents of other departments. Agents interact with each other by moving and colliding with each other and with 'information'. A collision means an upgrade of knowledge value. Knowledge can also be downgraded if agents do not collide. Different dynamics are being modelled, such as motivation, management control, openness, knowledge decay rate, information availability.

Self-organization, a characteristic of complex adaptive systems, is mainly accomplished in the model by a feedback loop in which an increase in knowledge will increase motivation, which in turn increases the chance of an increase in knowledge value. Emergence can appear in the simulations and will be identified as such if the pattern produced by the agents cannot be explained by the interactions between them.

## Departments and agents

The Netlogo model consists of six departments: Marketing (Mrk), Purchasing (Pur), Research and Development (R&D), Quality Assurance (QA), Bison Information Center (BIC) and Engineering (Eng). In addition, there is an external party, called EXT, which can be a vendor, a university or another external party that can be involved. Each department contains a number of agents (Figure 9.2). In the model, departments are represented by regions of contiguous patches. Agents move from patch to patch within a department, or between departments.

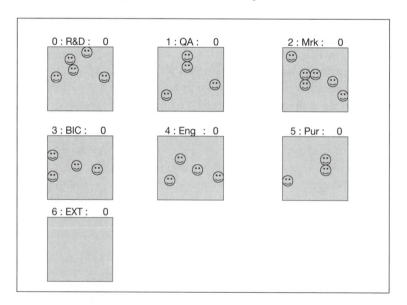

**Figure 9.2** *Example of the set-up of the simulation environment*

# Conditions and parameters of the Netlogo model

Some specific conditions and parameters are put into the procedures of the program. Others, where possible and applicable, were made so-called sliders so that the parameters could be varied.

The following conditions and parameters of the Netlogo model influence the behaviour of the agents:

1   Agents move within and between departments.
2   Openness affects movement destination. ('Openness' encapsulates both the job-required tendency to visit other departments, and the department's 'trust' of, or 'sociability' or 'compatibility' with, the other departments.)
3   Openness is represented by a matrix called the 'interdepartment movement matrix'. This matrix, arranged on the basis of interview results, is put into the procedures of the program.
4   The probability that an agent will move outside their own department (aside from the openness probabilities between the other departments) can be varied with a so-called slider.
5   Managerial control affects movement consistency. Each agent possesses a predetermined 'task list' of patches that it will visit, in sequence, and then repeat. The sequence is generated on the basis of the 'openness' matrix. Managerial control can be varied by using a slider. When managerial control is at a maximum, the agents follow the pre-set task list exactly. As managerial control decreases, the agents become more likely to deviate from the pre-set task list. In other words, they may select a different location, using the openness matrix.
6   Motivation affects movement frequency. Movement creates collisions which in turn cause knowledge exchange. Knowledge exchange affects motivation. This is called a feedback loop. Motivation increase is programmed as going towards a maximum value of 100.
7   Agents exchange knowledge with other agents. Each day, an agent will decide to move (on the basis of motivation) to the next task list patch or a random patch (based on managerial control and openness). After a collision takes place with another agent, the knowledge value increases by a certain value. That value (a percentage) depends on the other agent's department. The underlying assumption is that a collision with a department that has a large external network is more valuable than a collision with an internally

oriented department. All values are summed up in a so-called inter-department knowledge exchange matrix'. This is put into the procedures of the program.

8   Patch visit frequency visualization can be seen. The patches grow brighter each time an agent visits the patch. Over time, the brightness fades.

9   Agents are represented as 'smiles'. Smiles grow bigger when the agent gains knowledge, and vice versa.

10  Information availability increases knowledge. A second type of agent 'info-packet' is found in the model. Info-packets represent the presence of different types of information that may be incidentally encountered in the workplace. Info-packets appear in patches with a likelihood determined by each department's individual 'information availability' score, as well as a 'global information availability' slider. Each info-packet appears with a slightly varying value. Info-packets are displayed as a grey outline on the patch.

11  Knowledge goes stale over time. It is assumed that knowledge unused goes stale and is lost. So, agents who do not exchange knowledge experience knowledge decay. This is a percentage of the knowledge score that is lost each time an agent does not exchange knowledge. This occurs both when the agent moves to a location with no other agents, and when an agent is unmotivated to move.

12  Info-packets go stale over time.

13  Knowledge creation and sharing lead to project completion. Project completion enhances motivation (the extent can be varied with a slider).

14  The project completion thresholds were fixed at 200 for the agent and 700 for the department in all simulations. However, these are adjustable by means of a slider.

15  When the thresholds are passed, project completion occurs. The agent's 'projects completed' score is incremented by 1 and the agent's knowledge value is reduced. The latter is meant to model the exhaustion of 'creative energies' that is felt after completing a project, the effect of the dispersion of the project team, the idea that specialized knowledge that applies to one project may not readily apply to another, and so on. The amount of knowledge remaining after project completion can be fixed (resetting back to the base knowledge score), or variable, based on a simulation of 'experience'.

16  The evaluation of projects has an influence on the initial knowledge value of each agent. It can be varied with a slider.

The run length of each simulation can be varied with a slider but was fixed for this research at 4,000 'ticks'. This run length is assumed to be approximately five years but needs to be seen as a relative parameter.

In order to be able to compare the simulations with each other and with a 'norm', a standard successful NPD project was set up.

## Overall conclusions from the simulations

The simulations have shown that the company can be modelled as a complex adaptive system. The dynamic behaviour of such a system appeared to be present: a lot of parameters were involved and were influencing the agents in different ways. Linearity was certainly not present. No single parameter was found that led to causality. This confirms the validity of using the complexity perspective. Emergence was found in different simulations. Often there appeared to be one or two departments with unpredictable agent behaviour. That means that the assumptions for modelling complexity all applied.

Lack of openness of departments towards each other and to external parties appeared to influence the resulting project completions strongly. The level of influence was dependent on all other parameters. Managerial control led to decreased project completion if the openness was increased, and the opposite occurred when openness was decreased. The influence of managerial control became weaker with the original openness when motivation and information availability were increased.

Emergence appeared which occasionally caused an extreme increase in knowledge for one or two departments. However, it was found that extreme knowledge peaks did not necessarily lead to more successful project completions.

The sum of the mean department knowledge did not vary much. Base knowledge did influence the result a little. Nevertheless, enormous variation in project completion was found. That means that successful project completion does not necessarily mean that the total knowledge in the company needs to be at a higher level. Effectiveness of interactions seems to be of much more importance.

Interactions are stopped by lack of openness, and in those cases managerial control will force interactions, which eventually leads to more successful projects. If the openness behaviour changes positively, managerial control needs to be loosened immediately, because then the opposite occurs.

Information availability is crucial too. Both information availability and base knowledge were poor for all cases. The simulations have shown that a slight increase in both parameters has major positive effects on the results.

Another major impact was seen concerning the evaluation bonus and experience bonus. Those values accelerate the project completion rate if parameters such as motivation and information availability are poor.

## Conclusions

The following conclusions can be drawn from this research:

- Knowledge, learning and innovation cannot be seen separately from each other.
- Knowledge processes need to be distinguished from business processes.
- The company's problem with knowledge, learning and innovation can be seen from the complexity perspective. It has been proved that this company can be modelled as a complex adaptive system.
- Knowledge at this company is created and shared in different places within the organization. There is no formal structure for the way new product development (NPD) projects are organized and managed.
- Most NPD projects do have minor managerial control. Self-organization can cause continuous adaptation to the internal and external environment. However, the existence of barriers between departments (lack of 'openness') causes lack of knowledge exchange.
- Parameters that were found to have great diversity among the cases studied were global managerial control, global information availability, global motivation, openness between departments, project evaluation, base knowledge and involvement of specific departments.
- Poor information availability is a general characteristic of NPD projects.
- Lack of externalization and internalization of knowledge causes a lack of extension of the existing knowledge base after NPD projects have been finalized.
- Evaluation of projects does not take place and causes a lack of organizational learning.

- Unexpected behaviour by project members concerning knowledge exchange was found to emerge in the multi-agent simulation, mainly in the case of a high degree of managerial control and strong motivation.
- Successful project completion does not necessarily mean that the total knowledge at the company needs to be at a higher level.
- In the situation of normal and equal openness between departments, knowledge exchange decreases when managerial control increases (when at the same time information availability and motivation are adequate). This is consistent with complexity theory.
- When openness is low (together with low motivation), managerial control has the opposite effect: it increases project completion. This was proved by the multi-agent simulations as well.
- Peaks in knowledge at one or two departments do not imply that more successful NPD projects are completed.
- Multi-agent simulations have proved to be appropriate to simulate knowledge processing adequately.

## Human interaction

As a last illustration, I would like to briefly summarize a research project that combines the quantum interpretation of organizations with insights from political science (peace and conflict management) (van Starkenburg, 2004; Baets, Oldenboom and van Starkenburg, 2005). The working hypotheses concerning the polemological issues are still themselves under research. In fact, our goal is only to evoke the potential of this new paradigm to illustrate real, serious problems in sustainable (peaceful) development.

The project tries to visualize the dynamics of the processes of 'conflict'. In truth, we could apply this concept to polemology (the domain in which it is applied here), but also to everything which concerns the behaviour of organizations, or the interaction between humans. The project was titled 'treatment of conflict'. In a number of different scenarios we simulated an agent system whose members interacted, exchanged ideas and so learned from each other. All the agents were subdivided into groups which had different values (out of seven differentiated characteristics; remember the quanta of my approach). We had to define different groups just as we had to define the rules of interaction.

The research hypothesis in the project is the following. If we leave people to exchange freely between each other, without expressing themselves clearly as a group member (and sticking to the characteristics of that group), learning and the exchange of ideas take place very quickly but evolve towards self-organization without conflict. If, by contrast, the exchanges are based not on the convictions of the separate individuals, but instead on the values of the group to which the people claim to belong (religious or ethnic group, etc.), these populations do not reach a system without conflict (or at least, not without great difficulty).

Translated into polemological terms, we can imagine a number of major conflicts behind this research hypothesis. Although individuals belonging to different ethnic groups (as in Yugoslavia) may have lived side by side for years without major problems, as soon as the ethnic groups become dominant in the society, the situation is completely destabilized. Although the Israelis, the Palestinians and the Lebanese lived together in Lebanon for many years, when the groups identified themselves clearly, a civil war broke out. These are only two typical examples and they have not been studied. Here we are only looking at the mechanism.

Without claiming that the detail given is sufficient for scientific quality, I limit myself here to describing the project as an illustration, without giving too much detail.

Imagine a town or a country in which a certain number of people live. The people make up part of one of four groups in the country. These groups are defined on the basis of a combination of values based on seven characteristics: peacefulness, spirituality, religion, economic situation, degree of responsibility, rationality and a sense of justice. The four groups identified are called the pragmatics, the fanatics, the fair (who love justice) and the peace-lovers.

I illustrate the different characteristics of the groups in Table 9.1. The values are chosen on a scale of 1 to 10, 1 being not important and 10 being very important. Then it is important to note that rules of interaction have been defined comparable to the ones described for the previous project. We have defined two types of simulations. In the first type the individuals exchange by using their own values (individual). This simulates the situation in which individuals are not actively part of a group, or at least not to the point of increasing the value of the common values more than the individual values. At least during the exchange, they exchange as they wish, immediately. If they are football enthusiasts, they go to matches for the pleasure of the sport. A beautiful goal is considered beautiful independently of the team which scores it. In the alternative case, that is to say the case of a supporter who is there as a fan of one

**Table 9.1** *Characteristics of the four groups*

|  | Pragmatics | Fanatics | The fair | Peace-lovers |
|---|---|---|---|---|
| Peacefulness | 5 | 1 | 5 | 9 |
| Spirituality | 2 | 4 | 6 | 7 |
| Religion | 2 | 9 | 1 | 1 |
| Economic situation | 7 | 7 | 4 | 2 |
| Sense of justice | 1 | 2 | 9 | 8 |
| Responsibility | 3 | 4 | 7 | 8 |
| Rationality | 8 | 5 | 3 | 2 |

team rather than primarily to appreciate the quality of the football, the protagonist will defend the group values even if they are different from his or her own. In the second series of simulations the exchanges between people no longer happened with individual values but rather with the average values of the group to which the person belonged. The first group is called simulation type A, the second type B.

The exchange between values happens as follows: when two individuals meet, all the values change for the two individuals. The one who has the stronger conviction will diminish it a little, and the other will increase it to reach harmony for the stronger argument. It is a means for all the individual values to decide the amplification of the different changes. This, in effect, simulates the rather holistic concept of the combination of values and decision-taking of the person. If the two individuals have equally strong convictions, they both reinforce their beliefs.

The simulation software program used was SWARM, developed by the Santa Fe centre of complexity.

Then we did multiple simulations such as changing the chance of 'success' in the exchange and/or letting this chance be 10 per cent to 33 per cent with a lot of different people in different groups: for example, simulations with more fanatics, or more 'fair' people. Although it is still too early to be able to reach definitive conclusions, two observations can be made on the basis of the provisional results:

● This approach in effect shows (visualizes) the dynamism of this process in a unique fashion not yet demonstrated by other methods. It therefore allows us to study polemological as well as polemical problems completely differently and with remarkable depth, for example problems like sustainable development.

- The first results seem to confirm the research hypothesis. The position taken by the group (political party, religious groups, ethnic groups) seems not to facilitate the organization of a society at peace. Although this observation has many repercussions, in polemology it leads us to thinking about possible solutions to violent conflicts.

On the basis of a number of different simulations, a few observations can be made. Despite the limitations of the experiments, this is to our knowledge a first successful attempt to visualize a phenomenon that is known in political science, but of which the organizational implications are not well understood. Complex adaptive systems seem to be able to contribute to a better understanding of (artificial) social societies, in areas where other, more classical approaches have not been able to contribute a deeper insight.

The results of the simulations shown here give an interesting insight into the role that the different values play in the creation or avoidance of conflictual situations. The study went much further and has studied the different subgroups, and can now be used to study many more scenarios. Indeed, what this research has illustrated is the potential use of this tool (or tools of this kind) in the study of peace and conflict. Whereas most of what is done in the area of conflict study is causally rational, this approach is radically different and allows for the illustration of emergence. Emergence allows us to understand more deeply the creation and history of conflictual situations. Further research will be needed to confirm the role of these tools in conflict studies.

A second conclusion is that the same people, depending on whether they interact on the basis of individuals' values (A simulations) or perceived shared values (B values), create a dramatically different situation. First of all, it is clear that the B simulations take very much more time to converge, which might give sense to the observation that certain important political conflicts seem to take for ever to resolve (the Palestinian problem, the Northern Irish one, etc.). Second, this observation suggests that it is extremely difficult to find solutions as long as people negotiate via perceived groups and their representatives. Peace is clearly something that could be found more easily on the 'battleground' (via individual interaction, and of course without fighting) than around the 'table' (where clan representatives interact with so-called shared values). This observation supports the approach of certain organized education, sports, music, etc. in areas where important conflicts have taken place, with the aim of fostering individual communication. It looks as though this increased individual exchange might be a very constructive element in a conflictual situation. On the contrary, when groups (or countries) officially support groups (or countries) against others (and by doing so, restore a lot of perceived shared values), the usual result is more conflict. Comparing the A simulations with the B simulations also shows that they converge on other variables to other values, and the B simulations converge to more specific values than the A values. In the B simulations, 'values' seem to matter.

From a political science point of view (and even more broadly from an organizational behaviour point of view), the simulations suggest that conflict emerges out of opposed group values, rather than out of opposed individual opinions. At the least, the simulations suggest a different emergent behaviour in the two cases, leading to different group behaviours. More detailed research will be needed to confirm this.

The simulation done in this research seems to contradict the commonly held fear that religions (and of course, depending on the observer, they might differ) are a major cause of instability and potential conflict. Again based on these simulations, comparing what happens in most of the B simulations, it is suggested that religion, even for the B simulations, converges to relatively low values. It is also clear that it partly contributes to, and can be used for, the creation of a group identity (the values remain somewhat high), but in all cases it is much less significant than the other values. All this seems to suggest that when we consider conflictual situations (say the B simulations), religion is not a main factor responsible for the creation of a non-viable situation concerning conflict. Other variables seem to play a more devastating role (the feeling of justice, the economic situation, responsibility, etc.). Though this needs more research, these first runs seem to contradict the existence of a rational ground for fear of religion as a source of conflict.

Finally, though this research has dealt with conflict in societies, it is clear that it is an approach that could easily be used in order to study organizational conflict. The ontological assumptions on which this study is based are clearly much closer to corporate reality in conflict management than most of what we know today. With some careful consideration, we can easily observe that an evident source of conflict in companies will also be the perceived group values and the way exchange and learning do not take place in such a situation. It would be interesting to research whether this approach could, in a real-life case, illustrate some of the claims that are made in the 'learning organization' literature.

I do not want to claim any final validity for this study. I only want to illustrate the fact that this paradigm and the approaches proposed in this work offer us (I would say for the first time) the possibility of having a detailed and dynamic view into 'the internal ingredients of conflict'. To our knowledge, no other method could give us that before. Evidently, if we want to put sustainable development on the agenda, then the management of conflicts is an important aspect. I want to draw attention to the enormous potential of the research proposed in this work. Sustainable development is a research agenda of prime importance in itself as long as we can deal with it using the adequate paradigm.

## Conclusions

Evidently these projects do not give definitive responses, either on the subject of the theoretical concept presented, or on the subject of the possibility of simulating this concept with the CAS. What we can say is that these first results are encouraging. We are developing, on the basis of this new theory, and by using simulations, situations which are recognized at least as real. That is already encouraging and suggests that we can at least show what happens in practice. First of all, we need more research in these sorts of simulations and, if possible, also in the approaches based more on people (such as brainstorms) in order to be able to check and eventually validate the theoretical framework. This refers to my concern, already expressed, about obtaining better understanding in the emergence of markets and more general phenomena.

A second aspect which calls for more research is the use of CAS. But above all, this research must specifically be geared to the application of these approaches in companies. If we get to the point where companies start to use these approaches, the change of paradigm will gradually take place.

# 10 Let us start learning now: what can you do yourself?

*Erna Oldenboom*

- Focus on the individual
- Focus on the network
- The human in his or her world
- A first step

A new paradigm needs an adapted set of competencies for managers who want to manage in this new paradigm. Management *in* complexity (not *of* complexity), management *in* diversity, management *in* respect for multiple solutions and multiple truths, and management *in* paradoxes – these are the necessary skills of the manager of today. 'Wave or particle?'; it only makes a difference in the eye of the observer, the manager. Machines cannot realize values and cannot make intuitive choices. Machines cannot choose between multiple possible truths; managers who behave and think as machines cannot, either. Personal development: that is what I want to discuss in this chapter.

I could write a lot or little; eventually, every individual will have to take their own responsibility for developing themself. It is all related to activities and experiences, and it is not easy to write about it, or, even worse, to explain how somebody should do this. This is not easy to do in a book, despite the fact that many books have been written about the subject. The only thing I can do here is give some ideas, some suggestions, which might help individuals to start their exploration. Those suggestions can never be solutions. No instrument, no matter how good it is, is able to replace the necessary experimentation and change process a human has to go through: one eventually has to lay down the path in walking, always. Keep this in mind while reading this chapter: what is described here is only intermediary to reaching the goal – that is, becoming a learning individual. While learning, human beings advance in their personal development.

In many dictionaries a 'person' is often brought into relationship with theatre, and a person is then a role that is played. Only secondarily does the 'individual', the personality, come across. It is good to remember Varela here when he defines enacted cognition. Enaction is typically what a good theatre player does: actors do not put on an act, they *become* the identity, the personality, of the person, the role they play. Development is often interpreted as 'giving growth, bringing to its full potential'. Educating, transferring knowledge, are other ideas that are related to development and can be found in a dictionary. The duality between the individual and the 'role' that the same individual plays in the network of people surrounding them, proves to be very important, and will be discussed further. Working at personal change processes will always have to take place within the given framework of reality and within the existing human network. A person is only the personality they are within their context.

If we continue with the theatre metaphor, we could translate personal development as follows:

> Developing and bringing to full potential of the roles that the player plays (or could play) in the big theatre play (drama or comedy) that is called life.

However, in a play in the theatre we can anticipate with some certainty how it will evolve. The set does not change all the time, and the different roles are distributed and do not change during the play either. During the rehearsals the roles and the interaction of the players are fine-tuned, and in general we expect the players to stick to their respective roles. The play itself and the ending are known by the players and the managers beforehand, at least in most plays. The ambience can be different, players can act well or not so well, but we do not expect actors to suddenly start doing different things from what is expected. A theatre play takes place within the framework and the structure decided up front. A theatre play is not really a complex system. The play of life, on the contrary, is a complex system, an ever-changing, dynamic and non-linear system.

One could regard the life in which we are actors as a big play; there is nothing against doing so. But a theatre play can always be stopped, either during the rehearsals or during the performance. We could rearrange the set, or even adapt the roles slightly, and after repetitive rehearsals we will get the desired results.

Why this theatre metaphor as an introduction to personal development? The answer is that both the set (the context) and the actors are important, but even more so is the interaction between the different actors within the dynamics of the 'playing field', and all this within the given limits of the play chosen. In real life the play is not written yet.

The individual will have to explore and become aware of the possibilities and limitations of the play in which they are an actor, before being able to play a really active role and a role that is possibly ever-changing. Without any new insights, personal development does not really progress. We will highlight that when we talk about a possible learning structure for supporting personal development. The combination of new insights on the one hand, and the experience of a different learning approach, internally oriented (reflexive) instead of externally (transfer) oriented on the other hand, is key to personal development. The insight element (the externally oriented, the transfer oriented) refers to the right-hand part of Ken Wilber's holistic diagram (Figure 2.1). The focus on internally oriented learning has everything to do with the left-hand side of the same figure, i.e. the interpersonal as experienced by the individual and the highly subjective enaction of the 'I'.

If we want to do something with the ideas of this book, hence, we have to start searching for more holistic understanding of different learning situations. As already suggested, we can only give some sketches of such possible actions, but keep in mind that life – and, in particular, corporate life – gives plenty of possibilities for such experiences on a daily basis. Instead of creating them artificially, we could also use reality as a large experimenting field. Certainly at the beginning, some coaching, and acquaintance with some self-coaching techniques, are very useful. This support could be organized, for instance within the framework of a workshop if the aim is to create a more learning team, or in a more individual setting of personal coaching if the idea is more of a personal development trajectory.

In order to make our ideas accessible, let us cluster the possible actions in three phases that are ideally parallel programmes. We start with the focus on the individual. In fact, it is an individual who is reading this book, hence we can immediately tackle that individual. Next we consider some potentialities of the individual within their network, and in practice that will be the organization or the company in which the individual is active.

But even that organization or company cannot avoid a logic of complexity that is omnipresent. Being a learning individual within a non-learning organization only leads to frustration. Therefore, it is necessary to touch upon some aspects that have to do with the organization or the company: we refer here to some fundamental choices that need to be made.

# Focus on the individual

The prevailing paradigm, fitting a reductionist rational view of reality, which we want to get rid of, is the following. One invents a learning path (or a learning plan) with fixed learning goals that uses well-defined means in order for the learner to reach the set goals after a set time, after which we expect the learner to became measurably smarter or better. In contrast to the case of the theatre play, we presume that we can anticipate the final result from the very beginning and that the roles are fixed. In doing so, we try to block as much as possible our way of thinking and the conception of our learning itself, and we keep it as closed as possible: that is what we often call personal development or renewal. We teach the individual to keep as closely as possible to the predefined play within its given set.

A more holistic approach, though, starts with the learner themself who is able and willing to identify their learning goals and who wants to keep the freedom to continuously adapt those goals, and in doing so keeps the possibility to continually learn. The deepest inner emotion of the individual then becomes the driver for possible change. A person takes responsibility for their own learning. There is no stagecoach driver sitting up front on the box; every individual chooses their own path.

This also implies that if a manager (a person) is no longer able to get close to their inner emotions – which unfortunately often happens in the West – the starting position is already very difficult. The design of one's own learning goals cannot be dictated by the world, the environment or what the company would like you to learn: the imagined hoped-for behaviour, or the desired competencies that somebody should possess.

We cannot presume that somebody will walk the path that we have imagined for them, supported by those means that we have identified as being helpful and important and that will definitely lead to better results. Even the goal that we have for another person is often clearer to us than to the individual.

We should not underestimate how extremely implicitly this process becomes internalized. As already discussed, we collectively keep such a system alive and under continuous reinforcement. Schools, youth clubs, social meeting places, television programmes, newspapers, radio broadcasts flood our daily environment with messages that are consciously and subconsciously stored and metabolized in our bodies and that are so many expressions of the culture in which we live. We seem to live in full freedom without realizing that this is only a 'dependent' freedom, a relative freedom. Philosophically we could question whether we are at all able to think out of 'our' box. But in that case, all potential for continuously adapted learning, what I would like to call real learning, would become obsolete.

The learning human therefore needs to return first to their own inner feelings and sensation. In the West, this is close to a kind of mission impossible, since we strongly underestimate the potential of the embodied mind (as described earlier), a mind/body driving energy. In the Western world we often mix the power of thought with an extreme application of the analytical brain function.

Our actions (or our non-actions) are very much driven by our thoughts. Those thoughts are much more consistent than we often think. We are continuously searching for arguments to reinforce our thoughts and give them a higher level of truth. In doing so, we create our own world of thoughts and we keep it alive as much as possible.

If we think that the world will collapse (as Jehovah's Witnesses do), then we will see everywhere conflict and problems, violence, disasters, etc. On the other hand, if we think and observe in term of progress (growth) and if we define progress from a purely economical and technical viewpoint, we start considering countries as developed and less developed, or even underdeveloped. If we pay more attention in our actions and thinking to the rational side of our consciousness, we will observe the world in a more reductionist manner. If we prefer objectivism to subjectivism, we again choose another angle. In saying this, at least I presume that there is something like dualism, and that dualism means a difference between two things or viewpoints.

In Eastern cultures, people pay more attention to personal experience (to the subject), since the objective side simply exists, and is factually the same for everybody. The individual's interpretation is what makes the difference. That personal sensation gets more attention, and therefore there is less of a difference between the inner and the outer world.

For sure, it will be difficult for the learning manager to get close (enough) to their own inner feelings. Indeed, (guided) meditation is a possible way to get in touch with, and to rediscover, the inner self. Experience has shown that it is extremely difficult to make the first steps on this learning path. Not only do we not have much experience with exercises like meditation (though the old ritual prayer is not necessarily very different), but unfortunately there is also a lot of esoteric movement around techniques like these that does not always serve them well. In our world, the search for the inner self is highly discredited: we pay a high price for this. Do not forget, however, that thought invariably leads to action. If you want to become a learning individual, you will have to start by focusing on your own learning goals.

> You are where your thoughts are.
> Assure yourself that your thoughts are there
> Where you would like them to be.

Once this first obstacle is overcome, one cannot understand personal development independent of the culture or environment from which someone emerges. Personal development has to do with how someone considers their culture or environment. These thoughts give security and structure to our existence, but at the same time they limit our learning, and/or they can make someone a prisoner of their own life. The 'we' experience (say culture) refers to the lower left quadrant in Wilber's holistic picture.

Still the personal learning aims are central, but now we consider them within the network in which a person operates; very often this is the company. For simplicity, we can call that the external sensation of personal learning, but then we refer rather to the fact that this part can be 'shared'. What is learned remains highly personal, just as people's experience of that learning is personal. But part of the learning goals and part of what has been learned can now be shared. There is a common context.

In order to support this process we have developed a methodology and have even made it, in certain real-life cases, available via electronic support, e.g. using electronic learning platforms or corporate intranets. Particularly for companies and larger groups, this latter variant is interesting and allows working on a somewhat larger scale while keeping the necessary flexibility.

The aim is that the participants (managers, learning individuals) learn in order to realize their individual learning goals, based on personal responsibility (which we should have developed by now). The result anticipated is that managers are better able than before to manage their personal development plan (beyond this organized course). The methodology consists of a number of steps, and though I briefly describe them here, this description is in no way the methodology itself, nor does it give real insight into the experience that the learner gains when applying this method.

At the start of the learning trajectory there is an intake interview that roughly deals with the following questions, with the aim that the participant explores their own current feelings:

- Who am I?
- What do I want to reach or what do I want to learn?
- What do I need for that?
- How do I anticipate reaching that?
- When do I want to have reached this?

In fact, the aim is to translate in a very detailed and down-to-earth way a number of individual wishes, intentions and expectations. On the basis of the results, a personal learning coach is appointed. Next, the participants start working on the more content-driven parts of the course (in fact of any course, though some are more adapted to the purpose than others), though always using a learning-by-doing approach. A course in this context can never be a knowledge transfer, teacher-driven course. As already indicated, personal development can only flourish when learners are confronted with new and, preferably, challenging insights. This combination of new insights and personal development will return all the time. The trinity insight, form and meaningfulness (science, art and spirituality), identified earlier, is the guiding principle for the entire methodology and the course.

During the intake, one could use competency criteria and behavioural criteria in order to facilitate the interview. The knowledge and innovation approach advocated in this book is clearly and exclusively one based on competency development. Possible interesting competencies for a manager that could be reviewed are courage, initiative, independence, the capacity to deal with stress, the capacity to convince, organizational sensitivity, cooperation, flexibility, ambition, energy, etc. Of course, these criteria need to be adapted to each different company or organization and to what each individual wants to learn.

During the progress of the assignments, what we could call projects, the participants can share different (virtual) meeting places (we could use the metaphor of a house), in which different groups of participants can be each other's mirrors and sounding boards concerning their own learning. All this takes place in a self-organizing way. Within the different 'houses' there are different 'rooms', and the people inside decide who to allow in. Hence, somebody knocks on the door, and possibly someone opens it. The further details of the organization are less important here.

The sounding board function needs to be understood as follows. We consider here a triangular situation in which somebody is confronted with what they consider to be a problem (to be compared to the 'problematique' in soft systems methodology). That is the base of the triangle (Figure 10.1). A third person comes into the game and that person can take a number of roles. The first classical role, indicated by the arrow on the right, is that the third person gives their advice concerning the problem. The third person takes the role of the consultant and in fact takes over the problem instead of allowing the person to learn. The second possible role that the third person can take is indicated by the arrow on the left and is that of therapist. The third person gives their advice on the behaviour and decisional power of the person in question. Often this does not help the person to learn, since the therapist (consultant) again takes over, but now the therapist takes over the learning potential. The role as learning coach that we suggest is illustrated by the central vertical arrow. The coach spurs on the person in the person's learning-by-doing ability to solve their problem by themselves. The coach

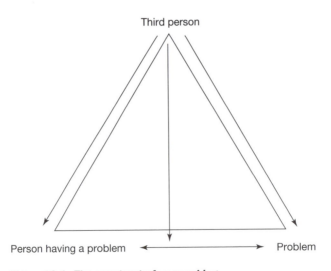

Figure 10.1 *The construct of co-coaching*

leaves the full responsibility to the person and only mirrors certain observations, contextual information, etc. for them.

This approach of being or becoming a learning coach is not self-evident and needs to be trained. Therefore, such an approach, which has been used successfully for many years in certain 'schools' of personal development, needs some initial training or coaching from a professional, after which in principle anyone could take this role of learning coach among their peers. The attempt of the professional is not to stay in the picture for the entire learning loop, but rather to pass on the competencies needed in order to become a learning coach.

Students choose any particular room, depending on their learning targets and their chosen learning path. One can always change rooms, but in order to do so one should have good reasons, and those reasons should be clear to the other participants. In the hypothetical case that one reaches all learning goals, the whole process starts all over again, on a higher level of consciousness.

The role of the coach is, I hope, clear now: to stimulate, to activate, to motivate, to inspire, and to raise enthusiasm. The pillar of this approach is, and remains, the responsibility of the learner for their own personal learning. The learner decides where to go; they take the steering wheel in their hands; the learner reacts on what is offered, but also creates (first); the learner respects others' opinions; the learner listens to the others; the learner contributes to the learning processes of each and every other participant; the learner respects the privacy of the others. In practice this list is longer, but this gives some insight into the basic rules of the game.

This rather external approach to personal learning and development can succeed only if we do not ignore the emotional component in this learning and developmental process. Learning without emotions is like training a monkey for the circus.

## Focus on the network

While we have paid much attention to the person themself (let us say the personality of the manager), personal development cannot be seen independently from the structures in which the individual operates. This book has highlighted these concepts many times. What can be done by a manager in order to avoid becoming a learning individual within a non-learning environment? What can a manager do in order to create a learning environment? A few ideas could help to give orientation to the manager, in line with the paradigm developed in this book. The dimension dealt with here is the one of the person 'manager' in the game that is called a company.

In general we observe that people rapidly jump to solutions without really listening to the problem, and without using the power of the people around them. Managers are immediately ready with their answer, their solution. There are very many procedures for solving problems, and there are even emergency procedures in case the first set does not work out. Queensday 2001, isn't it? Depending on the target selected, an optimal path is automatically deduced. And the target itself is almost automatically generated by the question or the problem. This is indeed a rather mechanistic way of organizing, but from observing managerial practice I would say that it seems to be the practice of the day. Add to this the hierarchical organization form and you quickly end with fixed, non-learning organizations. In the best of cases the improvement of a procedure will often lead only to a marginal increase in efficiency. In the worst of cases it is counter-productive. What can be done in such a case?

First of all, we have to observe that, given the rather strict mechanistic basis of Western management thinking, it is extremely difficult to radically change such thinking. Therefore, and certainly in the beginning phase, some coaching, training or education might be a necessity and will pay off. The possible ways of dealing with this are multiple and they need to be considered case by case. Again this will depend on the people involved and the context within which they work.

What needs to be learned is the rules of the game of the network. The previous chapter has elaborated in detail on these rules of the game, but I will summarize them here. In order to allow a network to come to autopoiesis, a number of minimal conditions need to be fulfilled. A fence needs to be put around the network, in order to (technically) avoid divergence of the system and elements disappearing to infinity. In practice it means that if we want to play soccer, we had better first define the soccer field in order to avoid starting to play another game (do not forget that the field is an integral part of the game). The boundary does not necessarily need to be very restrictive, making the playing ground very small, but it has to be clear for all players. For soccer players it is clear that soccer is played within the marked-out area of the field. If we moved the boundary (and made the field larger, for instance), we would not have the same game on a larger field, but would instead create a different ball game altogether. The larger the field, the more possibilities there are, and the more 'potential' the game contains. Hence, the first task of the manager is to define the boundary and the size of the field.

Next it should be clear for all players that they have to attempt to optimize their own interest. It is the role of the manager to bring together the players, who, while optimizing their respective interests, contribute to a larger common purpose. That common purpose is not easy to decide and it is certainly not the same thing as the path to be followed. But we shall come back to this a bit later. Since each individual optimizes their own behaviour, the manager does not need to give a lot of direction, or to exert a lot of control. This is easier to say than to do.

Finally, we should agree on a minimum set of interaction and communication rules. In soccer the rules of the game are that one should not touch the ball with the hands; one should not kick other players; etc. In business this would refer to rules like: people should respect each other; we should keep our colleagues sufficiently and continuously informed (and here knowledge management could again play a role); etc. It is the role of the manager to identify these rules in consultation, cooperation and co-creation, but above all to facilitate them. In optimal conditions this communication should be easy and productive. As has been discussed in detail in earlier chapters, this leads us rapidly into knowledge management as a facilitator for continuous learning.

In summary, the manager has three main tasks:

- Define the boundary and make sure that everybody knows it.
- Motivate everybody to optimize their personal interest as much as possible, while making it possible for individuals to contribute the best of themselves.
- Identify clear and simple communication rules with the aim of promoting communication as much as possible.

In practice one could work at this in different work forms, though workshops have proved to be the most straightforward.

However, there is a small 'but'. We should all know where we would like to go. When Alice (in Wonderland) asks the Cheshire Cat which path she should take, the cat asks her where she wants to go. And since she does not know, the path does not matter much. If one doesn't know where to go, every path is a good one. That does not mean that a set target needs to be reached. But without a target, we cannot make choices right away. Imagine you arrive at a roundabout and you can take either of two roads.

If you do not know where you would like to go (even if you eventually never arrive there), you cannot make a choice at this particular roundabout and you are going to stay there for the rest of your life.

## The human in his or her world

The goal, in turn, has everything to do with what the company is aiming at. In many cases a company does not really have a vision. Most company 'vision statements' are the same: service clients, growth, internationalization, quality, etc. They are almost interchangeable. And from that vision, managers immediately transform it into a path: what steps need to be undertaken in order to realize that vision?

However, very often there is a step before all that, which is concerned with the paradoxes and often mutually exclusive choices. Next we should consider how the network could be organized (the minimal network requirements) to realize the choices made. That is what I would like to call a business architecture: it is a first sketch of the network organization that we want to grow, to cultivate.

It is clear that all this can only be reached by putting people around the table. In order to avoid falling immediately back into defining the path, external facilitation is highly desirable. The following are some examples of fundamental choices that should be addressed in such workshops:

- Are we looking at short-term orientation (shareholder value) or longer-term vision (sustainability)?
- Are we in search of 'simplicity' (limiting and controlling the complexity and hence the possibilities) or complexity (creative potential)?
- Is the management approach one of control (spreadsheet management) or rather one of stimulating initiative?
- Do we consider diversity to be a creative force or a disturbing factor?

Concerning the design of a business architecture, different methods exist, though most of them are not based on the self-creating and self-organizing power of a network. As regards choosing a methodology, it seems important to us that it should be based on a well-thought-out paradigm, in line with the identified aims. And let us keep in mind that here too, order will lead to chaos.

## A first step

We have made an attempt to briefly describe what a learning manager or learning human more generally could do in order to realize some of the ideas described in this book. Particularly since the proposed paradigm goes strongly against the prevailing ideas in the Western world, it is not easy to realize it, though this does not make it less important to do so – on the contrary. Often external help will be necessary.

While we like to start with the company, we have to stress that the most important step is the 'de-learning' of the individual. First of all, we have to train the learning manager from a holistic perspective. Afterwards, this spider-in-the-web can then continue gradually his or her work.

Good insight into your thoughts increases the possibilities for further development. Theoretical concepts can further help to increase your understanding, to which an inner journey into one's personal world of beliefs and feelings, for instance via music, art or (guided) meditation, could be a welcome complement. The reason for this journey is that the major problem of the learning manager, and a problem that also concerns one's personal development, is that the blocks are almost always inside the person. The learning human needs to invite themself to return to their own creative and creating potential. Learning is in the first place a 'meeting with oneself'. For most of us, this meeting is easier within an adapted context.

This context is one that is based on a holistic view of the human; a person who thinks, feels and experiences. An interesting first step for a company is therefore often a three- or four-day workshop highlighting these different aspects. In such a workshop we need to continuously seek a balance between understanding, creation and sense-making, which should show themselves via different work forms and subjects. Only as an illustration, a possible example of such a seminar could be as follows.

The participants begin the seminar with at least one specific case of their own experience and corporate environment. Before the seminar, each participant needs to write down some personal experiences that they are willing to share during the seminar, and identify a learning agenda with some specific learning aims, around the theme of the learning human. This pre-workshop assignment is discussed with the learning coach before embarkation.

## Welcome and introduction

After a first round of presentations with the coaches and the participants, the 'welcome and introduction' session deals with the prepared learning agendas and the expectations concerning the workshop. The idea is to focus in particular on some practical dilemmas and/or paradoxes that are recognized by the participants in their daily practice and that could be used as an ongoing case during the workshop.

## Thinking about thinking

The 'thinking about thinking' session analyses the philosophical frame of the reductionist and rational scientific approach prevailing in the United States and Europe. Particular attention is given to the link between these philosophical assumptions and our view on the development of managerial competencies. Starting from some classical views on the philosophy of science, a number of alternatives are discussed, like more postmodern ideas, constructivism, or Varela's autopoietic (self-organizing) paradigm. Since the way we think about thinking is crucial for our scientific development, we have to make this understanding apparent first.

## Djembee and rhythm workshop

In the djembee and rhythm workshop the participants experience, by playing the djembee, an African (or Afro-Cuban) drum, how order emerges out of chaos and how a manager or leader can play a stimulating role.

## Thinking about doing

Now that we have an idea of how our mental framework can either support or limit the development of new ideas and hence of learning, it is time to consider how systems operate. The participant is given insight into the new paradigm of complexity and chaos. In fact they are introduced to the behaviour of non-linear dynamic systems – in other words, to the behaviour of all systems in which humans cooperate (companies, markets, organizations, etc.). It is explained why such systems cannot be forecasted and how they behave and emerge. Here we deal with such theories as Prigogine's irreversibility of time principle and the theories of Lorenz, Holland, Mandelbrot, etc. All the time, the participants' cases are used to illustrate these theories, and in return those theories are used to enrich the participants' understanding of their cases.

# Walk in nature

## Guided fantasy (revival of the walk in nature)

Most of the time, managers do not pay enough attention to acquiring new information, or, even worse, they do not spent the time needed to acquire new emotions. We seldom take the time to distance ourselves from reality in order to allow emotions to have an impact on us. If we took more time and distance, it would be easier to generate new ideas, since if all input falls away (or is filtered out), then it is almost impossible to learn anything new.

## Doing about thinking

As a next step, we can investigate how further insights based on complexity theory could work out in real-life cases. We deal in detail with how networks (of individuals) become self-organizing and self-referential. Varela's philosophical framework is translated to the practice of self-organization, but equally some intriguing ideas of Gödel pass by. With lots of practical examples, human networks are explored, with a particular focus on the organizing principles. From the new insight acquired already, it will be easy to understand all kinds of different network properties and it will be possible to learn to be able to apply them differently. The paradigm of the new economy (the network economy, or the knowledge economy, or the quantum structure of economy) is grounded here. We investigate how complex adaptive systems and artificial intelligence can be supportive and illustrative, particularly since they are based on the same organizing and learning principles. A short but passionate voyage though artificial intelligence rounds up this workshop. Throughout this workshop also, there will be a lot of attention paid to the continuous feedback of these ideas to individuals' cases. The same ideas are used in order to prepare the other parts of this seminar.

## Practitioner's examples of complexity

Managers who claim to use complexity theory as their guiding principle in their daily management can recount their experiences and share some of their lessons learned.

## Doing about doing (1)

Now that we have understood the new paradigm and its possible applications, the time is right to introduce the holistic concept of the learning manager. This is based on the holistic framework of Ken Wilber, discussed earlier in this book. This framework illustrates the potential for the continuous learning of both the managers and their employees. If we could bring the holistic image of the human back into our daily management practice, we create not only a deeper and larger implication of humans, but also the potential for creativity and innovation. From this holistic perspective, personal development and coaching are almost automatically generated.

## Doing about doing (2)

Now that we have created the necessary conditions and elaborated new insights, this session deals with the practice of knowledge management and management learning in a corporate context. The potential for (e-)learning, corporate (virtual) universities, communicative technologies, etc. is discussed. How can a company organize itself in order to facilitate knowledge exchange and to use knowledge and learning creatively? What are knowledge platforms and how do they operate? How can we really integrate knowledge management and (e-)learning? Many examples of companies are debriefed.

## Assignment

The participants are sent back to their companies with an individual assignment. The participants should prepare a return day a few months later. In fact, we ask the participants to update their earlier preparation work, using the new insights and experiences they have acquired. They should identify the dilemmas (choices) and paradoxes (apparent oppositions; they appeal on acceptance) that hinder one's learning, on the basis of the newly acquired ideas. Next they should design an application plan for the learning manager: what am I going to do tomorrow?

## From assignment to action learning

The return day, a few months later, starts with debriefing on the individual assignments, making an inventory of possible and/or common dilemmas and paradoxes. This list is used during the day as illustration, with the aim of bringing learning as close as possible to daily practice. After the inventory phase, action learning is developed as a concept and a possible attitude of the learning and (re)searching manager: managing while learning.

## Workshop action learning

Based on the previous session, the method of action learning is practised in order to develop an answer to the remaining dilemmas and paradoxes. This workshop allows the manager to refine their action plan (assignment) in order to make it even more applicable.

## Final evaluation

A workshop can take all kinds of different forms, different durations. It could involve more or fewer people, and could be animated for a different duration, locally or virtually (in the case of a multinational company). But invariably we will have to take responsibility for our own learning.

> The way to happiness and suffering is a decision of the mind.
>
> (Sogyal Rinpoche)

The aim of this chapter has been to give an introduction to possible learning paths, and possible ways in which a manager or a company could foster managerial learning. In no way are the suggestions exhaustive or limiting. But the realization of the quantum potential of any company or organization will invariably happen via the learning manager and their learning colleagues, within the context of a self-organizing learning network. This book invites the responsible and creative manager to make an informed choice that is eventually going to make the difference for their company and themselves, deploying the creative potential of any individual person and any group of humans.

The choice is yours, but at least you are aware of the potential now.

# 11 Epilogue: some poems of Erna Oldenboom

## Dream Catcher

Magnificent particles separated in space and time
Not necessarily desperately looking to combine
Freedom and the joy of liberation
Contributing to yours and mine

Floating waters of all different names
Crystal clear drops of laughing tears
Dancing in the endless space and time
Attracted by the divine

Single sounds in the world of hearing ears
Breathtaking views of vibrating melodies
Composed of universal rhythms
Reflected in creators' eyes

Dying in unforgettable moments
Living tinkling possibilities
Unbounded in the field of the spectacular
Source of all existing circles

Share with me the miracles of wisdom
Flying on the wings of peace
Melting significantly, together for ever
Blowing in the wind

## Subtitles

I really want to let you know how much I care
You are always in my heart
I close my eyes and think of you
And we were never meant to be apart

My words cannot cover all the deeper
Levels of my conscious thoughts
Blessing whispering sounds of loving
Warmth is showing in my eyes

I always knew you in the timeless
Space of unique moments
Silent fragments almost disappearing
In the world of sound

Show your talents as an invitation
To all that is around
Touch the field of high potential in the
Ocean of ever-changing movements

I will be always part of you
Only separated by external meaning
Of the sequential mind
Close enough to be your other part

## Wholeness

I cannot reach you in the world of separation
You're too far to hear my voice
Ocean water drifts us apart in unknown directions
Blindness born in desert storms

Building blocks instead of clear blue skies
Somewhere in forbidden cities
Untouchable by warmth and love
Frozen hearts of bleeding pain

Order necessary to control chaos in a
War and constant battle of unfulfilled desires
Voices crying in the wilderness
Full of lonely individuals

In the world of combining cells
Networking for a higher purpose
Creative wisdom in an intelligent flow
Where synchronic miracles occur

Masterpieces simplified by reduction
Crying to be free again
Spread your wings to look behind
The horizon of space and time

## Related

When we first met I was unknowing of
Your past and it made me aware
Of the 'miracle' of the present
The awareness of the self

From all over the world we gathered
In the magic field of combining experiences
And sharing values like diamonds in a
Colourful spectrum in the gardens of discovery

I looked into your beautiful faces
And it touched my heart like the smile
Of the upcoming sun as a
Promise of the fulfilment of hope and dreams

Magnificent blowing wings brought
Energy from different places
Surrounded by the expression
Of a global view

I am grateful for the inspiring melody
Of your inner music
Composed by the willingness to learn
Through the golden mirror of respect

# Powerful Meaning

Whenever you want, I will be with you. Whatever you do I will
applaud so that everybody is able to hear the applause from many
miles' distance.
Forgive me, my darling, for not recognizing you when we first met.
My mind was too busy with unimportant aspects of a boring life.
I went too fast just passing by.

I thought your smile was meaningless, your eyes just lit by the
upcoming sun, your body moving by the wind.
I was not aware that all body parts of you were inviting me to dance in
the flashing rhythm of life.
I will show you how much I have changed.

I will let you feel how much I care.
You will discover the fragrance of pure love making entering your
nostrils.
I will cover your body with my soft, shining body in the unbounded
world of paradise.

Standing in front of you I let you taste my juice.
Sparkling champagne in a firing surrounding.
Come with me my God of love.
And enter my door to heaven.

Spinning around in a magnificent source of divinity
Fantasies are coming truth.
Flying with our wings in endless space
Liberated in a world of ecstasy.

# 🌀 Bibliography

Apostel, L. and Walry J. (1997), *Hopeloos gelukkig: leven in de post-moderne tijd*, Meulenhoff

Argyris, C. and Schön, D. A. (1978), *Organizational Learning: A theory of action perspective*, Addison Wesley

Arthur B. (1998), 'The end of certainty in economics', in Aerts, D., Broekaert, J. and Mathijs, E. (eds), *Einstein meets Magritte*, Kluwer Academic

Baets W. (1998), *Organizational Learning and Knowledge Technologies in a Dynamic Environment*, Kluwer Academic Publishers

Baets, W. (ed.) (1998), Special issue of *Accounting, Management and Information Technologies, Complex Adaptive Systems and Organisational Change*, Elsevier (8)

Baets, W. (1999), *A Collection of Essays on Complexity and Management*, World Scientific

Baets, W. (2003, 2004), *Wie orde zaait zal chaos oogsten: een vertoog over de lerende mens*, Van Gorcum

Baets, W. (2004), 'Une interprétation quantique des processus organizationnels d'innovation' (A quantum interpretation of innovation), Thèse d'Habilitation à la Direction des Recherches (HDR), IAE Aix-en-Provence, Université Paul Cezanne, Aix-Marseille III

Baets, W. (2005a), *Knowledge Management and Management Learning: Extending the horizons of knowledge-based management*, Springer

Baets, W. (2005b), 'Une interprétation "quantique" des processus organizationnels d'innovation', in *Proceedings of Intelligence de la complexité: Epistémologie et pragmatique* (Cerisy)

Baets, W. (2006), 'Complexity theory: dynamics and non-linearity are the only reason for knowledge management to exist', in Boughzala, I. and Ermine, J.-L. (eds), *Trends in Applied Knowledge Management*, Edition Hermes Penton Science

Baets, W. and van der Linden, G. (2000), *The Hybrid Business School: Developing knowledge management through management learning*, Prentice-Hall

Baets, W. and van der Linden, G. (2003), *Virtual Corporate Universities: A matrix of knowledge and learning for the new digital dawn*, Kluwer Academic Publishers

Baets, W., Oldenboom, E. and van Starkenburg, T. (2005), 'Emergence of peace and conflict: an experiment with agent-based simulations', in EGOS Colloquium 'Unlocking Organizations', Berlin

Blommaert, S. (1992), *Niets is mogelijk, alles kan*, Kritak

Bogdanov, I. and Bogdanov, G. (2004), *Avant le Big Bang*, Editions Grasset & Fasquelle

Cahoone, L. (ed.) (1996), *From Modernism to Post-modernism: An Anthology*, Blackwell

Caro, M. and Murphy, J. (eds) (2002), *The World of Quantum Culture*, Greenwood Press

Checkland, P. (1981), *Systems Thinking, Systems Practice*, Wiley

Chopra, D. (1990), *Quantum Healing: Exploring the frontiers of mind/body medicine*, Bantam Books

Clauser, J. F. and Shimony, A. (1978), 'Bell's theorem: experimental tests and implications', *Reports on Progress in Physics*, 41: 1881–1927

Clippinger, J. III (ed.) (1999), *The Biology of Business*, Jossey-Bass

Cushing, J. (1998), *Philosophical Concepts in Physics*, Cambridge University Press

Dalla Chiara, M. L. and Giuntini, R. (1999), 'Quantum logical semantics, historical truths and interpretations in art', in Aerts, D. and Pykacz, J. (eds), *Quantum Structures and the Nature of Reality*, Kluwer Academic

de Geus, A. (1988), 'Planning as learning', *Harvard Business Review*, 66 (2), March/April: 70–4

Dirac, P. (1958), *The Principles of Quantum Mechanics*, 4th edn, Oxford University Press

Einstein, A., Podolsky, B. and Rosen, N. (1935), 'Can quantum-mechanical description of physical reality be considered complete?', *Physical Review*, 47, reprinted in Wheeler, J. A. and Zurek, W. D. (eds), *Quantum Theory and Measurement*, Princeton University Press

Epstein, J. and Axtell, R. (1996), *Growing Artificial Societies*, MIT Press

Feyerabend, P. (1975, 1993), *Against Method*, Verso

Gleick, J. (1987), *Chaos: Making a new science*, Heinemann

Harkema, S. (2005), 'Emergent learning processes in innovation projects', in Baets, W., *Knowledge Management and Management Learning: Extending the horizons of knowledge-based management*, Springer

Harkema, S. and Baets, W. (2001), '"Customerized" innovation though the emergence of a mutually adaptive and learning environment', *European Journal of Economic and Social Systems*, 15 (1): 111–29

Heisenberg, W. (1927), 'Über den anschaulichen Inhalt der quantentheoretischen Kinematik und Mechanik', *Zeitschrift für Physik*, 43. In English translation: Wheeler, J. A. and Zurek, W. D. (eds) (1983), 'The physical content of quantum kinematics and mechanistics', in Wheeler, J. A. and Zurek, W. D. (eds), *Quantum Theory and Measurement*, Princeton University Press

Hoebeke, L. (1994), *Making Work Systems Better*, Wiley

Hofstadter, D. (2000), *Gödel, Escher, Bach*, Penguin Books, (reprint)

Holden, N., Cooper, C. and Carr, J. (1998), *Dealing with the New Russia*, Wiley

Holland, J. (1998), *Emergence from Chaos to Order*, Oxford University Press, 1998

http://euromed.blogs.com

Klein, M. J. (1964), 'Einstein and the wave–particle duality', in Gershenson, D. E. and Greenberg, D. A. (eds), *The Natural Philosopher*, vol. 3, Blaisdell Publishing

Latour, B. (1987), *Science in Action*, Harvard University Press

Le Moigne, J. L. (1980), *Le Constructivisme*, EME, Editions Sociales Françaises

Le Moigne, J. L. (1999), *La Modélisation des systèmes complexes*, Dunod

McDermott, J. (ed.) (1973), *The Philosophy of John Dewey*, University of Chicago Press

Mandelbrot, B. and Hudson, R. (2004), *The (Mis)behaviour of Markets: A fractal view of risk, ruin and reward*, Profile Books

Marcuse, H. (2002), *One-Dimensional Man*, Routledge Classics (reprint)

Martens, B. (1999), 'Innovation, increasing complexity and the need for a new paradigm in economics', in Heylighen, F., Bollen, J. and Riegler, A. (eds), *The Evolution of Complexity*, Kluwer Academic

Maturana, H. (ed.) (2004), *From Being to Doing: The Origins of the Biology of Cognition*, Carl-Auer-Systeme-Verlag und Verlagsbuchhandlung

Maturana, H. and Varela, F. (eds) (1980), *Autopoiesis and Cognition: The realization of the living*, Reidel

Maturana, H. and Varela, F. (1992), *The Tree of Knowledge*, Scherz Verlag

Merry, U. (1995), *Coping with Uncertainty*, Praeger

Mingers, J. (1995), *Self-Producing Systems: Implications and applications of autopoiesis*, Plenum Press

Mitchell, E. and Williams, D. (1996), *The Way of the Explorer: An Apollo astronaut's journey through the material and mystical world*, Putman's Sons

Moten, A. R. (1996), *Political Science: An Islamic Perspective*, Macmillan

Nagel, E. and Newman, J. (1958), *Gödel's Proof*, New York University Press

Nicolis, G. and Prigogine, I. (1989), *Exploring Complexity*, Freeman

Orwell, G. (1990) *Nineteen Eighty-four*, Penguin Books

Pauli, W. and Jung, C. G. (1955), *The Interpretation of Nature and Psyche*, translated from German, Routledge & Kegan Paul

Pirsig, R. (1974), *Zen and the Art of Motorcycle Maintenance*, The Bodley Head

Polkinghorne, J. (1990), *The Quantum World*, Penguin

Schrödinger, E. (1935), 'Die Gegenwärtige Situation in der Quantummechanik', *Die Naturwissenschaften*, 23. English translation Wheeler, J. A. and Zurek,

W. D. (eds) (1983), 'The present situation in quantum mechanics', *Quantum Theory and Measurement*, Princeton University Press

Senge, P. (1990), *The Fifth Discipline*, Doubleday

Senge, P., Kleiner, A., Roberts, C., Ross, R. and Smith, B. (1994), *The Fifth Discipline Fieldbook*, Nicholas Brealey

Sheldrake, R. (1995), *The Presence of the Past*, Park Street Press

Sheldrake, R. and Bohm, D. (1982), 'Morphogenetic fields and the implicate order', *ReVision*, 5: 41–48

Stacey, R. (1992), *Managing Chaos*, Kogan Page

Stacey, R. (2000), *Strategic Management and Organisational Dynamics: The challenge of complexity*, 3rd edn, Prentice Hall

Stewart, I. (1989), *Does God Play Dice?*, Basil Blackwell

Stowell, F. (ed.) (1995), *Information Systems Provision*, McGraw-Hill

van den Bersselaar, V. (1997), *Wetenschapsfilosofie in veelvoud*, Coutinho

Teubner, G. (1993), *Law as an Autopoietic System*, Blackwell

van Diessen, S. and Gommers, R. (2005), 'Knowledge management at Akzo Nobel Car refinishes R&D: improving knowledge creation ability', in Baets, W., *Knowledge Management and Management Learning: Extending the horizons of knowledge-based management*, Springer

van Meijgaard, H. (2002), 'Wolfgang Pauli centennial 1900–2000', PhD thesis, TU Twente

Varela, F. (1979), *Principles of Biological Autonomy*, Elsevier-North Holland

Waldrop, M. (1992), *Complexity*, Penguin

Whittington, R. (1993), *What Is Strategy and Does It Matter?*, Routledge

Wilber, K. (2000), *A Brief History of Everything*, Gateway

Wilson, B. (2001), *Soft Systems Methodology*, Wiley

Wolfram, S. (2002), *A New Kind of Science*, General Science

## PhD thesis supervised by the author

Harkema, S. (2004), 'Complexity and emergent learning in innovation projects', Nyenrode Business University

## MSc dissertations supervised by the author

Braaksma, F. and van Liere, G. (2004), 'Telemedecin: a systemic research into ICT innovations in the medical care market', Nyenrode Business University

van den Broek, S. (2004), 'Innovation in SMEs: a network structure', Nyenrode Business University

van Diessen, S. and Gommers, R. (2004), 'Knowledge management at Akzo Nobel: improving the knowledge creation ability', Nyenrode Business University van Jooren, C. (2005), 'Investigation on the knowledge processes of Bison International: a complexity approach', Nyenrode Business University

van Starkenburg, T. (2004), 'Conflict treatment: an experiment', Leiden Institute of Advanced Computer Science (LIACS), Leiden University

# Index